THE ADMINISTRATION OF TELEVISION NEWSFILM AND VIDEOTAPE COLLECTIONS

A CURATORIAL MANUAL

THE ADMINISTRATION OF TELEVISION NEWSFILM AND VIDEOTAPE COLLECTIONS

A CURATORIAL MANUAL

Edited by

Steven Davidson
> Louis Wolfson II Media History Center

and

Gregory Lukow
> National Center for Film and Video Preservation
> American Film Institute

American Film Institute
Los Angeles
Louis Wolfson II Media History Center
Miami

American Film Institute
Los Angeles, California 90027

Louis Wolfson II Media History Center
Miami, Florida 33130

Library of Congress Catalog Card Number:
    97-70587

ISBN   0-9649097-0-7

The Editors:

Steven Davidson has been the Director of the Louis Wolfson II Media History Center in Miami since its establishment in 1987. Prior to that, he was the Director of Library Services at the Museum of Broadcasting and Associate Director of the National Jewish Archive of Broadcasting. He has served on the Executive Board of the Association of Moving Image Archivists and co-chairs its News and Documentary Interest Group. In addition, he has organized presentations at a variety of public, professional and academic forums, including meetings of the Broadcasters Educators Association, Radio-Television News Directors Association, Society of American Archivists and American Library Association. He has also consulted for moving image archives and served as an advisor for a number of archival based documentary productions.

Gregory Lukow is Director, Administration of the National Center for Film and Video Preservation at the American Film Institute in Los Angeles, where he has worked since 1984. He is the National Center's delegate to the International Federation of Film Archives (FIAF) and International Federation of Television Archives (FIAT), and is a member of The Film Foundation's Archivists Advisory Council, and the Sony Pictures Film Preservation Committee. Since 1992, he has served as the founding Secretary of the North American Association of Moving Image Archivists, and is a member of the association's Executive Board. In 1987 he was project director for the NHPRC grant that funded the first national conference of local television news archives.

CONTENTS

Chapter 14
Outreach *199*
by Karan Sheldon

Appendix A
Bibliography *221*

Appendix B
Photo Directory *231*

Index *243*

FOREWORD

from the National Historical Publications and Records Commission

Television newsfilm collections contain unique documentation. Unlike traditional paper records, these research materials move and talk. They provide multiple insights into historical events and engage the viewers' imagination and emotions in a special way. And yet, like their paper cousins, television newsfilm and other visual materials are subject to deterioration and neglect in the absence of procedures and programs to foster their care and preservation. They present a constant challenge to those individuals and institutions in whose custody they are found.

The National Historical Publications and Records Commission (NHPRC) first acknowledged the importance of the preservation of television newsfilm as an historical medium when, in 1984, it made its first television newsfilm grant to the University of Baltimore to preserve its A. S. Abell Collection. A Federal funding agency affiliated with the National Archives and Records Administration, the NHPRC supports projects relating to the preservation, access, and use of historical documents of all types relating to the history of the United States. To date, the Commission has provided over $500,000 in assistance to ten institutions in nine states to deal with specific film and video collections projects, and for special projects to benefit the broader community.

The first of these special projects was undertaken in 1987 when the Commission funded a national conference plan for the improved care and availability of local television newsfilm collections. One of the needs identified by the conference was a curatorial manual, written by and for television newsfilm and video caretakers. The Commission, keenly interested in assisting with archival education covering all collection areas, recognized the need for the manual and offered financial assistance. The result is now in front of us. Although geared to television news, this curatorial manual should be of use to anyone with responsibility for care of film and video materials. The manual codifies for the first time the procedures for caring for these distinctive materials and supplements the published work of such broadly based professional organizations as the Society of American Archivists, the Association of Moving Image Archivists, and the National Center for Film and Video Preservation at The American Film Institute.

The Commission applauds the National Center for Film and Video Preservation and the Louis Wolfson II Media History Center for their efforts in coordinating the publication of this manual and looks forward to seeing it used in a wide variety of archives as a means to ensure the continued preservation and use of moving image materials.

Nancy Sahli
Acting Executive Director
National Historical Publications and Records Commission
October 1995

FOREWORD

from the Association of Moving Image Archivists

On behalf of the Association of Moving Image Archivists, I wish to thank everyone who planned, wrote for, edited and otherwise contributed to *The Administration of Television Newsfilm and Videotape Collections: A Curatorial Manual.* Special debts of gratitude are owed Gregory Lukow of the National Center for Film and Video Preservation at The American Film Institute and Steve Davidson of the Louis Wolfson II Media History Center for serving as project coordinators. I also want to thank the National Historical Publications and Records Commission for providing necessary funding and welcomed encouragement.

This manual is not an AMIA publication – the project actually began before AMIA was formalized as a professional association. Nevertheless, it is of great significance to us for two reasons.

• One, it speaks directly and comprehensively to the needs of our largest and fastest growing constituency. The past fifteen years have seen a remarkable growth in the number of archival news collections and the level of activity associated with them. Now for the first time, archivists and administrators will have a written guidebook to use in dealing with the unique conservation and curatorial issues characteristic of these collections.

• Two, it reflects the spirit of cooperation and mutual support which is the hallmark of AMIA and which increasingly must become the guiding principle of the archival moving image community as a whole. By my count, at least forty individuals representing sixteen institutions worked on this project, each contributing his or her knowledge, experience and unique perspective. The finished product is all the richer for it.

Today, no one doubts the enormous value of newsfilm and video as modes of communication, records of historical events, and documents of social customs and cultural experiences. This manual will help insure that these resources are managed with an eye toward both use in the present and preservation for the future. All associated with this project are to be congratulated for an important job well done.

Eddie Richmond
President, 1995
Association of Moving Image Archivists

PREFACE

This manual is the product of genuine collaboration. It would not have been possible without the cooperation and contributions of many people. We are especially grateful to the National Historical Publications and Records Commission for helping fund the project and for the Commission's ongoing support of the archival community. The association of both editors with the NHPRC dates back to the 1980s, when the AFI National Center for Film and Video Preservation organized the first national conference of local television news archives with NHPRC support in 1987, and when the Louis Wolfson II Media History Center received a newsfilm project grant from the Commission in 1988. Our experiences on those projects were vital forerunners to this one. For all their help, the AFI and the Wolfson Center would like to thank Laurie Baty, Lisa Weber, Nancy Sahli, Gerald George and all at the NHPRC.

In Miami, the Wolfson Center would like to extend special acknowledgments to Lynn Wolfson for her ongoing generosity and support; to Margaret Pelton, past Executive Board President, for her unwavering commitment; to Dr. Paul George, Executive Board President; to Louis Wolfson III, former Vice President, and the other members of the Executive Board; and to the Wolfson Center's sponsoring institutions, Miami-Dade Community College, the University of Miami and the Miami-Dade Public Library System. For their continued support of the Center and its activities, thanks to the Metro-Dade Cultural Affairs Council, the Florida Humanities Council, and the Florida Department of State Division of Cultural Affairs. Also to be commended are Wolfson Center staff past and present who contributed to the Center's progress and, as a result, this manual

In Los Angeles, the National Center would like to thank Radha Thampi for his invaluable contributions in completing the project; to Janice Mabry, Tracy Papazoglou and Christopher Reiner for their important work in the early stages of the project; to Tony Gonzalez for his continuing assistance; to AFI Associate Director Bruce Neiner for his role in administering the grant, and to AFI Director Jean Firstenberg and NCFVP Vice Chair Ken Wlaschin for their encouragement and support.

The editors would especially like to thank the many friends and colleagues in the field and all the contributors and advisors to this project whose dedication and scholarship made this publication possible. Finally, on more personal notes, thanks to Regina, Aaron and Jodie in Miami, and to Rachel, Lauren and Anne-Marina in Los Angeles.

Steven Davidson
Louis Wolfson II Media History Center
Miami

Gregory Lukow
National Center for Film and Video Preservation
American Film Institute
Los Angeles

December 1996

ACKNOWLEDGMENTS

Project Directors and Editors
Gregory Lukow
Steven Davidson

Production Coordinator Radha K. Thampi
Layout and Design Christopher Reiner
Administrative Support Amy Gurowitz, Lou Ellen Kramer
Photography Steven Davidson
Cover design Lee Kline
Cover photograph Steven Davidson

This publication was funded in part by a grant from the National Historical Publications and Records Commission. Additional support by the American Film Institute National Center for Film and Video Preservation and the Louis Wolfson II Media History Center.

Project Advisory Committee
Larry Viskochil, Chair
Dan Den Bleyker
Linda J. Evans
Alan Lewis
John Lynch
Jean MacNichol
William T. Murphy
Wendy White-Hensen
Helene Whitson
Bonnie Wilson
Gerry Yeager

All photographs in this manual courtesy of the Louis Wolfson II Media History Center, with the following exceptions:
pp. 60, 62, 64 courtesy State Historical Society of North Dakota;
p. 74 courtesy Chicago Historical Society;
pp. 141, 145, 146 courtesy San Francisco State University.

For information or inquiries about this publication contact:

Louis Wolfson II Media History Center
101 West Flagler Street
Miami, FL 33130
Phone: 305-375-1505
Fax: 305-375-4436

National Center for Film and Video Preservation
American Film Institute
2021 North Western Avenue
Los Angeles, CA 90027
Phone: 213-856-7637
Fax: 213-856-7616

CONTRIBUTORS

Louise M. Benjamin
George Foster Peabody Awards, the University of Georgia, Athens

Steven Davidson
Louis Wolfson II Media History Center, Miami

Dan Den Bleyker
Mississippi Department of Archives and History, Jackson

James A. DeVinney
Documentary Writer/Producer, Boston

Ernest J. Dick
Consulting Archivist, Granville Ferry, Nova Scotia

Jane Dunbar Johnson
UCLA Film and Television Archive, Los Angeles

Alan Lewis
National Archives and Records Administration, Washington, DC

William T. Murphy
National Archives and Records Administration, Washington, DC

Gerald G. Newborg
State Historical Society of North Dakota, Bismarck

Kenn Rabin
Fulcrum Media Services, San Anselmo, California

Brian Rose
Fordham University, New York City

Karan Sheldon
Northeast Historic Film, Bucksport, Maine

Barry L. Sherman
George Foster Peabody Awards, the University of Georgia, Athens

Helene Whitson
J. Paul Leonard Library, San Francisco State University, San Francisco

Gerry Yeager
Harford Community College, Harford, Maryland

INTRODUCTION

Local television newsfilm and videotape are among the most pervasive and fundamental records of twentieth century American life. They form an invaluable record of the day-to-day events and activities that have shaped the social and cultural fabric of both urban and rural communities across the United States. They provide regional perspectives on national and international events, as well as detailed coverage of historical issues and controversies before they become part of the national agenda. They stand as primary source materials documenting specific historical events, while at the same time revealing the more intangible moods, beliefs, fashions and attitudes of our times.

Archives and educational institutions have already demonstrated the many ways in which these collections can be actively used by researchers, students, university and secondary school educators, film and video makers, and the general public. The extraordinary historical value of the materials has been further highlighted by their use by historians and scholars in a wide range of local and national research projects, and by their appearance in high-profile historical documentaries produced for television and theatrical release.

Ironically, despite their historical value, local news materials are among the most endangered of our moving images. Institutional mechanisms are already in place for the retention and conservation of nationally broadcast television news. But until recently the situation with regard to local television news was comparatively undeveloped and chaotic. Many stations had already disposed of decades worth of historic news coverage, and conservators of material that had found a way into archives were scattered throughout the country working largely in an informational vacuum. Hard information and basic guidelines on key archival questions regarding the appraisal, preservation and documentation of these materials was lacking.

While *The Administration of Television Newsfilm and Videotape Collections: A Curatorial Manual* may be of interest to all who collect moving image materials, it was written specifically on behalf of the broad range of local news archives throughout the United States. Beginning in the late 1970s and early 1980s, institutions acquiring local television newsfilm collections became the largest and fastest growing constituency within the American moving image archive community. Their number grew rapidly from a handful of institutions in 1980 to nearly 100 today. The number of collections housed in archives will no doubt continue to increase, given that there are more than 1,500 television stations across the country that may at some point donate some or all of their materials to public archives.

The relatively sudden appearance and development of the local news archival constituency within the past fifteen years had very specific historical causes. It was the direct result of major changes in the way television news was produced by the broadcast industry, namely, the switch in the mid-1970s from 16mm newsfilm production to more cost-efficient production on magnetic videotape. With this switch to electronic newsgathering (ENG), many local television stations began to look for ways to rid themselves of the storage costs attendant to maintaining many years and millions of feet of 16mm film. Unfortunately, tales of these historic collections being thoughtlessly thrown away are all too common. Yet a significant amount of this material has now been donated to a broad range of state and local archives, historical societies, libraries, and universities across the country. In some cases, materials were donated by conscientious television stations. In other cases, collections literally had to be rescued from the dumpster.

In the mid-1980s, a core group of local news archivists began to meet on a regular basis within the context of annual meetings of the Film and Television Archives Advisory Committee (F/TAAC), a gathering of preservationists later reconstituted as the current Association of Moving Image Archivists (AMIA). The Visual Materials Section of the Society of American Archivists was also helpful in providing information and networking opportunities during those early years. The American Film Institute's National Center for Film and Video Preservation served the important role of coordinator and advisor for many of these efforts.

At about the same time, the National Historical Publications and Records Commission (NHPRC) began to recognize the historical value of television news collections, a recognition that proved crucial to the development of the new constituency. The first NHPRC grants to support these records were awarded in 1984 to the Mississippi Department of Archives and History and the University of Baltimore. Since then, additional NHPRC preservation and access grants have been made to the San Francisco State University Library, the Southwest Collection at Texas Tech University, the State Historical Society of Wisconsin, the Louis Wolfson II Media History Center, the Oregon Historical Society, the Southwest Film/Video Archives at Southern Methodist University, the State Historical Society of South Dakota, and the Vanderbilt Television News Archive.

In 1987, the NHPRC also supported the first national-level conference of television news archivists held in Madison, Wisconsin. Organized by the AFI National Center for Film and Video Preservation and hosted by the State Historical Society of Wisconsin, this meeting was attended by representatives from over 50 archives and organizations in the United States and Canada. The Madison conference was an important step forward in the development of the television news constituency. It generated a dialogue that interfaced established preservation practices long-utilized by the larger film archives with the special problems of local news collections. It was at this conference that the magnitude of issues and the range of concerns unique to newsfilm collections was first articulated. Initial recommendations and practical suggestions for the care and handling of newsfilm and video materials were made. In this way, the conference began the process of building a consensus on appropriate curatorial procedures.

Yet despite the strong early history of federal support for preserving television news in public archives, the criteria for judging these projects and awarding funds for them were made for the most part on a case-by-case basis. A written manual providing an overall perspective and recommended practices for the proper administration of these collections was still missing. The Louis Wolfson II Media History Center and the AFI National Center for Film and Video Preservation, with initial consultation from the Chicago Historical Society, prepared a grant proposal to produce such a manual. It was, again, the National Historical Publications and Records Commission that provided much of the support and the impetus for bringing about the completion of this manual. Accordingly, it is hoped that the information in the manual will not only assist archives in the day-to-day handling of their collections, but also assist all funding agencies in the evaluation of future grant applications received from these archives.

The purpose of *The Administration of Television Newsfilm and Videotape Collections: A Curatorial Manual* is to guide archivists and librarians – many of whom may have no previous experience with moving image collections – through all the questions and issues that arise in acquiring and managing television news materials. The administration of these collections has been likened to getting married or buying a house. One can observe others in those situations, but unless you've gone through it yourself, you don't know what you're in for. The administration of television news material is a complex process involving millions of feet of film or thousands of hours of videotape, as well as a challenging array of legal and financial concerns.

This publication is not meant to replace any of the other valuable technical and reference books on moving image preservation that are available for archivists to consult. Many of these are listed in the bibliography at the end of the manual. Instead, it is meant to serve as a primer and companion to those other works written from the perspective of locally-based film and television collections. It sets forth, for the first time, guidelines and criteria which cover the theory and practices necessary to process and administer these collections. It does so by drawing on the invaluable experiences and generous contributions of moving image archivists and other experts who have been pioneers in the field.

The manual addresses the needs of newly established or emerging archives as well as those that have held materials for some time. Some of the chapters may be useful immediately while others may help archives plan for the future. Individual institutional considerations, mission statements, budgets, and staff are factors that must be considered before moving image collections can be housed in any archive. For these reasons, the manual has been written not only for those who have accepted materials and are now ready to process their acquisitions and become involved in all facets of archival operations, but also for those who may be considering the offer of a donation of material from a television station. Indeed, it is hoped that the manual will help facilitate relations between archives and television stations – the producers of these collections – by giving both parties a better understanding of the work involved and the resources necessary for an archive to accept these materials.

The production of this manual has been a collaborative effort carried out in the spirit of cooperation that has been a hallmark of the moving image archive field since its beginning. Each chapter has been written by a different contributor, and the editors have tried wherever possible to let these contributors retain their own voices and styles. This approach provides a variety of valuable perspectives on a range of topics, rather than simply filtering all issues through the experiences of a single institution.

The manual also has been published with the realization that the field is rapidly evolving and new technologies and archival standards are continually being developed. Moving image archivists themselves have always played the most crucial role in keeping the field informed of new developments. With this in mind, the editors both hope and expect to receive from our many colleagues in the field any comments and suggestions for possible future editions of the manual.

TV As History: The Importance of Television Preservation

Dr. Barry L. Sherman and Dr. Louise M. Benjamin

College of Journalism and Mass Communication

The University of Georgia

From television's inception, the public has relied on the medium as a source of information and today more people watch the news than read newspapers. Though often considered ephemeral – old news – and not worth saving by the very stations that produced it, this chapter sets forth the importance of television and television preservation.

Dr. Barry L. Sherman is Director of the George Foster Peabody Awards program and Professor of Telecommunications at the Grady College of Journalism and Mass Communication, University of Georgia. He is the author of a number of books, including *Telecommunications Management: Broadcasting/Cable and The New Technologies*, Second Edition. (New York: McGraw-Hill, 1995), and *Broadcasting/Cable and Beyond: An Introduction to Modern Electronic Media*, Second Edition (New York: McGraw-Hill, 1990; 1993).

Dr. Louise Benjamin is the Associate Director of the Peabody Awards and an assistant professor in the Department of Telecommunications at the University of Georgia. Her published work has appeared in the *Journal of Broadcasting and Electronic Media, The Historical Journal of Film, Radio, and Television, Journalism Quarterly*, and *Free Speech Journal*. In a previous lifetime, she was a writer/producer/director for a middle market television station.

TV As History: The Importance of Television Preservation

Introduction

The effort mapped in the pages ahead — specifically the techniques of acquisition and preservation of images mainly produced for television — raises two significant and interrelated questions. The first, simply put, is why preserve television? What historical significance can be attached to television images? Is television deserving of the kind of effort documented in this manual?

In this brief essay, we begin with the rationale and justification for the field of television preservation. Like film, books and objects of art, we maintain television is an important (and often seminal) vessel for the transmission of history and cultural meaning.

The second question inherent in the effort to preserve television and related materials relates to their value as historic artifacts. What can we learn from television materials? How do they differ from other relics of human interaction, commerce and culture? Having made the case for the historic preservation of television, we inventory some of

A technician at the controls during a news broadcast in the 1950s.

the advantages and pitfalls of using television imagery to describe and explain historical, social and cultural events. We begin with the primary concern: why save TV?

Most historians embrace Santayana's oft-quoted maxim "those who cannot remember the past are condemned to repeat it." This is a primary impetus to preservation: to develop a collective memory, a record of our experience. For centuries, books, letters, and paintings, sculpture and other "plastic arts" have been painstakingly preserved, cataloged and made available to varying degrees, to succeeding generations.

How many contemporary historians, however, are willing to make the leap to the artifacts of the electronic age, specifically television? Indeed, the very terms used to describe a second look at television materials—"rerun" and "repeat"—seem pejorative and suggest diminishing value over time. The argument that broadcast programming, particularly the output of commercial television, is deserving of the preservation and curatorial efforts traditionally accorded print materials, is often a difficult one to make. It strikes at the nature of archives, libraries and museums, and their proper function in society. It dredges up long-standing debates about the relative importance of moving images and the spoken word when contrasted with the presumed preeminence of books. It kindles philosophical and ideological arguments around such topics as cultural bias, commercialism, "high" versus "low" culture and the amorphous issues of "impact" and "effects." And it presents perilous technical and personnel problems: from obsolete format standards to issues of signal degradation; from the need for curators and scholars to the essential expertise of engineers and editors.

Some years ago, a former advertising executive presented four arguments for the elimination of television.[1] Essentially, his main points were that the medium is by nature impersonal and separates people from actual experience; that its images stultify imag-

Television Among the Arts

TV Preservation: As Deserving as Film

Checking out equipment prior to broadcast.

ination and generally dim the brain; and that the medium is inherently biased against accuracy, subtlety, and difference.

Like many broadsides, there is a kernel of truth in each argument which makes the manifesto compelling. But it is precisely these reasons which make TV preservation essential. It's not "just television." With all its presumed faults, limitations, and biases, the TV image is above all, an invaluable and irreplaceable history of our life and times.

One good reason to uncover and preserve vintage television is to address the common misconception that film predated the development of television, and is therefore, in some measure superior. Because of the commercial success of the kinetoscope and nickelodeon parlor and the mass production of celluloid prints and negatives (plus paper prints made for copyright purposes), many films survive from the medium's early days. However, save for some rickety old equipment in the hands of a few collectors, the product of TV's progenitors has largely disappeared. As a result, there is a persistent celebration of the primacy of film over the television image; a sense that somehow celluloid is better, more artistic and more worthy of preservation than is television. This conceit is often reflected in the archival community as a predisposition to preserve film over videotape.

It is important to appreciate that experiments which led to the development of film and television were simultaneous. Both media sprung from common ancestry; the advent of photography and advances in physics, electronics and optics in the mid-19th Century. While one set of experimenters and entrepreneurs moved into motion pictures (e.g. Muybridge, Edison, Méliès, Porter) a second group of lesser known inventors was making attempts to transmit pictures through the air.

In 1882, an Englishman named William Lucas described an electronic television system.[2] By 1884, a primitive form of television had been successfully demonstrated in Germany by Paul Nipkow.[3] As film moved from sideshows and music halls, into prominence as a legitimate (if silent) art form, early forms of television were being developed and publicly demonstrated. By the 1920s, even as the first radio stations were being built, television receivers were being marketed by John Logie Baird in Great Britain, and by

Charles F. Jenkins in the United States.[4] And, at the same time *The Jazz Singer* was revolutionizing motion pictures (1927-28), television plays were being produced in Schenectady, New York, and in California, Mary Pickford's film *Taming of the Shrew* was already a staple of young hobbyist Philo T. Farnsworth's television broadcasts.[5]

The point is that the archival value of film has been demonstrated somewhat ironically, due to its photographic basis, its record of mass production and the happenstance of the tenacity of celluloid stock. Television, on the other hand, was conceived from the beginning as a live electronic medium (like radio), was not mass produced or distributed until the late 1940s and perhaps most importantly, lacked a sufficient means of preservation until a quarter-century after the emergence of sound movies.

The historical argument for television preservation is not that TV is inherently better or more artistic than film. Rather, the idea is that TV development was conterminous with film and radio. Like those media, TV history deserves to be uncovered, restored, preserved and retold.

Television newsfilm cameramen and still photographers, 1950s.

Of course, as historic artifacts, TV images are rife with limitations (as are written and oral histories, photographs and other primary sources). There are issues of gatekeeping and control: that an editorial decision was always made to point the camera in one direction, and not another; that one angle of view was chosen, and not another; that some images were kept in the edit room, while others were left out.

The Television Artifact

Unlike film preservation, in which the narrative form, from short subject to feature-length, presents an ideal preservation and restoration goal (the restored print, the original release, the director's cut, and so on), TV archives range from whole programs, to individual stories or "packages," to silent "B-rolls," to raw footage. Yet it is precisely this diversity which is the compelling force for preservation. Many of the medium's inherent biases have been imposed on the archival matter: especially the pressures of deadline and broadcast schedule. By preserving as much original material as possible,

(Right) WTVJ reporter on assignment in Havana.

(Far right) Sorting through a typical donation of television newsfilm materials.

including outtakes, a more comprehensive historical record is now available for historians and filmmakers to follow.

First Witnesses to History

Filmmaker Jim DeVinney, whose work with archival television materials can be seen in *Eyes on the Prize* and *The Kennedys*, spoke eloquently on this point to an audience of TV news producers and reporters at the Wolfson Media History Center's Awards Program ceremonies in Miami:

> You are...first witnesses to history. I go back and I look at the work that reporters like you, and not just reporters...the camera crews and the sound people and the editors and the news directors...I do the job that historians are responsible for. We make connections. We try to connect what you have done in the past with how you have looked at the truth, re-examined that truth, tried to update that truth in light of subsequent revelations.[6]

The Commercial Nature of Television

One reason for a persistent bias against television preservation has been the medium's commercial nature. Somehow television programming has been deemed unworthy since its basic function, at least at the time of message creation, was simply to keep audiences attentive for commercial breaks.

While this assertion is basically true, the same case can also be made against film and other forms of popular entertainment, from comics to dime-store novels. Advertising has long been the driving force behind public mass communication. In fact, magazines and newspapers have been rife with ads since their introduction. At the same time, they have been dutifully acquired, inventoried, cataloged, copied and preserved by libraries and historical societies as an invaluable record of the culture and time in which they were produced. In a very real sense, television newscasts and documentaries have become the "hometown newspapers" of the mid-twentieth century and beyond. As such, these moving images deserve our attention and effort.

Television
equipment from
the 1950s.

Now that we've made the case for the historic preservation of television and related materials, we turn to the second set of salient questions. What kind of history is television? In other words how good is the evidence culled from the small screen as a primary resource for the study of history and culture?

Media collections comprise only one of numerous primary sources available to historians, students of popular culture, and television and film producers looking for materials documenting the past to be used in new creations. Others include documents of record, such as government sources and business records; family and personal resources; reference works; literary and artistic sources; and oral histories. Each brings rewards and problems to scholars and producers. Use of media collections, visual and aural artifacts developed and presented over popular media such as radio, television and the cinema, can enrich the understanding of the past.

To illustrate this point, think of ways to expose college students to the events of the McCarthy era. One exercise made possible through media preservation is to have them read accounts of confrontations between Joseph McCarthy and Edward R. Murrow on *See It Now*. Then, one can play tapes of the actual broadcasts. The tapes will undoubtedly have more impact than the printed word. Emotion conveyed by both Murrow and McCarthy in delivery, nuance and inflection gives students insight and understanding far richer than that communicated by written word alone.

In the same fashion, using media collections can therefore enhance research, current productions, and understanding of the past. But difficulties can arise in using these collections to present elements of yesterday.

The Perils and Pitfalls of Television as History

First, in utilizing television collections, one has to recognize a seemingly obvious point — a media artifact is a source for the period in which it was produced, not for the period about which it is produced or purporting to represent. Take, for example, recent television programs such as *Dr. Quinn Medicine Woman* or *The Young Riders*. Such programs will often tell more about contemporary attitudes towards gender roles than

A Point in Time

7

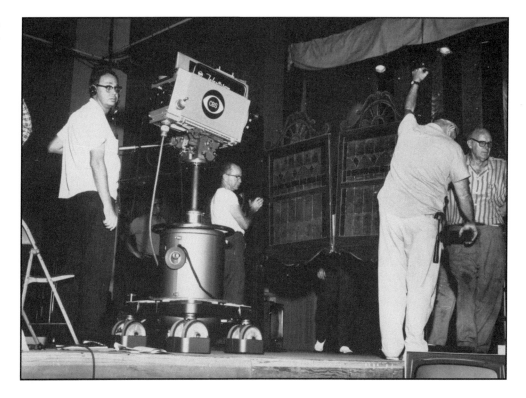

On the studio set in
the 1950s.

about the attitudes and beliefs of the nineteenth-century American West. Westerns of the late 1950s such as *Cheyenne* or *Rawhide* will tell more about America in the height of the Cold War than about the American West. Entertainment shows reflect concerns of their times.

So, too, programs of news and other information shows also reflect the concerns of their times and the technology then available to record those times. When they are used, care must be taken to recognize both technological developments and the context in which the artifact was produced.

Thus, television collections provide imperfect and often only fragmentary evidence. Other materials are needed to supplement and complete the picture drawn. Think again of the McCarthy/Murrow confrontation. Powerful by themselves, these programs are only fragments of the Red Scare and McCarthyism that existed after World War II. Print materials and other artifacts augment and enhance the aural and visual record present in television collections.

The Need for Time and Immersion in the Materials

A third concern of using television collections is the time-consuming nature of this research. One must first watch or listen to program material to understand its basic structure before delving into deeper questions. Researchers and producers must temporarily set aside these specific questions to address only the most simple questions: How is the program organized? What are its major points, briefly summarized? Beginning with this overview, researchers and producers are less likely to take a part of the program out of context, amplifying its importance at the expense of the rest of the program or historical accuracy.

The Grammar of Production

In establishing an overall understanding, a program's significance often depends upon the circumstances in which it was made, so scholars, researchers and documentarians must approach programs with production values and producers' expectations in mind.

For example, was the program recorded in segments and edited together, or was it recorded "live" — that is, recorded in studio without stopping tape or as the program was sent out over the air? Simple program production techniques must be understood to construct and reconstruct program context.

This context may also be established in part by asking what the program might have presented but did not. In identifying the wide range of alternatives in any situation, researchers and producers gain insight into why one presentation method was chosen over another. In determining these alternatives, it is often necessary to analyze a film or tape, and that requires breaking down the visual artifact into sequences, and sometimes scenes and shots. One must recognize the different types of shots; the use of different lenses; comprehend the grammar of dissolves, fades, and cuts; and be conversant in the ways sound tracks are dubbed and music or sound effects deployed.

Program Purpose and Intended Audience

Two other elements researchers and producers must establish in using television collections are the original purpose and intended audiences of the programs studied. What were the overt purposes of the show — to educate, to entertain, to inform? Who were its intended audiences? How did they and unintended audiences perceive the production? What reaction did they have to the program? Was this reaction expected? Did producers achieve their purported purpose? Researching such audience and program effect questions adds to the overall analyzation of the program's impact.

Publication and Copyright

In using audio-visual material as basic pieces of evidence, researchers and producers will want to play or present portions of these materials to illustrate or exemplify whatever critique they are advancing. With today's CD-ROM technology researchers can imbed text with visual and aural material to augment arguments, analysis, and interpretations. That capability leads to two major, interrelated problems — publication and copyright.

For the traditional historian, scholarly journals generally do not incorporate moving visual or aural materials as examples. Journals do not employ the computer technology that could integrate print and non-traditional evidence for distribution to readers. Thus, scholars will find themselves using a thousand words to describe one sequence, shot, or the interplay of pictures and music in their interpretations. Even if editors can use these non-traditional materials in their publications, they will hesitate because of potential copyright problems.

Under current copyright laws, researchers and producers can use copyrighted materials under "fair use" provisions. But just what constitutes "fair use" for using non-print materials still needs to be defined, and no editor, scholar or documentarian wants to be the test case. Therefore, before "publication" researchers and producers must track down copyright permissions for visual or aural materials. As we will see, many television collections do not hold copyright; they are simply repositories for artifacts. The task of obtaining copyright permission is compounded by the fact that many businesses may no longer exist — they could have gone out of business or been bought out by another company.

Sometimes royalties or other conditions for use are attached to obtaining copyright or even permission to use collections. Research fees can be assessed to use the collection, and researchers must follow all archive regulations. At times, donors attach conditions to their collections that limit accessibility or use.

Ralph Renick of WTVJ-Miami conducting an interview in the 1950s.

The Last Word   Yet preserving television artifacts is critical. Such collections enhance scholarship, education and production. Their use augments our understanding of the past, and provides critical visual evidence of our life and times for future generations of filmmakers and scholars.

Footnotes   1. Jerry Mander, *Four Arguments for the Elimination of Television*. New York: William Morrow, 1978.

2. See Joseph H. Udelson, *The Great Television Race*. Tuscaloosa: University of Alabama Press, 1982, p. 16.

3. Erik Barnouw, *Tube of Plenty*. New York: Oxford, 1974, p. 5.

4. See David T. Macfarland, "Television: The Whirling Beginning," in Lawrence W. Lichty and Malachi C. Topping, *American Broadcasting*. New York: Hastings House, 1975, pp. 46-52.

5. Barnouw, op. cit., pp. 60-78.

6. James A. DeVinney, Keynote address, Louis Wolfson II Media History Center Awards, Miami, Florida, 1991.

2

A History of Television
Newsgathering Formats

Alan Lewis

National Archives and Records Administration

This chapter surveys the history of television and television newsgathering formats and outlines the components of television newscasts. From 16mm film through television news' transition to videotape through recent video formats, it provides perspectives on the make-up and components of moving image collections and their contents.

Alan Lewis began his professional television career in program production and administration with WEDU-TV, Tampa (ten years), and PBS in Washington (ten years) where he "backed into" the media archives profession. CBS News was his next venue (four years) where he headed the Film and Videotape Archives. He then began his own independent media preservation consulting business (four years) until the National Archives beckoned him to return to Washington as its Supervisory Audiovisual Specialist.

A History of Television Newsgathering Formats

Some Basics   Modern television didn't spring up overnight from the mind and hands of a single fertile-brained inventor. It evolved from nineteenth and early twentieth-century developments in physics, electronics, optics, and photography. Likewise, within the overall field of television, its news coverage owes much of its form and substance to its forebears: print journalism, illustrated journalism (principally photo journalism), the motion picture and radio news broadcasting.

Many early U.S. commercial television stations were owned by newspapers which already owned radio stations. The flow of news orientation from the parent company to the broadcasting outlet(s) was a natural evolution, especially when coupled with the Federal legislation that controlled their broadcasting licenses and mandated in the Communications Act of 1934 that stations operate "...in the public interest, convenience and necessity." This tie to print journalism provided an intellectual base and brought with it a newsgathering structure of syndicated sources, assignment editors, writers,

Newsfilm and still cameras covering a rocket launching in 1958.

etc., a whole institutional structure that was used to providing daily news coverage on deadlines to meet press runs and on-street sales.

From illustrated journalism came something of the idea of a news picture being worth a thousand words; of showing people, places and things; the newsmaking personalities, the locales and the events that were newsworthy. It put the eye of the beholder into the hands of the sketch artist or the still photographer, seeing events as they happened (or sometimes as they might have happened or perhaps even as they were restaged to happen!). This concept of what makes something visually newsworthy is one that has been discussed at great lengths.

From the motion picture, television news inherited a part of its initial technology, using a film camera to get out of the television studio, as well as some of the visual characteristics and style of film, but with a limited size and postage stamp shaped screen. There were also concepts of shot selection (wide establishing shot, close-ups, reverse angles, etc.), editing, pacing to sustain interest, natural sound as well as added sound,

Technicians in the WTVJ remote truck, circa 1960s.

etc. Inherited, too, were bulky cameras and sound equipment with their technical dependence on lighting, film sensitivity (speed), camera positioning, camera movement and microphone placement.

Television newsgathering is a direct descendent of the theatrical newsreel. Indeed, early television newsfilm might very well have been shot on 16mm film by the very same people who were also filming in 35mm for the newsreel companies.

Finally, from radio news broadcasting came the sense of personal immediacy, of instant coverage of evolving events; of airtime deadlines and tight schedules; of story length criticality and a relationship to commercial inserts; of live, on-the-spot coverage; etc. It also brought some of its on-the-air talent, taking them out of a face-less radio studio into the visual TV setting. Radio news broadcasting also brought with it the relationship of national and regional networks and local broadcasting outlets.

Some TV History

Most textbooks credit the beginning of modern television broadcasting in the U.S. to an event that was a news story: the introduction of commercial television at the RCA Pavilion at the 1939 World's Fair in New York. The texts then relate that development of the medium was forestalled by U.S. entry into World War II and then further delayed until 1948 by the large number of players who sought to get into the new medium and flooded the airwaves with competing broadcasting signals.

It thus can be argued that "real" television began in the U.S. following the end of the Federal Communications Commission's "television freeze" in 1948. The "freeze" was a period following World War II when the electronics industry moved from military to consumer production and the television industry moved from an over-the-air novelty of the late 1930s to a full blown industry.

The first national television entities were largely new divisions created within the radio broadcasting networks. At the local level, it was independent radio stations and newspapers that already owned radio stations that led the way into television broadcasting. Part and parcel of the program services of these national and local entities was news and public affairs. Whether this non-entertainment programming was done to build viewership (viewers = advertising revenue = profits) or because the FCC required stations to deal with matters of public interest can be debated, but the record is clear that in the late 1940s the fledgling television industry at all levels got into news and public affairs broadcasting.

The terms "news broadcasting" and "public affairs broadcasting" are sometimes confused with one another. They are really somewhat different entities. For convenience, we might define them as follows:

• News broadcasts are programs or segments of programs dealing with the events of the day (literally) in brief form and containing stories that rapidly go stale if not used immediately. A current TV station's or network's evening news broadcast typifies this

14

type of programming. "Hard news" is a term often used to describe this type of programming. From these news broadcasts, it is usually the snippets of film that were made to show the people, places and things of the day that have survived the rigors of time and economics to become the stuff of the television newsfilm archive.

•   Public affairs broadcasts tend to be weekly rather than daily programs, are often more "talking heads" in one-on-one interview or panel discussions settings, etc. rather than visualized stories. All too often they are not seen in the prime viewing hours. The various local and national Sunday morning talk shows are public affairs programs, not news broadcasts.

The fact that television journalists often are seen on both types of programs adds to the confusion. For all practical purposes, this manual deals with news broadcasts and not public affairs programs because the latter typically used little if any newsfilm.

What's in a TV Newscast?

A typical news broadcast, whether it's from years gone by or even today's local station news, contains a number of elements that need to be identified. This identification allows the materials that survive to go into an archive for preservation and be understood in its context. In some chronological order as they might be seen on their air, the broadcasts include:

• Teasers: brief spots featuring station news personalities and/or graphics promoting featured events on an upcoming news broadcast.

• Opening credits: Graphics, montages, etc. that serve to introduce the news program. They are often uptempo to set a tone of excitement and anticipation.

• Commercials and/or "non-commercials" (public service announcements, also called "PSAs"): Messages that were used to sell products or services or support worthy causes in the community, region or nation.

• News anchor persons or newscaster (a radio term): The studio host or anchor person of the program. The role of the anchor is to link all of the news program elements together, doing "intros" and "outros" for each story and leading into commercials and PSAs. Some stations used multiple anchors, giving rise to the term "two-headed newscast."

• Reporters: The field newspersons who cover stories, often working with a field producer and a field camera crew.

• Roll-ins: The filmed story elements that are used to illustrate a verbal descrip-

16

tion of a story. The final version of a roll-in is an air cut and the terms are often used interchangeably.

• Closing credits: Graphics, montages or other visual devices used to close a program, often listing the names of persons involved in the broadcast. Air credit is most often given only to persons or production positions for whom credits are required by a labor or personal contract.

• Spot promos: Another element that might be found from time to time are promotional announcements supporting the stations news coverage in general or specific programs. While not an integral part of a newscast and its internal elements, they are a part of the news image of the station and are worthy of accessioning, describing and preserving.

Some Technical Matters - Film

Television newsgathering might be defined as the ability of a television news entity to get out of the TV production studio with transportable equipment to capture the people, places and things that were thought to be newsworthy. This transportable equipment at the beginning of the television news era ranged from live TV mobile production units, typically mounted in trucks ranging from twenty to forty feet long to much more portable, "man-carried" film cameras. Since magnetic tape recording was not yet developed in the 1940s, film was the recording medium of the period.

Television newsgathering was initially based on the equipment available at the time. The theatrical newsreel used 35mm cameras, both silent and equipped with sound recorders, because it was the film gauge that was the standard of the theater industry. Only 35mm film provided the image quality that was suitable for projection on the screens of the period. The other common film gauge of the period, 16mm, was considered suitable for small screen uses like school audiovisual projection. Another, 8mm film, was a home hobbyists format.

This mobile television unit cruised the streets of Miami.

Exterior view of the WTVJ remote truck.

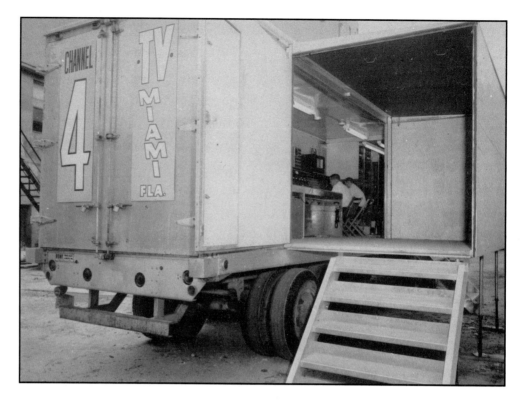

Silent and sound 35mm cameras were readily available but they were generally big, heavy and dependent on reliable line or generator power although some battery equipment was available. Power inverters running off auto batteries also could be used.

The cameras required mounts, usually tripods, and were equipped with multiple lenses mounted in a revolving turret on the front of the camera which offered a selection of fixed focal length lenses, each producing a different field of view. The variable focal length lens, the zoomar (zoom), had not yet been developed.

Filming in 35mm sound required at least a two person crew for most set-ups. On the other hand, 16mm film equipment was even more readily available and had virtues that far outweighed 35mm film when applied to television news use:

•   16mm film was easily accepted by television news producers because its image was suitable for the small home TV screen of the period.

•   The equipment was cheaper to purchase including cameras, editing equipment and the devices needed to project film into the TV system (a "film chain").

•   Raw film was considerably cheaper to purchase than 35mm film.

•   The smaller gauge film was cheaper to process than 35mm film.

•   Film cores, reels, cans and storage shelving were considerably less expensive for 16mm film.

•   Processing equipment could be installed in a TV station, which meant a station did not have to send its material out to a commercial film lab. Indeed, most TV stations set-up their film labs as separate profit centers and sought outside film processing contracts.

•   16mm equipment was more compact and was thus easier to transport, setup and use.

•   Film chains, the devices that included one or more film projectors mated to a TV pick-up camera, were equipped with polarity reversing circuitry that enabled negative film to be shot in the field, processed, edited quickly and then projected on TV using polarity reversing to electronically create a positive image.

•   Later, when color television arrived on the scene, color reversal film stocks were available that produced a positive image from the same strip of film that had passed through the camera and was broadcast-ready after a one-step development process.

•   And, finally, 35mm newsreel cameramen shooting for theatrical newsreels could also piggyback a 16mm camera along and do some filming for TV news with the smaller equipment at the same time.

For all of these reasons, 35mm film was never a serious contender for TV news coverage. Among many kinds of 16mm cameras used for news production, a few stand out: the Bell and Howell DR70, a spring-wound silent camera with 100' roll film capacity; the Bolex H-16, another spring motor device that had some features unavailable on the B&H; the Auricon Cinevoice and Pro models, electrically driven sound cameras, and the Cinema Products CP-16, a magazine-loaded sound camera often mounted on a shoulder brace rather than a tripod for greater portability. Many were equipped with turrets mounting a selection of lenses to provide the wide shot, medium and close-up shots associated with visual story-telling process. In later years, the variable focal length lens was introduced and came down in price to the point that cameras with lens turrets became obsolete. The zoom lens added a new flexibility to the technology and a new filming technique, the zoom shot.

Getting to the story.

Sixteen millimeter film, first using black-and-white film stock and later switching to color as the TV networks and local stations "colorized," was the standard for television newsgathering beginning in the 1940s until it was replaced by a different technology in the 1970s. The film, once exposed and processed, could not be reused to capture other images and the result became a massive amount of material, some used on the air, some not. This gave rise to TV news department film libraries and to them adopting and adapting motion picture and newsreels terms to describe collections. In the TV news context, there are some terms to be remembered:

•   Air cut: The final edited version of a filmed (later videotaped) news story as seen on the air. Air cuts might be intended to be narrated by a studio-based reporter or anchor person, could have some sound, perhaps what has come to be known as a "sound bite" or be a full sound-on-film story. It is these air cuts that have most often survived to become part of newsfilm archives. Air cuts are sometimes called roll-ins.

•   Trims: These are unused portions of scenes that appeared in the final air cut. In essence, these are the bits and pieces of non-critical story elements that were removed

Each of these 3/4-inch cut story tapes contains 30-50 individual news stories.

from the story to "tighten" it, due to time constraints, journalistic clarity or the quality of the photography.

If you're lucky, the tapes come with a log or rundown for identification.

•　　　Outtakes: Scenes that were filmed (or videotaped) as a part of a story but not used at all in the final air cut.

•　　　Newsgathering: In the context of this manual, the going into the field with television news production tools, in this case film (later videotape cameras and recorders), to record events as they happen or scenes that followed up on an event or activity.

•　　　Film-in-the-field: The act of doing news production outside the confines of a television studio on motion picture film stock.

•　　　Videotape-in-the-field: The act of doing news production outside the confines of a television studio on magnetic videotape stock.

•　　　Standuppers: Segments in which a reporter in the field stands before the camera and tells a story. Often a standupper is done following the filming of a story to give the film of an event or activity a journalistic context. Having the reporter do a stand-upper in the field rather than having the studio anchorperson do it gives the story the feeling of validity, excitement and the sense that the news broadcast is doing what the viewer would have done if s/he were at the site.

•　　　Roll-in: A prepared visual segment illustrating a story. They are used with standuppers or studio anchorperson telling a story.

By the 1970s, technological advances in video recording technology and in the design and manufacture of relatively small and lightweight cameras made videotape-in-the field a feasible alternative to film-in-the-field. By the mid-1970s, the television newsfilm era had come to an end to be replaced by magnetic videotape, chiefly the Sony-developed 3/4-inch U-matic videocassette format. With the decline of film in TV stations, something of a "golden age" of moving image history came to an end. Those 30 years were "golden" because many of the images which have survived did so because the film wasn't reusable. Videotapes are reusable and that recyclability means that their potentially historic images are lost forever.

Non-Station Newsfilm in Collections

In the very earliest years of local station news broadcasting, before stations were tied into their networks by cable or microwave links, national and international stories were often prepared by the networks or by commercial syndicators, duplicated in quantity and shipped to local affiliates for inclusion in their local broadcasts. It is therefore very likely that archive staff members will find network or independently syndicated non-local stories intermixed with local material.

This national-to-local distribution of stories continues under different technological arrangements in the current era when a local station's image in its community is shaped by its news operation. Thus local news programs are often well sprinkled with regional, national and international stories acquired by the station from its own remotely located bureaus, fed to it by regional newsgathering consortia or by the national network news department with which it is affiliated.

Some Technical Matters - Videotape

Magnetic recording had a long developmental history and reached a level of commercial acceptability for audio recording in Germany during World War II. It reached the TV industry in the 1950s when Ampex Corporation developed the first practical system for recording television signals. The system used tape moving at 15 inches per second past a revolving wheel with four magnetic heads that rotated at right angles to the tape path. The recording medium was two-inch wide flexible tape developed by 3M Company

A kinescope of the *Kate Smith Show* (second from the bottom) among the local television kinescopes at the Wolfson Center.

ON THE RECORD (KINESCOPE)

HURRICANE AUDREY - TIDAL WAVE (KINESCOPE)

TVK 016   H-9 KITTYHAWK

Public Affairs   HURRICANE - TIDAL WAVE (KINE)

H-17 TOUCHING THE UNKNOWN (KINE, 1956) 2/13/91

TVK 021   T-4 THIS IS RUSSIA (KINESCOPE)

TVK 022   T-5 THIS IS RUSSIA (KINESCOPE)

TVK 024   NBC KINESCOPE: KATE SMITH SHOW

TVK 025   H-30. KNOW YOUR CONSTITUTION (KINE).

specifically for the purpose. The format was technically known as two-inch quadruplex recording ("2-inch quad") and was the standard of the broadcasting industry for high quality production and editing purposes from 1956 until the early 1980s.

WTVJ cameramen in the studio.

The two-inch quad format machine was expensive, large, heavy and basically transportable only by truck. The equipment had to be coupled to the bulky cameras and support gear of the period and never was a serious contender for spot news gathering except in planned major events that allowed these large vehicle-mounted television production systems to be placed in position hours if not days in advance of the event or story.

Although smaller formats were quickly developed for non-broadcast uses in the late 1950s and 1960s, the formats did not meet the FCC's requirements for broadcast uses. Producers' needs for a compact device that produced broadcast quality images and distributors' needs for interchangeability between machines of the same type were finally met by the mid-1970s through the parallel developments of the 3/4-inch U-matic videocassette format and of the time base error corrector, a "black box" which when combined with the U-matic (and other) machines created a small format video system that could replace "film-in-the-field."

An older but still in use 3/4-inch U-matic deck.

With the advent of a small videotape format that was acceptable for broadcast purposes, the concept of newsgathering in the field changed. Although video camera/recorder units for field use were considerably more expensive than film cameras, a video unit was complete and produced an "edit ready" news recording. Coupled to this was the development of compact microwave transmitters and receivers that enabled a field crew to produce in the field and either record a story on-site or transmit it back to the news headquarters where it could go on-the-air live or be recorded for later review, editing and then broadcast. Small format video with its microwave component thus eliminated the need for couriers to take the raw material back to the TV station's film laboratory and eliminated time consuming and expensive chemical processing.

The advantages of 3/4-inch U-matic videotape included:

•   Production speed: because no chemical processing was needed, images were ready to edit or broadcast as soon as the tape could be delivered to the studio, rewound and cued.

3/4-inch U-matic editing system.

- The images were in color.

- Editing is a faster electronic process, the original tape is not physically cut.

- Blank videocassettes are inexpensive when compared to film stock on a cost-per-minute minute basis. This excludes the start-up costs to equip a field news crew with videotape gear and a supporting editing room at the station's news department, however.

Erasable videotape, unlike "one-shot" film, is a completely different technology with strengths undreamed of in the newsfilm era. It has a downside though; its recyclability

Videotape can be erased and reused.

which has spelled the end to the volume of news images that survived the newsfilm production process and, years later, have become the basis of television news archives.

By the 1980s, the 3/4-inch U-matic videocassette had been replaced for newsgathering-in-the-field by the single unit "camcorder," a device that combines into a single shoulder balanced unit the optical and electronic visual pick-up devices, a microphone, and the tape transport/recording system. Power for the unit is supplied by onboard recharge-able batteries or from a belt battery pack worn by the cameraperson. There are a number of professional camcorder technical formats, almost all incompatible with one another, mostly using 1/2-inch videotape in different sized cassettes. They include the formats known as Betacam (and an upgraded Betacam SP); MII; and S/VHS (Super Video Home System), an upgraded version of the ubiquitous 1/2-inch home VCR system. Following closely on the heels of those formats is Hi8, an 8mm wide videotape-in-cassette which developed from the Video8 home system. A Hi8 cassette is slightly larger than an audio cassette.

Video formats used at television stations over the years eventually make their way into archives.

The strength of this entire videotape-in-the-field technology lies in the ability of news producers to record material in the field unobtrusively and with it, rapidly route the material to a broadcast or satellite transmission point for eventual consumption by the news audience.

Videotape-in-the field does have some weaknesses, both from a production and certain-ly from an archival point of view:

• Camera crews shoot far more footage than their film counterparts did in previous years, making more and more non-essential tape available to the news editor and, perhaps ultimately, to the archivist for appraisal.

• Contrary to the above, the erasability of videotape coupled to tight budgets means less and less material survives to become available for archival appraisal and preservation.

•   The rapidly changing video formats mean that archives must also become "machine museums," maintaining equipment, spare parts, manuals and trained technicians to keep the equipment in operating condition for playing back those tapes in its possession for description, preservation and reference purposes.

•   The technological aspects aside, it is unclear whether videotape has better long term keeping qualities than did the film it replaced. Newsfilm, especially when stations turned to color film and added magnetic stripe sound recording, seems to be highly subject not only to color dye fading but also to the vinegar syndrome, a chemical decomposition in which the acetate film base begins to revert to its acetic acid origins.

Returning to two-inch quadruplex videotape, it was replaced in high quality production uses by a completely different system, one-inch Type C recording. One-inch uses a narrower gauge tape with a different recording system and has distinct advantages over its predecessor in its technical quality, editability, compactness and economics.

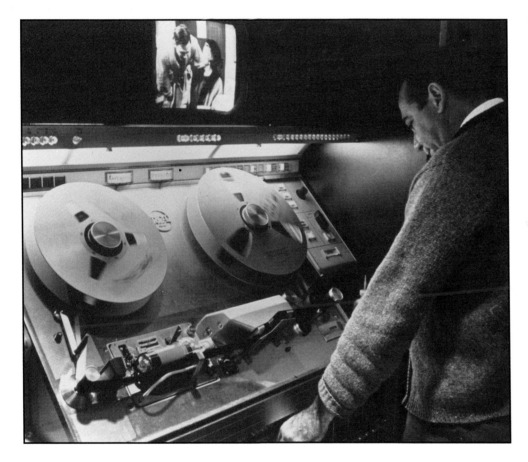

The two-inch quadraplex format, once the standard of television stations.

One-inch Type C is itself giving way to digital formats using even narrower tape in self-contained cassettes: D-1, an all digitalized system; D-2, a digital recording system that is "plug-compatible" with existing analog production and editing equipment and others. As this chapter is written, there are proposed D-3, D-4 and D-5 systems either recognized as being in production or in development. They all tend to be billed by their proponents as being of high quality; of closing the gap between field quality and studio quality; of being less costly initially and in tape stock over the life expectancy of the format; of having greater flexiblity in various uses; etc.

In short, the formats continuously change, get smaller, better and use thinner tape. All of this change is the curse of the television newstape archivist.

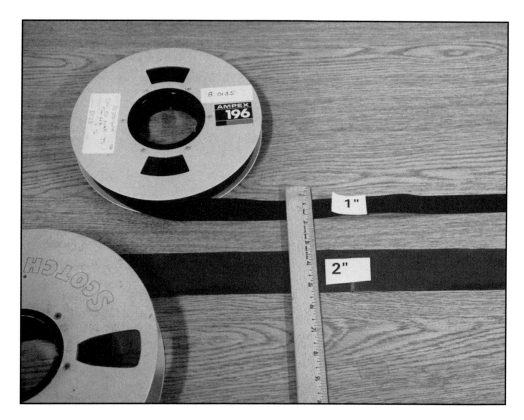

Open reel one-inch and two-inch video formats.

A Motion Media Newsgathering Technological Timeline

Noting that newsgathering began with film cameras and evolved to videotape, a chronology might be useful at this point:

The beginnings of the motion media industry to the 1950s:

• 35mm newsreel film for theatrical distribution

1950s to the 1960s:

• 35mm continues in theatrical newsreel use while 16mm black-and-white negative and reversal film come into wide use in television news coverage.

Mid-1960s to mid-1970s:

• 16mm black-and-white film phases out, replaced by 16mm color reversal film as the TV industry goes to color broadcasting.

Mid-1970s to mid-1980s:

• 3/4-inch U-matic videocassette format almost universally accepted. More compact production recorders developed to use twenty-minute long videocassettes.

Mid-1980s to mid-1990s:

• Smaller format videotape cassettes gain wide acceptance, especially Hi8, Betacam and Betacam SP.

1990s-onward:

• Wider use of Hi8, Betacam SP and, increasingly, digital formats.

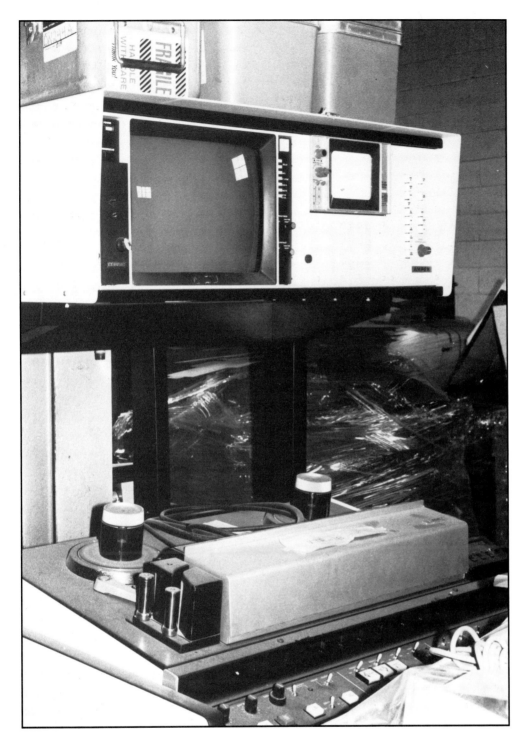

Operational two-inch equipment is getting harder to find, as are the technicians who can operate it.

In any particular news gathering organization, the dates of transition from one technology to another varied due to individual economic conditions, special financial arrangements made between manufacturers and users, the entity's production requirements, the inertia of sticking to old ways, the training of personnel, etc. There was also an overlap period during which the older technology and the personnel skilled in its use were being phased out and the newer technology and personnel were being phased in.

Since the 1980s, with the advent of readily available satellite time and changes in corporate structure at the national networks (and therefore in their news divisions), the structure of event coverage has changed. The division of labor that once existed in which local stations covered local events and national news organizations covered regional,

What Does the Future Hold?

national and international events has become a thing of the past. More than ever before, and on an increasing basis, "local" news will become more and more a mix of local, regional, national and international news. The production of local segments, those segments that are of value to local historical agencies and archives, will be intermixed with more and more acquired footage from local amateurs and from syndicated sources. The task of the local television news repository will thus become more difficult in pinning down the source of material and its local value.

If present trends continue, equipment will become smaller and with this miniaturization, the recording medium, whether magnetic tape or disks, laser devices, etc., will decrease in size and increase in complexity and sophistication. Preservation requirements for the material may become more complex because of tighter tolerances used in the manufacture of the recording systems and the recording media. It seems that the need for "machine museums" will be even greater than in the past as more and more formats come on line.

The gap between professional and amateur quality equipment, already made smaller by the use of the time base error corrector, will lessen and more and more players will enter the local news production field, covering events for various broadcast and non-broadcast distribution entities.

This writer also thinks that more and more use will be made of moving image archival material. Academic institutions will recognize that their students are becoming more and more "visual" and scholarly research and publication will make more use of the visual media, including the production of visual theses and dissertations. Likewise, the production industry that supports distribution entities with programs will make more and more use of existing material in some form because it is cheaper to produce continuing series by doing "compilation films" rather than in creating wholly new productions.

3

Appraisal of Collections

Ernest J. Dick

"Are we going to accept this collection?" is the question all moving image archives have asked – at least once. Though many institutions may ask the question more frequently, each time it's posed archives must consider the consequences of that decision. This chapter reviews the criteria that may help provide the answer.

Ernest J. Dick is currently a Consulting Archivist based in Granville Ferry, Nova Scotia. He was most recently Corporate Archivist for the Canadian Broadcasting Corporation, coordinating archival policy throughout the Corporation. He began his archival career as a sound archivist with the National Archives of Canada in 1974, joining the CBC in 1989. He has been a founding member of the Association of Canadian Archivists, the Association for the Study of Canadian Radio and Television, and the Association of Moving Image Archivists, where he was a past president. He has written widely on sound and moving image archives and prepared exhibitions on Canadian film, radio, and television.

Appraisal of
Collections

**Why Do an
Appraisal?**
Television news collections have curious and diverse ways of coming to archives. Urgent last-minute rescue calls to the archive from TV stations warning of massive and immediate disposal are more common than carefully negotiated and scheduled transfers. Television news collections can consume more time and resources in bringing them into an archive than ever imagined. Making television news collections accessible can be fraught with technical, legal and logistical questions that archives have often not dealt with previously.

Television is our own popular culture and therefore, we don't quite know what to make of it yet in archives. Television is exceedingly ephemeral, both figuratively and literally, and therefore quite unlike most of what archives hold. It generates great quantities of information and programming that daunts the most rigorous of archival philosophies.

Therefore archives have to take that simple question "are we going to accept this collection?" very seriously. Appraisal of television is a difficult theoretical and philosophical exercise with enormous practical implications.

Television is still a relatively new communications medium which continues to evolve rapidly, both technologically and in program formats. Technical limitations and possibilities, formats and media, staff, and programming concepts have all undergone radical changes in the fifty years of the evolution of television. Similarly, the orientation and nature of the television news collections has evolved and continues to change.

News collections can, therefore, be considered highly important to ongoing programming one day and be abandoned the next by the station because of technological, staff or programming changes. Archives will rarely be considered while the television news libraries/collections are being utilized. But then, archives may be called upon to respond very quickly when collections are being threatened. Appraisal, therefore, becomes an urgent art and archives may respond hastily before all the appropriate questions are asked and answered.

Television news collections can pose challenges that conventional archives have not faced before. These collections are invariably voluminous, in chaotic order, and moreover require specialized equipment to "read" or play-back the collection. Television news does not lend itself to easy or natural selection within the collection. News collections may contain considerable duplication and can include banal and poorly shot footage. Television news collections may not be what they appear to be, in that past

Appraisal is not an easy matter; often we must consider video formats for which we don't have playback equipment. . .

. . .or newsfilm with no documentation.

usage and extensive editing may have removed the most useful and frequently-referred-to portions over the years. Extensive, if also cryptic and idiosyncratic, indexes and finding aids may have once been created for these collections but now may be almost impossible to understand, let alone reconstitute. Television news collections are not easy to work with.

Television news collections document relatively recent events that may not otherwise be venerable enough for archival consideration. It can document events, locations and

personalities powerfully and eloquently and is widely held to be the dominant source of information for citizens since the mid-twentieth century. Therefore archives are coming to realize that they must do something with television. What archives should do, however, is not at all clear or self-evident.

Television news collections offer commercial or research opportunities that can be both enticing and frustrating. Television news collections offer the promise of bringing other archival collections up to date and once preserved, they guarantee users access to television. They appear to banish forever the stereotypical and cliched image of archives as dusty and irrelevant. Entering the pressures of contemporary communications media, however, can be a double-edged sword. The demands of television producers in using archives can often be more insistent and urgent than those of conventional researchers.

The challenges and opportunities of television news collections make archival appraisal problematic. Institutions raise the importance of appraisal because the resource implications of television news collections are greater than most conventional archival collections. The urgency of the appraisal of television news only exacerbate the difficulties of these questions.

34

Archival appraisal also involves evaluating the archive's mandate and determining whether television news complements the institutional mission. A new archival medium and format such as television news may well challenge and confound an institution's mandate. This is perfectly natural and healthy. If archives are to be dynamic and responsive organizations their appraisal criteria will naturally evolve over time. This chapter will outline the factors to consider for television news in that evolution of an archive.

The communications context within which a television station existed first needs to be understood and appraised before the collection can be considered. When the television station is the single, or predominant, communications medium in an area then its television news collection will obviously be of greater import in reflecting and shaping the community's issues.

A useful way to think about television news is to compare it with the research potential of newspapers where we have had much longer experience. Any comparison of the

Appraisal of the Television Station

3/4-inch tapes prior to inventory.

number of readers/viewers and editorial resources between newspapers and television simply and effectively demonstrates the research potential of television.

Also, an advisory committee of historians and broadcasters may be helpful in appraising the communications context of television for an archive. Such experts will invariably be delighted to serve on such committees and their representation of their communities will invariably serve the archive well. Such scholars and broadcasters will, however, tend to bring their immediate projects and preoccupations to such deliberations. Archives need to know and understand these requirements, and indeed to serve them. But archival appraisal also seeks to serve posterity, and archives must bring a broader perspective to such advisory committees.

Logging videotapes.

Communications environments with competing media or television news operations may offer potential parallel archival collections from a variety of sources. Such collections will undoubtedly include coverage of the same events and will often include similar footage in their holdings. For some research purposes such parallel coverage may be of particular value in documenting a more comprehensive coverage of a community. Also, different media and stations may have taken very different perspectives and covered very different events within the same community.

Archives need to determine whether available news collections are unique and comprehensive. Limited archival resources may require that the more comprehensive and authoritative television news collection be acquired and conserved before parallel material can be accepted. Nonetheless, parallel collections will have different research and archival potential and they should never be rejected out of hand.

This appraisal of the communications context of a community may lead an institution to approach other stations to determine what they have retained and whether it might also be available for archival deposit. The first station that approached the archive may not hold the richest collection and an understanding of what other broadcasters hold will be essential. This knowledge will also strengthen the archivist's negotiating position and introduce some skepticism in accepting broadcasters' claims - notorious for their self-promotion.

Archivists are next advised to understand the role of the particular television station offering the material. The geographic orientation of the station, the quality and extent of its news reporting, and the ideology or mission of the station should be known by the archivist undertaking the appraisal.

The orientation of the station to regional rather than only local news might enhance the archival value of the collection for a regional archive. However, a rich and coherent local collection will be equally valuable to the particular community.

The extent of news gathering resources and the editorial position of the television news operation during formative events should be known. The importance of the station over time in originating news programming of community, regional and national significance will be of fundamental importance in appraising their news collection. The station's network and syndication relationships need to be understood and analyzed.

The political or ideological perspective of station ownership or staff should never disqualify a television news collection from archival consideration. Moreover, a distinctive editorial position, which may balance other media or archival holdings, could well enhance the archival value of a television news collection.

There may be no single right or wrong answers that arise from this appraisal of the context of the television station. Nonetheless, these appraisal questions will strengthen the institution's resolve in accepting or rejecting a collection. Also, some obvious conclusions will present themselves as a consequence of such an exercise.

Broadcasting Context

The broadcasting context of what is actually being offered must be clearly understood. Rarely do television news libraries or collections contain comprehensive runs of news programming as broadcast. In the days of film local stations rarely had the capacity to make a recording of programming as broadcast. Broadcasters never expected that they would re-broadcast the news as originally transmitted and therefore rarely bothered to keep such complete programs.

**Appraisal of
What is Being
Offered**

For a variety of archival research purposes, however, the complete broadcasts as transmitted will be exactly what is requested. Such complete programming, when it exits, is often on formats such as kinescopes (a 16mm film image shot directly from a television monitor) or 1/2-inch VHS cassettes. These formats are invariably of inferior visual and audio quality to the original footage that constitute the bulk of television news collections. Nonetheless, the comprehensive and contextual perspective of programming as broadcast makes such materials valuable.

Weekly current affairs series, or special documentaries, were often prepared in advance and these, therefore, stand a better chance of surviving as broadcast. Similarly, other programming that was not as quickly dated as news might be retained longer. Children's programming, variety entertainment, and even television commercials may well have been retained somewhere within a television station. Also, such programming is not as likely to be edited and reused as was the news film and is more likely to exist in its entirety than television news. All programming should be part of the appraisal process and can usually be evaluated on a series-by-series approach.

Indeed a series-by-series appraisal is strongly recommended for all television programming collections. The concepts, program objectives, and technological formats will usually be relatively coherent throughout the duration of a program series and allow one to assess whether the series warrants archival retention. Admittedly, long-running series can evolve and change substantially but since broadcasting organizations and personnel are structured by program series it is reasonable to approach archival appraisal similarly.

Within a program series random selection may well be necessary and justified for non-news programming. Certainly a minimum of one program sample per broadcast season of all series originated by a station should be retained as an archival record. Delaying final selection is often found to be prudent because of the surprising uses that are emerging for a wide range of past programming.

Television programming and news collections in languages other than English obviously require expertise in those languages for appraisal to be undertaken. Such materials should not be rejected simply because the language expertise is not readily at hand. They may provide an alternative perspective on the same events or period and could be valuable to an archive.

For news programming either random or informed selection within a program series is fraught with difficulties and is guaranteed to frustrate future researchers. Moreover, it takes a great deal more time and more sophisticated expertise to make a program-by-program or item-by-item selection. Admittedly, limited archival resources may require some hard choices about which television news series can be acquired, conserved and cataloged. Even so, selection within a television news series can rarely be justified, given the time and effort required, and the high probability of making the wrong choices.

Original television news footage collections already represent significant "weeding" or selection both intentional and random. News cameramen were rarely documenting complete events but rather capturing enough sound and visuals for a news story to be prepared. Meeting the daily deadline may cause footage to be borrowed and never returned, re-edited, or simply erased. Personal and particular circumstances may cause footage to be erased or appropriated for private collections. Space or blank tape requirements may cause older footage to be junked or recycled. Long before archives come to appraise television news collections much may already have been discarded for a variety of reasons.

Original television news footage can be found organized in a variety of ways in such libraries/collections. Often the film elements actually used in a broadcast will be found edited exactly as they were transmitted with, or without, accompanying sound. These film elements will often be painfully short with the reporter or news anchor providing the context as the report was being aired. The accompanying sound may be missing, may be found elsewhere in the collection, or may never have been recorded (in the case of a live voice-over during broadcast). These film clips may therefore even be pithy and colorful but if the date and location is impossible to discern their archival value is seriously reduced.

The films in this box came without any identification or inventory numbers.

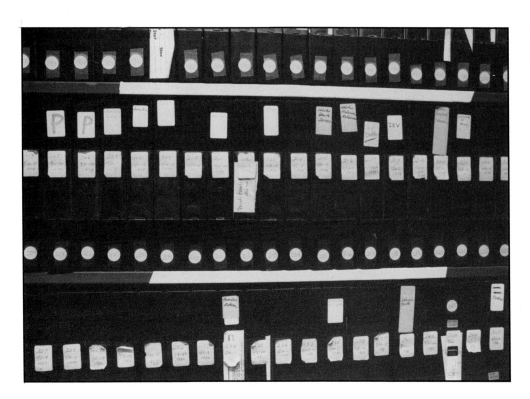

These "edit packs" or cut story tapes only have a date reference.

The film footage not used for transmission may have been junked, retained as "trims" and "outs," or retained as stockshots. Reuniting such film footage with the transmitted portions of news reports to reconstitute the original camera footage is usually much too tedious and time-consuming to attempt. However, some notable and historic events might well justify such restorations of news footage.

Combined with original news footage shot by, and for, the station may well be a variety of other material. Invariably network or syndication footage of national and international events will have been used by the station for the coverage of these stories and this footage often is incorporated into the television news collection. Similarly, over the years, the station will have received promotional, instructional and other completed productions that may have been edited for use as newsfilm. This context may or may not have been retained in the numbering, labelling and description of the footage. Also, the station will not own the same rights to such footage as they do for the footage that they originated. Such productions and outside footage may well be preserved in other archives, or might well consist of unique footage. Archives should make neither assumption and need to carefully verify whether such footage is duplicated elsewhere or whether it is unique. If such footage is well preserved and accessible in its broader context elsewhere then a good case can be made for the elimination of such material.

Stock footage components of news libraries/collections were frequently used by the stations themselves. They consisted of the generic shots that would not be quickly dated and therefore could be inserted into a variety of stories to add visual interest. Consequently stock footage may be of the least archival interest. However, if date and location are reliably provided, or can be identified, then stock footage collections need to be examined for the unique events, personalities, and locations that might be documented.

The advent of electronic news gathering meant that physical cutting and splicing of original film footage was no longer necessary - this was now done electronically on videotape without impairing the original footage. Therefore the original recordings from which the edited stories have been assembled, known as "field tapes," may often be found in such news collections. Even more common will be the edited reports, known as "edit-packs," often organized in chronological order or by particular reporters.

However, changing circumstances within television news rooms and budget constraints may have caused such field tapes sometimes to have been erased and recycled.

The field tapes will usually contain the actual sound of the event being recorded (often referred to as "wild sound" or "actuality sound") whereas the edited reports may contain a reporter's voice-over (sometimes on a second audio track). Also, any electronic graphics on news programming such as those identifying locations or personalities are usually inserted at the point of broadcast and are not found on the edited reports in news libraries/collections.

Physical Contents

The actual, as opposed to the presumed, contents of a news collection have to appraised. The policies and practices in the news library have to be understood. All the news that a station originated or transmitted may or may not be held in their library. For example, a station may have originated historic news footage for network syndication that was forwarded to or duplicated in the network libraries. Also, the inflated prices being offered briefly in the mid-1970s for silver caused some film collections to be recycled for their silver content. A variety of technical, logistic, administrative and practical factors combine to determine which footage has been retained or not.

In some cases the only identifying information on film cans is the date. Each of these cans spans several days.

The varieties of film and video formats found in news libraries/collections need to be identified and understood. Each format may require its own playback technology and may have been differently organized within the television station. Invariably library inventory and cataloging systems evolved as new formats were introduced. These finding aid systems may not have been applied consistently, however, due to changing staff and station priorities.

Reorganizations of such libraries/collections by station personnel can be helpful or frustrating for the institutions. For example original film outtakes, or edited stories, are often found wound tightly in individual rolls with as many as twenty-five to thirty inside a single large film can. This "chocolate box" phenomenon can appear chaotic but

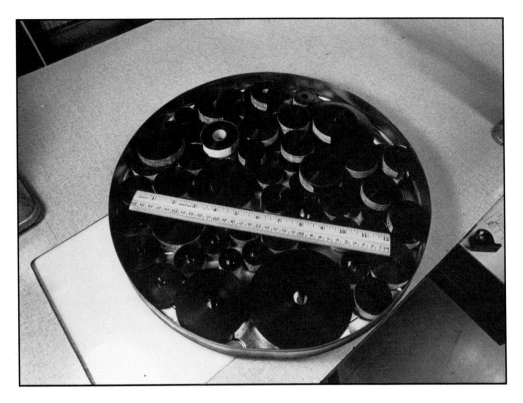

Rolls by any other name. . .chocolate box, hockey puck, rollette. Over fifty individual news stories are in this can.

it may be preferable to having individual stories spliced together in a random sequence. On the other hand, compilation reels where footage has been brought together because of a consistent theme or a clearly-established date-range can be very useful. Nonetheless, this subject organization can cause technological problems in playing back film of different formats.

A common practice with newsfilm was to re-cut and re-edit original footage as required for second and subsequent uses to the point where the footage literally could be used up. And, of course, this meant that the most frequently used footage (and often the most

Even with the best of records, each individual can and its contents must be identified, viewed and inventoried.

valuable for archival purposes) would also be the most abused. This practice can seriously erode the archival value of a news library/collection. Certainly, this practice confuses the accurate identification of the date and location of the original footage. In such cases it may be advisable to work through collections from the most recent footage backwards in time, rather than the more conventional forward chronological approach.

Labels on film/video containers are often illegible or cryptic at best. Also, one cannot always trust that such labels reliably refer to the contents of their containers. And with film such labels often consist of sticky adhesive tape that has left an unwelcome residue on the film itself. Nonetheless, the existence of any such clues may be helpful to later identification, organization and conservation of a television news collections. Any labels should be noted in an appraisal and their internal logic or relationship to inventories or catalogues should be evaluated.

Finally, news footage has to be screened on appropriate playback equipment for an appraisal to be completed. Labels on tape and film containers are notoriously misleading and over time they tend to fall off or become obscured. Also, it is always easy for films

and tapes to become separated from their original containers. Given the fragility of older film, and the technological rarity of some formats, transfer to conventional video formats may be required before screening is possible. Such transfers are invariably expensive and time-consuming and can hardly be justified if the film will subsequently be rejected. Appraisal must therefore be thorough and critical before transfers on selected samples should be undertaken.

Operational and Administrative Records

News programming always required extensive research and preparation that was often documented on paper or, more recently, in electronic data form. Given that the final product of a television news operation was their on-air programming, much of this documentation was compiled very roughly, on the poorest quality paper, in the shoddiest style, and filed hastily, if at all. Therefore it may well not be available or may appear to the archivist's eye to be hardly worth serious archival consideration.

Indeed, such documentation is by definition preliminary. If the programming itself is complete, well-identified and cataloged, much of these scripts, cue-sheets, program

The Wolfson Center's newsfilm scripts date back to the early 1950s.

logs, and research files can be safely jettisoned. Then, only samples need be retained to document the television newsgathering and reporting process. Also exceptional events, or the coverage of controversial issues, would warrant more extensive archival retention of such research materials.

In most cases, however, television news collections rarely contain complete programming or arrive at an archive well identified, let alone already cataloged. In these cases related documentation becomes indispensable in allowing the archivist to organize the collection. Also, such related documentation will then become invaluable to the researcher reconstituting complete reports or newscasts.

Research files with background notes, newspaper clippings, press releases, etc., quickly became voluminous if retained within a television news operation. Sometimes such files were cross-indexed, or even microfilmed, because of their ongoing utility to newsgath-

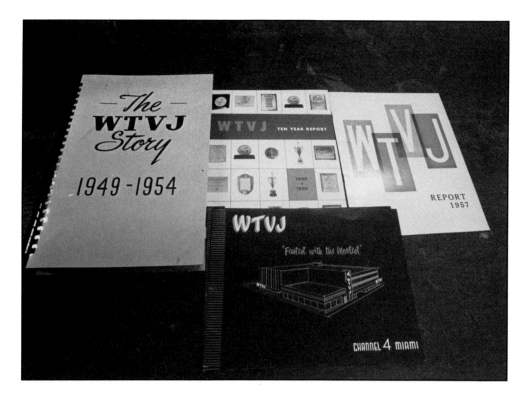

Station history records received with the WTVJ collection.

ering process. However, aside from the sampling suggested above, or the exceptional/controversial events, such research files probably are of little archival value.

If the administrative records documenting the editorial process within television news operations can be available together with the news collections, this will enhance the archival value of the collection. The files of the news director and executive producer are particularly valuable. Station management may well require restricted access to such

Labeling varies from cryptic to detailed with no guarantee of accuracy until the film or tape is viewed.

records but as long as the duration of such access is reasonable such restrictions should not inhibit archival acquisition.

Such operational and administrative records may be disappointing for what they do not document about the television process. Much of the decision making in the process of preparing television news programming is made so hastily with looming deadlines that conventional written records document little of what actually transpired. Broadcasting is a visual and oral culture with less reliance than usual upon written communication. Electronic data communication and word processing will only intensify these trends.

For this reason, oral history interviews of station personnel should be considered by archives appraising television news collections. They may be the only way to answer many of the appraisal questions that need to be asked. Such interviews may also supply evidence about the evolution of the newsgathering process that otherwise would be lost.

Appraisal of Station Collaboration

Ongoing station support for the archival acquisition of a television news collection will be essential to the appraisal process outlined. If the television station merely wants to devolve its responsibilities and has lost interest in the collection, an adequate appraisal will be impossible to carry out. Often one of the most mutually beneficial ways to ensure good cooperation is for the archive to use station personnel, or past personnel, to work on the collection. Television news personnel invariably move from station to station quickly over the years and, therefore, long-standing staff become a valuable asset to the archive.

The potential for ongoing transfers from the television station to the archive should be considered in the appraisal process. Just as the 16mm film became available to archives in the early 1980s, 3/4-inch U-matic videocassettes will become available in the 1990s. As long as a format is in daily use stations will naturally need to retain the collection to facilitate the immediate access that archives may have difficulty satisfying. Nonetheless, provisions for the eventual transfer of collections, once formats evolve, should be discussed.

Given the archival value of the total newscast in its context, off-air taping might also be considered in the ongoing relationship between the archive and the television station. The complete broadcast as seen in the home with advertisements, graphics inserted, credits, and interruptions will have undeniable value to many communications researchers. Admittedly, any recording outside the originating station will suffer quality degradation because of transmission and recording technology limitations; but the margins of these quality differentials is narrowing in recent years and off-air taping is becoming more and more economical.

Archives may need to organize their selection process according to the extent of collaboration offered by the station. If the station is able and willing to collaborate, the archive should be prepared to be willing to accept station requirements in their selection. On the other hand, the station's disinterest may prompt the archive to be much more rigorous in what they decide to retain. Certainly archives have to retain the right to reject some of the collection that may have been transferred to them. However, this should never be done unilaterally and a mutual decision-making process can be educational for both institutions.

Nonetheless, the television station invariably will become the primary researcher and user of the collection once deposited in the archive, even if it does not expect to. Access to the news collection within the archive might well improve for the television station because of the identification and cataloging undertaken at the archive. But expectations need to be reasonable and well-outlined. Television production tends to expect immediate access and rarely can indulge time delays that other researchers may be prepared to live with. This recall or reuse by the originating television station can become mutually frustrating and troublesome if not carefully understood at the outset.

The demands of television production in reusing the collection also present opportunities for the archive. With appropriate credit it allows the archive to demonstrate its relevance to contemporary communications. Secondly, when archival footage is required for production purposes, resources can sometimes be supplied by the station for conservation that might otherwise not be justified.

Appraisal Conclusions

All of the above complexities and considerations are not intended to discourage the acquisition of television news collections. Indeed, they are intended to assist and facilitate the appraisal of television news collections. The appraisal principles are not unique and adopt the documentation strategy well understood in archives generally.

What is unique about appraising the records of television is that we are bringing our archival expertise and knowledge to bear upon our own popular culture. Archives cannot afford to wait the normal period to allow time to winnow the records of television. Technological change has been so dramatic and rapid within the fifty years of television, and the programming itself so ephemeral, that little would survive the usual vagaries of time. The records of television, if neglected for a couple of generations, could be as fragmentary and difficult to decipher as archeological evidence from prehistoric civilizations.

Many of the archivists required to appraise television may well themselves recall a time before television. Our personal perceptions and experiences may therefore play a stronger role than is usual in our professional capacities. Because we are so close to television—we use it so extensively ourselves—we cannot yet begin to imagine the archival uses that might be made of it.

Therefore it may be prudent for us in appraising the records of television not to be too selective. Usually it is undeniably good and responsible archival practice for archives to accept only those records that they can conserve, catalog and make accessible. The storage space, budget, staff size and expertise, technological capacity and ambitions of

VHS off-air recording system at the Wolfson Center.

the archive are practical factors that cannot be denied in undertaking an archival appraisal. Nevertheless, acquiring a television news collection can also present opportunities in improving all of these.

The resources that are available today to catalog and conserve the records of television are admittedly very limited because our society does not yet value highly the artifacts of our own popular culture. However, we would risk a most draconian selection process if we were to limit our acquisitions to what we now can fully handle in our archive. With records of our own time we may want to give another generation of archivists a second chance.

Finally, there are no definitive right or wrong answers to the appraisal process. Posterity will undoubtedly benefit if different archives answer these appraisal questions quite differently. And archives should evolve their own mission and appraisal criteria over tim, should they change their minds. Thereby, researchers of the future will have a wonderful variety of collections to access for widely differing purposes.

4

Station-Archive Relations

Steven Davidson

Louis Wolfson II Media History Center

Acquiring newsfilm and videotape material often takes more than a clearly defined collection policy. The donors – the television stations – will have their own concerns and motivations, which may be different than the archives. The chances of negotiating successful agreements from the perspectives of both sides may be increased with informed and realistic dialogue among the parties. Timeframe is another significant matter. Sometimes agreements are reached in relatively short order; at the other extreme, it may take years to do so. This chapter provides considerations to keep in mind both before and after the donor agreement is negotiated.

Steven Davidson has been the Director of the Louis Wolfson II Media History Center since its establishment in 1987. Before coming to Miami, he was the Director of Library Services at the Museum of Broadcasting and the Associate Director of the National Jewish Archive of Broadcasting in New York. Davidson has served on the Executive Board of the Association of Moving Image Archivists and Co-chairs its News and Documentary Collections Working Group. He actively works to promote the efforts of newsfilm and video archives to other groups around the country and has organized presentations at the Broadcast Educators Association, Radio-Television News Directors Association, the Society of American Archivists and the American Library Association. He is the editor, contributing photographer and co-project director of this manual.

Station-Archive Relations

Television newsfilm and videotape collections may be found in a variety of institutional settings including museums, historical societies, public libraries, colleges, universities, state archives and independent organizations. How these collections are acquired and the terms of the donor agreements with television stations vary, even within the same institution. Any number of factors may shape newsfilm and video acquisition policies.

If the moving image archive is part of a larger organization, collection policy may already be defined in accordance with institutional mission statements or by curatorial committee guidelines. The institutional setting of an archive may also shape the collection policy and/or the context in which these materials will be used. For example at San Francisco State University, newsfilm collections are acquired to serve the academic and student communities. The Mississippi Department of Archives and History's collections are acquired to serve the citizens of the state, providing a historical record. At the Wolfson Media Center, there is more a broad-based mission to collect and

Part of the newsfilm collection at the Mississippi Department of Archives and History.

Note labeling on masking tape.

make accessible film and video materials produced in or about Florida and to provide access to the general public and educational, cultural and research communities. In some institutions newsfilm/video collections are complementing other print and/or photographic records, as is the case at the Chicago Historical Society. In other instances, such as at the Wolfson Media Center, it has been the moving image materials that have lead to the acquisition of paper records and photographs which support the study and understanding of the newsfilm and video materials.

These unprocessed news stories are wound on larger cores, most often two large reels per can. Note masking tape label and splices.

Collection policies may also define specific parameters. For example, an archive may determine that they will collect only newsfilm (Mississippi Department of Archives and History), or both newsfilm and video (Wolfson Media Center). Other factors may be geographic range, collecting materials from one city or region (San Francisco State University Archives) as opposed to stations from around the state (State Historical Society of North Dakota), time frame (span of years) limiting the number of newsfilm/video collections, or type of material — full programs, or documentaries, not individual stories. Policies may also address copyright status (some archives won't accept materials without transfer of copyright) or be shaped by considerations of space, staff and funding necessary to process these collections.

These factors and resulting decisions may be guided by both policy and an institutional awareness of the consequences of accepting a collection. Larger institutions may have a curatorial committee, while other organizations may have an advisory board comprised of historians, educators, broadcasters and archivists working with a development/fundraising committee. It's one thing to choose to accept these collections, another to find the funding to do the work required.

An institution should also be aware of the nature of these collections—from the demands that will be made for immediate access (by ill-informed or well-intentioned users), to the educational process for other staff members or departments within the institution. For example, if an archive is located within a university, faculty may expect the same kind of access to the archival material as they have to the resources of the library or audio-visual department (and would likely handle the materials in the same fashion), informing you that all their students will be in to do research for their final projects. Meeting such demands is certainly not possible early on, but within time (and with proper resources) this should be a goal. In the interim, policies should be developed to provide limited access.

How Are The Collections Acquired?

There have been and will continue to be cases where frantic calls are received by the archivist about coming to get a collection before it is thrown out by a local station. At the other extreme, collections are acquired through long protracted negotiations until an agreement is reached. Experiences gained from acquiring a first collection may also have an effect on the acquisition of others. Institutions that have already gone through the process of negotiating with a television station for donation of a collection and/or the experience of preserving one, may rely on those experiences next time.

While every situation is different, if circumstances permit, the archivist/institution is advised to reach an agreement with a donating television station outside of a "crisis" or rushed situation. As long as there is no danger of the collection being discarded or erased by the television station, time should be taken to work out an agreement that should be beneficial to the archive and to the donating station.

Differences in Television Stations

Remember that all television stations are not the same and the differences may play a role in trying to work out an agreement. Stations have different network affiliations, others are independent (no network affiliation), some are O & O (owned and operated by the networks), many are part of other broadcast groups such as Post-Newsweek and ownership of the station is not locally based and the final decision by the station may rest with its owners in another part of the country. In any case a good relationship with one station could help in reaching an agreement with others. Television station personnel also tend to move around, and you may find yourself working with the same person you worked with at another station.

Negotiating Donor Agreements

There are many issues involved in working out a donor agreement and an institution may have different agreements with different stations for a variety of reasons. It may be that circumstances at stations may vary or lessons were learned after working out the first agreement, etc. In any case, it is very difficult to renegotiate the terms of an earlier agreement. It is therefore imperative to clearly research all the parameters and be

WTVJ in Miami began as an independent station, then became a CBS affiliate and most recently an NBC owned and operated station.

actively involved in the process. While it is likely that attorneys on both sides will play a role at some point, the archivist should make sure that the terms of the donor agreement are realistic and know what the obligations are for both sides. Board members, development committee members and all who may be involved also need to be fully informed in this process.

The Archive's Perspective

From the archive's perspective, favorable terms could include donation of materials with copyright transfer, provisions for ongoing donations at scheduled intervals, and cash or inkind contributions to defray some of the costs associated with the organization, preservation and storage of the collection or costs associated with provision of materials back to the donor. If collections are received with copyright ownership it allows the archive to license materials for use in new productions, generating revenue for the institution. (Another chapter in this manual discusses reference services and fees.) There may be cases, however, in which the station will not agree on any terms concerning outright copyright transfer. The archivist then must weigh the options. Perhaps the station may consider donating copyright ownership for part of the collection. For example, if the materials span several decades, they may agree to provide copyright ownership for the first twenty years. Another option may be that while copyright ownership is not initially granted, rights may be transferred after a period of time. The station may also agree to allow the archive to charge license fees without donation of copyright, provided the station approves each request for footage. Remember, too, that receiving these collections with copyright is certainly an asset, but it may be some time before license fees may be generated due to the amount of work required.

There are other considerations for the archivist, including the condition the collection is in, what formats are involved, and whether there is any documentation (cardfiles, scripts, notes) that will aid the organization and preservation of the materials. Don't be fooled; even collections that appear to be in good condition are all going to require

Organizing newsfilm collections may take thousands of hours of work.

hundreds or thousands of hours of work. Based on the experience of institutions around the country that have received NHPRC funding, this translates to a minimum of one year with at least two technicians to begin the organization and preservation process of these collections. With the best of intentions, many of those institutions who received NHPRC grants asked for project extensions because of underestimating the time involved.

While an archive may have a standard donor agreement, the television station and the circumstances surrounding the donation may require that the agreement be customized to the benefit of both archive and donor. There are a number of factors that must be considered in successfully negotiating such an agreement. These include the following:

Components of a Donor Agreement

Materials Proposed for Donation. One of the first issues is that of what materials are to be included in the donation. This is a matter of both the volume and type of material to be acquired. From the archive's perspective, existing institutional collection policies may shape the overall nature and extent of the donor agreement. Chapter 3 of this manual details issues of appraisal and collection policies, and an archive's initial interest in acquiring a newsfilm and video collection from a station may be based on those considerations.

However, there are any number of scenarios or variables which may come to bear, sometimes leaving the archive little or no choice in the acquisition process. In some instances the station may already have discarded most or all of its newsfilm and only videotape from recent decades remains. In other cases, a station may wish to keep all its video and may only be interested in donating its "obsolete" newsfilm for the time being. In another scenario, a station may have transferred newsfilm or early video material to a newer video format (such as Betacam SP), but in the process decided only to keep its final cut stories; in this case, all unaired trims and outtakes – often the most valuable part of a collection – may have been discarded.

Sorting a recent donation at the Wolfson Center.

Any of these video
formats can be part of
a collection received
from a television
station.

Station Access Requirements. But suppose the potential donor is a station that has kept all its newsfilm and videotape – several decades worth of outtakes and aired stories – right up through the present. In this case it is essential that the archive's collection policy be considered. For example, is the institution interested in acquiring all of this material, including recent video production, or just the more "historic "newsfilm? If the entire collection is sought, and if the station will want ongoing access privileges to their material, consider that the station will most likely continue to use its current material more frequently. This is one reason why it may be in the interests of both the station and the archive for the station to keep its most recent material – perhaps for five to ten years – before donation to the archive. This will prevent over-burdening the archive with frequent service requests from the station for footage in the collection.

Format Technologies. Archives must also consider ever-changing format technologies and their impact on the viability of the donation. Collections dating from the 1950s through the 1970s will be comprised primarily of 16mm film, although an archive may be "lucky" and discover that the station has also kept its two-inch videotape. Collections from the mid-1970s through the present will consist mainly of videotape, and while the majority of this videotape is likely to be in the 3/4-inch U-matic format, materials from the 1980s onward may be on other formats, including MII, Betacam, and Betacam SP. Format-specific equipment will be required to play back each one. If the station has such equipment that it will no longer need, the archive can ask that this equipment be included in the donation.

Inventory of Donated Materials. After the nature and scope of the material to be donated has been determined, an inventory should be prepared and included as an addendum to the agreement. The inventory ultimately should be as detailed as possible, but an initial preliminary inventory will suffice. Generally, such an inventory may characterize the material by a span of years and number of boxes; for example, thirty-six boxes of newsfilm material from 1952-1969.

Copyright Ownership. If the station is assigning copyright ownership to the archive, this needs to be specifically stated. If the station retains copyright, terms of the donation need to be specified, and procedures for the archive to follow in making material available must be addressed.

Restrictions on the Collection. If the donating station has specific or out-of-the-ordinary restrictions that it wants placed on a collection, these should be clarified. For example, some archives have received donations from stations who do not want material in the collection to be accessed by other competing television stations in the same city or market.

Role of the Archive Regarding the Collection. The traditional role, rights and responsibilities of the archive in processing, maintaining and using the collection should be stated. This encompasses preservation, duplication and access by the archive and its users, and by the donor.

De-Accessioning. The rights of the archive to dispose of any materials in the collection that it deems to have no archival or use value should be stated.

Future Donations. A television station may agree to continue providing the archive with updated donations of additional or more recent material. If this is the case, terms and schedules for these regular or ongoing donations should be spelled out. They may, for example, be on an annual or biannual basis.

Agreements in Perpetuity. The deed of gift should also state whether or not the agreement will continue in effect if the television station undergoes a change in ownership or network affiliation.

Do not become frustrated by the time it may take to complete the negotiation of a donor agreement. An archive and a station may reach agreement within a week, or it can often take much longer. For example, the Minnesota Historical Society signed an agreement with a St. Paul station following six years of discussion. Be willing to show the station model agreements from other archives so that they will have a sense of the possible.

Needless to say, everything agreed to must be put in writing. Oral agreements with "friendly" station managers or news directors can end abruptly if these individuals leave the station. In some larger cities and even in smaller markets, there is frequent turnover in these positions.

Maintaining Relations with Stations

Clearly, it is in the best interests of the archive and the television station to maintain good relations on an ongoing basis. This should be done with as many stations in your region as is possible, both before and after any donation agreements are reached. Invite station representatives over for a tour of the archive, let them observe first hand the work involved in maintaining news collections, and invite them to your public programs so they can see how the materials are used. Place station personnel on your mailing lists so they can keep abreast of your activities – and then keep these lists up-to-date. The more the station knows about your institution, the better chance of working out an agreement.

At the same time, stations should understand that when collections enter an archival institution they are handled in an archival fashion. In most cases, this handling and processing will be quite different from the way things operated at the television station.

A common concern of donating television stations is how they can get access to "their" materials and how long it will take. First, you need to set the record straight (diplomatically) about the material, even though it may take a while until it is referred to as "yours." As to when and how the station can have access, the answer depends in part on the condition of the material, on the amount of documentation received with the collection, and on available resources and staffing at the archive. The station should be provided with a realistic time frame for response, not given promises that will be hard or impossible to keep.

Soon after the donation is completed and the collection is received by an archive, there will no doubt be calls from film and video makers wanting to use the material. The donor agreement should have outlined procedures for making material available for such use. If the station retained copyright, it will make the decision as to whether or not material may be used. If the archive has acquired the copyright, a license agreement and fee schedule must be developed. Remember that if the station retains copyright but still permits material in the collection to be licensed to out side users, it will be the archive that performs much of the work in helping users research the collection and in making preservation and access copies. The archive should work out a rate schedule for these activities and collect fees to cover them, even though the station receives the actual license fee.

From the archive's perspective, it is vitally important to have a good understanding of how television stations operate and, more specifically, how television news departments function. Even with the best-negotiated agreements, if there is a breaking news story, stations may provide little notice in requesting back material. Often several people from the station may call at the same time and ask for the same material, not realizing that anyone else is working on the story.

Access protocols can be greatly facilitated in advance by specifying a contact person at both the television station and the archive. All requests from the station would be channeled through one individual and directed to a similarly designated individual at the archive.

5

A Case Study:
Newsfilm Preservation Project at The State Historical Society of North Dakota

Gerald G. Newborg

The State Historical Society of North Dakota

The State Historical Society of North Dakota submitted two unsuccessful newsfilm grant applications to the NHPRC before a third proposal was accepted and completed after a two-year period. It is interesting to note that the earlier proposals were rejected largely because they were too ambitious. This chapter reprints the final report of the North Dakota project, and provides an excellent description of the scope of work involved in successfully processing a television newsfilm collection.

Gerald Newborg has been the Director of the State Archives and Historical Society of North Dakota since 1981. Prior to taking his present position, he was State Archivist with the Ohio Historical Society and also worked in private business.

Newsfilm Preservation Project at The State Historical Society of North Dakota

The State Historical Society of North Dakota recently concluded a National Historical Publications and Records Commission (NHPRC) newsfilm preservation project. The final report of the grant project is included here in its entirety, with the addition of the following excerpt from the initial NHPRC report which provides some additional background information.

The present, successful project proposal was preceded by two unsuccessful approaches to NHPRC. Prior to the most recent submission, NHPRC granted funds to the agency to hire a consultant to advise on our approach to television newsfilm preservation and on this project. Our current project differs from previous proposals in two key areas. First, our earlier proposals included cataloging of newsfilm footage at various levels. Our consultant also emphasized that adding cataloging made our project too ambitious. The preservation activities included in our current project and cataloging needed to be done separately. The second major difference between the current project and earlier proposals is the extent to which film is transferred to videotape. Under our earlier proposals, approximately 100 hours of film, based on anticipated demand, was to be transferred to videotape for ease of reference. Other film would be transferred to videotape on a demand basis. Based on the advice of our consultant, our current project

At work on the WDAY/WDAZ collection at the State Historical Society of North Dakota.

includes the transfer of all newsfilm to videotape, both 3/4-inch U-matic and VHS copies. The videotape promotes preservation in that the film is projected only once. After that, copies can be made from the 3/4-inch U-matic cassettes and the VHS copies can be used for reference and future cataloging.

The purpose of this project was to preserve the television newsfilm collections of the State Historical Society of North Dakota. The collections, originally estimated to be approximately 2.5 million feet of 16mm film covering the period 1953 to 1978, are the product of three broadcasting companies in the state (six stations) and one independently produced news program. This project was to inspect, clean, and splice the film, assemble it on cores, identify the material, place the film in archival quality film cans, and transfer the film to videotape. The purpose of the videotape transfer was to prolong the life of the film by reducing the need to project and view the original film as well as aid in further identification and access. Cataloging was not part of this project, although every effort was made to retain all existing identification and add to available information on individual segments and the collection as a whole.

The project began officially on February 1, 1992. Two technicians were hired under NHPRC grant funds as full-time project staff. We were fortunate in recruiting two individuals who had worked in the division under a different project. Both were familiar with the agency and its general procedures and the collections. One had served as photo curator at an earlier period and had been the principal sound camera motion picture photographer for a local station. In fact, he shot a portion of the early film in the collections. Both individuals had demonstrated good work habits in the past and both were capable of recalling many of the events and personalities recorded on the film in the collections. We were also fortunate in retaining the same staff for the duration of the project.

In addition to the two film technicians, staff members engaged in the project included the project director, the deputy state archivist, archives specialist, and division secretary. One regular volunteer assisted with data entry and database revision, and two part-time summer workers assisted in film cleaning. Regular staff worked approximately 3,700 hours on the project during the official project period. Several hundred additional hours were spent before and after the project period both in preparation and in continuing video transfer, as will be discussed below. During the official project period, therefore, approximately 12,000 person-hours were invested. The pre- and post-project related activities have or are consuming an estimated 1,500 additional hours. The proposal foresaw the expenditure of about 10,400 hours. The difference in time estimates and reality are due largely to the fact that the collections were slightly larger than anticipated and to the enormity of the film-to-video transfer task. Although the additional time could be explained by the fact that the size of the collections is 128 percent of our original estimate (and project hours spent only 116 percent of those proposed), the fact is that video transfer time accounts for more of the difference.

Project staff met weekly to discuss progress and procedures, trouble-shoot, and plan future activities. These regular meetings proved beneficial throughout the project. The project team could engage in collaborative decision making, adjust procedures as necessary, and call attention to potential problems.

Staff also proved inventive in developing gadgets for working with the film. Plastic pipe cut lengthwise was used as a trough for holding and sorting the small tightly-wound segments of film. A small record turntable was a handy device for unrolling small segments of film, the record spindle being the same size as the opening in the tightly-wound spool. Weighing film segments provided a speedy, and surprisingly accurate, method for determining what would fit on any given thirty-minute core.

Equipment

Most equipment and supplies were in place prior to the start of the project, so there was little delay in getting the project underway. The basic pieces of equipment consisted of manual rewinds, Moviscope viewers, a Precision Sound Reader (magnetic and optical), synchronizers, tape splicers, Perf Fix sprocket repair equipment, and split reels. Our original video chain was replaced in mid-project with the contribution of a professional quality multiplexer and film projectors. Some other small items were added, including a third splicer to use at the cleaning or video transfer stations, and additional split reels. Most of the time-consuming equipment difficulties also concerned film-to-video transfer.

Cleaning

Film cleaning posed some difficulties initially. We began by using a freon-based cleaner which is less hazardous for the individual using it, but which is now unavailable because of its environmental impact. For most of the project, we used a standard film cleaner which requires adequate ventilation. After considerable experimentation and contact with other film repositories, we took our film to a conservation lab in the building and used the standard film cleaner under a power-ventilated fume hood. Because the cleaning area is physically removed from the project work space, all cleaning was done on a batch basis, i.e., a number of cores are assembled and then transported to the conservation area for cleaning. All cleaning was done using a staff-devised cleaning contraption which regulates the flow of cleaner to a pair of velvet cleaning tapes. This process is quite efficient and obviously safer for the staff.

A specific cleaning problem was a number of cores which had been taped together, using masking tape, across the edge of the core. The tape had either dried or become sticky, in both cases leaving a residue potentially damaging to both film and equipment. By rewinding the film using an even, tight wind, the tape itself was pulled off and the resulting flat, smooth surface could be cleaned without cleaner or tape residue being forced onto the film surface. This was mostly successful. However, on the worst examples, some evidence of tape residue will occasionally be found.

One discovery did disturb us. Each film segment was identified with a short white leader and a short red trailer, the latter being six inches in length. Each core then was given a longer leader and trailer. We discovered in a couple of our early cores that the

Viewing and identifying material from the WDAY/WDAZ Collection at the State Historical Society of North Dakota.

red trailer, where it came in contact with a section of white leader, had discolored the white leader, i.e., the white leader had a light red impression on it at the point of contact. This was not universal, but we were concerned enough to stop using the red trailer at the end of individual segments until we could determine that it would not fade to or damage any film. We initially suspected that the film cleaner may not have completely dried on these cores before the film was taken up on the rewind. Later in the project we discovered that it was in fact the red leader that was at fault. We stopped using it and when found on cores assembled early in the project, we remove the red leader.

Our experience indicates that each thirty-minute core took about ten minutes to clean on average. This figure includes a single pass through the cleaner and manual rewinding.

Work Plan

As indicated in the grant proposal, the project began with the WDAY/WDAZ-TV Collection because this was the largest and best identified. It also consisted almost entirely of individual segments tightly wound into "rollettes" without cores and taped with an identifying slug, either simply an identifying number or the number and a name or brief description. Each segment usually ranges from fifteen seconds to two minutes in length. The collection had an accompanying card file organized as a meager index (no more than one card per segment and not all segments identified) arranged by such categories as local events, local personalities, and national personalities. Although spartan, it was the best we had and we believed that as part of the recording and verifying process when the cores were assembled, this information could be incorporated on the technicians' forms without the need to re-enter slug information. The WDAY/WDAZ-TV Collection also has accompanying scripts used for the news broadcasts. These scripts have been extremely valuable and were used heavily by staff in identifying segments and verifying work form information. The WDAY/WDAZ Collection was actually fifty-six percent larger than anticipated, and activities related to organizing the collection took approximately twenty-five percent longer than planned.

The Meyer Broadcasting Company, KXJB-TV, and *Focus on the News* collections took about as much time as anticipated and were completed within a time frame close to that planned. Staff also discovered some Prairie Public Broadcasting film (KFME-TV) and some other miscellaneous materials which were preserved within the last two months of the project. The total film footage for all collections exceeded estimates by about twenty-eight percent.

Following the initial concentration on the WDAY/WDAZ Collection, our initial proposal called for film-to-video transfer to begin in the third quarter of the project. Other collections were to be taken in turn, moving from the best organized and described to the worst. Staff followed the basic plan, but failed to meet some aspects of the schedule. Film-to-video transfer did begin in the third quarter, but staff failed to meet a satisfactory production schedule due to scheduling and equipment difficulties. Transfer of film to video was most concentrated during the final six months of the project. By the end of the grant period 1,117 cores had been transferred to videotape.

Data Entry

Prior to the official start of the project, staff set up a database file using DBASE with fields for the basic technical information needed as well as essential identifying information. This included core and segment number, original (station supplied) number, length of segment, color or black and white, sound type, and identifying information on person or subject, location, and activity. Because the card file was segmented into "old film" and "new film" categories, it was possible to concentrate on entering the earliest card file information into the database prior to the time the technicians would be starting. Once entered, staff could organize the database by original number, check for missing

Finished product. The
WDAY/WDAZ
Collection.

Finished product. The WDAY/WDAZ Collection.

numbers, and insert records for these missing numbers. Staff then created a report format that, when printed, would serve as a work form for the project technicians. By setting up this database and printing out the technician work forms, the amount of information the technicians have to manually enter and the amount of information that is entered more than once is greatly reduced, thereby ensuring greater accuracy. As technicians assembled the cores they verified or corrected the information transcribed from the cards, added any missing data, and assigned core and segment numbers. The corrections and additions are then entered into the database which serves as the processing record for the project. The database could be updated with each successive activity, such as the addition of core numbers, segment numbers, and correction of any errors which may have been in the index. Transfer to video provides another opportunity to check a new printout of the database, although in practice the old work sheets might be used and the data entry done on a cumulative basis.

We also entered available information from the Meyer Broadcasting Company Collection. There are many more gaps in this data, but the report printouts still provided a basic framework for recording of data by the film technicians. Pre-entering of segment information was only possible for the WDAY/WDAZ-TV Collection and for part of the Meyer Broadcasting Company Collection because of the availability of station-provided finding aids. However, because the WDAY/WDAZ-TV Collection is the largest, this is especially significant for the project. For the KXJB-TV Collection and the *Focus on the News* collection, which lacked any finding aids, this procedure was of limited use. After an initial attempt to incorporate what little information we had on these latter two collections, staff moved to using blank forms. We largely limited the data collected to basic technical information and general dates for the latter two collections, although the technicians added content identification when possible.

The databases are still being completed and cleaned up. At present, they are being kept as separate databases, but they will ultimately be merged. Linking relational databases have also been established for the WDAY/WDAZ-TV and Meyer Broadcasting collections to hold additional personal names and subjects. We are grateful for the information and advice we received from other institutions, including report materials from the State Historical Society of Wisconsin. Our data entry and descriptive practices borrowed liberally from these institutions.

As indicated in our project proposal, appraisal of the collections was considered largely done at the point the materials were acquired and there was thought to be little in the collections that do not meet criteria for inclusion. One exception, in the *Focus on the News* collection in particular, is service bureau furnished segments which may not have been used. While these have not been disposed of, they will not be transferred to videotape and there will be no effort to do extensive content description of the materials. Within the WDAY/WDAZ-TV Collection, national news segments not filmed by the station were segregated and placed on separate cores. These will also likely receive a lesser level of description in the future and will be evaluated separately for transfer to videotape. Some may be transferred to VHS because of particular reference interest. Our practice is generally not to appraise individual film segments or categories of stories, but rather to provide a lesser level of description. We believe item appraisal to be contrary to accepted archival practice.

The WDAY/WDAZ-TV Collection appears to be as deep and rich as originally thought. The station benefited from a stable staff, with one news director in place from 1956 through 1989. The station also began with a system in place for organizing its film holdings, a system which lasted throughout the 16mm film era. Although tightly wound, the film was in very good condition, apparently stored in cans under good conditions. While some segments had been lost or strayed, the collections provide a good representation of aired news stories. The main difficulties encountered related to the large number of small segments, and the amount of curl in the film from being tightly wound. Most was good quality film, however, and had made only a single pass through the projector. There were only a couple of thousand feet of negative film. The collection, originally estimated to contain one million feet of film, actually contains over one and one-half million feet on 1,443 cores. Each core has, on average, twenty-five segments.

The Meyer Broadcasting Company Collection was more disappointing. The company suffered from frequent turnover in the news department. Although KFYR-TV is and was the dominant news station in the western part of North Dakota and probably produced as much newsfilm as WDAY-TV, the collection is less than one-third as large, with only 438 cores. Each core contains, on average, twenty-seven segments. KFYR's practice was to place its film stories in numbered slots. When the capacity of its film storage was reached, a slot would be emptied, the contents discarded, and the new film put in its place. As a result, little of the earliest film from these stations exists. The collection is very strong from the late 1960s onward, but disappointing for the earliest period. The film was in good condition, but not as well organized as WDAY.

KXJB-TV, a Fargo rival to WDAY, did not make as much of an effort in its early history to go out and gather news. While its studio equipment was often superior to its rivals, it spent less on other camera equipment. This collection was on cores or reels and that level of organization is primarily all that was available. The collection provides a different perspective from WDAY, and also reveals a different news organization. The collection is contained on 325 cores, but these cores average forty-five minutes in length because we did not want to disturb the existing order of this otherwise unidentified collection. Each core, on average, contains twenty-six segments.

The *Focus on the News* collection, produced by the North Dakota Farmers Union, includes film from both KFYR-TV (Bismarck) and WDAY-TV (Fargo), as well as film shot by the producer and received from service bureaus. The collection had been divided, due to a gift by a NDFU principal to the University of North Dakota. We preserved and transferred to video tape the ninety cores held by UND. Both holdings total 751 cores.

KXJB and, especially, *Focus on the News*, provided the greatest problems relating to their condition. Masking tape was used to hold cores together in many cases. Much of the *Focus* collection had been exposed to the elements. Unprotected reels of film lay piled in an unheated garage for a number of years. As a result, staff saw more dirt, tape, shrinkage, and brittleness in this collection than in the others combined.

At the close of the project, staff were more convinced than ever as to the enormous value of these collections. We are also more convinced than ever that they are complementary, with little overlap. Where stations did cover the same event, the difference in coverage has value as well.

Time and Cost

Our initial estimates, based on information received from other institutions, were that the total time spent would be in the area of seven to eight hours of staff time for each hour of film. This figure is a rule of thumb we have used in the past. Actual times come close to this, with some allowance for administrative and organizational time. For purposes of this project, we have attempted to divide the costs between core assembly, or basic preservation, and film-to-video transfer. We developed our figures around a thirty-minute core, although as noted above, cores in one collection were substantially longer than that. We still believe this to be a valid estimator, however.

Technicians spent an average of 2.38 hours (two hours and twenty-three minutes) per thirty-minute core for basic assembly. Cleaning added another ten minutes per core. This is basically a five-to-one ratio for the key portion of this effort. Data entry and record keeping added another forty minutes per core, bringing the ratio of labor time to film run time to more than six-to-one. Transfer of film to videotape averaged forty-eight minutes per core. By adding this task to the others, the ratio increases to more than eight-to-one, not counting administrative and organizational time.

The cost of each activity is complicated by the varying salaries. For purposes of this report, film technicians' salaries were used to compute the core assembly costs. (Core assembly consists of all tasks necessary to produce a clean thirty-minute core and place it on the shelf: cleaning, splicing, identifying, and so forth.) Film technicians received $9.73 per hour in salary and benefits during this project. Other costs use combinations of salaries. Data entry is based on the average of three salaries, film transfer on the average of two salaries, and so forth. Film-to-video transfer is based on a salary figure of $12.53 per hour.

Supplies were purchased in economic order quantities throughout the course of the project. Costs are averaged over the course of the project and include freight costs. As a state agency, the State Historical Society is not subject to sales taxes. A comparison of actual and estimated supplies purchases follows. Discrepancies are due to the fact that some supplies were on hand at the outset of the project in quantity and therefore it was not necessary to purchase as many as were used during the course of the project.

Material purchased:	Estimate	Actual
3/4-inch U-Matic tapes	1,200 @ 15.00	1,051 @ 15.67
VHS tapes	600 @ 5.00	870 @ 3.84
Film leader	60 @ 22.00	54 @ 27.37
Cores	2,000 @ .28	2240 @ .24
Film cans	2,000 @ 3.78	2,775 @ 3.90
Splicing tape	170 @ 2.95	290 @ 3.02
Cleaning materials	590.00	456.12

Some items, such as printed forms, were not used. Instead, we had computer-generated forms for most of the project and purchased several boxes of continuous paper.

66

Our original intent was to begin full-scale transfer to videotape beginning in the third quarter of the project. No transfer was planned for the first six months of the project because we wished to insure that misplaced segments would not need to be inserted into cores already transferred to videotape and because we wanted to concentrate on basic organization of the materials and entry of existing identification for the film. While transfer to videotape began in the third quarter of the project, the effort was not as sustained as anticipated and more time went into organization, data entry, and procedural refinements. During the second reporting period, 260 cores were transferred to videotape (both U-Matic and VHS copies). During the third reporting period, quarters five and six, an additional 380 cores were transferred. In the final six months of the project, 477 cores were transferred. An additional 243 cores have been transferred since the end of the grant period. The transfer of a thirty-minute core averages forty-eight minutes. Because we have only one film chain for film-to-video transfer, the real-time staff and equipment limitations are a controlling factor in determining the time frame within which transfer will take place.

Cores transferred to date represent approximately forty-six percent of the 2,957 cores contained in the four major collections. Because of the amount of service bureau film of national news stories within the *Focus on the News* collection, and to a lesser extent, the WDAY/WDAZ-TV Collection, we expect to concentrate on the transfer of 2,213 cores. Of that number, sixty-one percent has been transferred to date (fifty-one percent by the end of the grant period).

Video Transfer

Conclusion

During the course of the project, staff made various attempts to publicize the project and to experiment with methods to improve access. The project has been featured three times on news broadcasts. At the end of the first six-month period, we produced a brief newsletter, *News Update*, to distribute to anyone interested in the project. We anticipate issuing another one as a final public report on the project. Time did not permit issuing others during the course of the project. An article by a television news pioneer was published in an issue of *North Dakota History*, the quarterly journal of the State Historical Society. The issue was very well received, and the North Dakota Heritage Foundation held a reception in the author's honor in Fargo. The State Historical Society also presented a series of programs on the media in Fargo and Bismarck in April, 1994, to highlight in part the completion of this project.

Because of the value of the WDAY-TV scripts, we conducted a brief test to determine how well this material would scan for optical character recognition and how much time this effort might take. Our test was unsuccessful both in terms of time, which nearly approached rekeying, and in error, which was unacceptably high. The problem is a combination of uneven impressions from manual typewriters and script forms which added too many extraneous characters to the converted document. We may attempt the experiment again after gaining more experience with scanning and OCR.

KTHI-TV, a Fargo-based station which broadcasts throughout the Red River Valley region, recently transferred a first installment of news stories on videotape. They have agreed to donate their master tapes to us after five years.

This project, in addition to its primary objective of preserving these newsfilm collections, has also helped establish the credibility of the State Historical Society in its maintenance of film and video collections. As one example, KTHI approached us regarding the transfer of its videotape. We have also improved relations with one of our donors to the point where the station is coordinating its index to current news stories with our database, with the idea that their current materials will be deposited with the State Historical Society in the future.

The improved access to the collections is also extremely important. Although we have far to go in developing our finding aids, what we do know about the collections can be accessed rapidly. This is especially important as we expect use to increase significantly within the next couple of years.

The State Historical Society is extremely grateful to the NHPRC for its support of this project and we hope that you will find satisfaction with its accomplishments as well.

6

The Preservation of News and Documentary Film

William T. Murphy

National Archives and Records Administration

This chapter provides a comprehensive overview of 16mm film conservation and the equipment and supplies necessary for archives acquiring newsfilm collections. While archives may have both film and video material, it is usually 16mm newsfilm that is received first. The chapter includes basic information on equipment and procedures that will be important from the outset, as well as more technical data on film stocks and laboratory transfers that may seem esoteric within the parameters of newsfilm archives, but are critical when that information is needed.

William T. Murphy, a senior specialist in audio-visual archives at the National Archives and Records Administration, helped establish some of the broad archival programs relating to audio-visual records. His book, *Robert Flaherty: A Guide to References and Resources*, was cited by *Choice* as an "outstanding academic book of 1978." He is also a contributor to *Propaganda: The Art of Persuasion: World War II*, *The International Dictionary of Films and Filmmakers*, *International Encyclopedia of Communications*, as well as the author of articles about documentary film history and audio-visual archives. He is past president of the Washington Film and Video Council and founding president of the Association of Moving Image Archivists. In 1991 he received the Preservation and Scholarship Award of the International Documentary Association.

The Preservation of News and Documentary Film

This discussion of motion picture preservation is aimed at archivists, librarians, and others who undertake the management and care of historical collections of television news and documentary film. It attempts to provide basic knowledge for a general plan of operation, describing the key steps that are used to bring such collections under archival control, and the conditions and repairs that will extend film's useful life. It also provides guidance on restoration and copying onto newer film and videotape.[1]

In the years when they were using film, television news and documentary units used the 16mm gauge. The predominance of 16mm film dated from the late 1940s to the mid-1970s. In the early years of television news there was still some limited use of 35mm film, marking the transition from theatrical newsreels, and indeed 35mm was used by documentary film units on rare occasions. In the mid-1970s 16mm film along with its cumbersome sound equipment followed parchment and quill into extinction as a means for recording and reporting news. The upstart electronic device that caused the untimely demise of 16mm film and a veritable upheaval in news gathering and broadcasting was the 3/4-inch U-matic cassette, which, not incidentally, transformed industrial and other professional uses of moving images.

The videocassette brought about significant changes that affected the collection of news footage and its status in film libraries, changes that appear fairly typical from one broadcast organization to another. Film equipment was left in disuse or disrepair and eventually surplussed, especially film processing tanks with their pungent chemicals. Personnel skilled in the use of film equipment eventually retired, or made the transition to ENG or Electronic News Gathering. Even the making of a proper film splice became something of a lost art.

The upheaval also affected news film libraries. Relegated to storage rooms or other poorly-suited off-site storage areas, the film libraries were used with lesser frequency due to the failure or impracticality of integrating film footage of past events with videotape. In some cases, the absence of finding aids compounded this disuse of company assets. Retrieval depended on the memory of long-time employees, at least until they retired. Newsfilm libraries became remote from the daily broadcast operations with their ever-urgent deadlines. In the ceaseless succession of corporate takeovers and mergers, some cost-minded but myopic owners authorized wholesale destruction of film libraries. Happily, more prudent owners kept their libraries intact, and, one prefers to think, made the responsible decision to donate their collections to archival institutions in recognition of their historical value. Which, more or less, brings us to the present discussion of what to do with the massive quantity of film that has landed or will land on our doorstep.

This chapter focuses on the 16mm film record with several important assumptions. One is the need to preserve the original film for as long as possible; the original, after all, is the copy with the best photographic resolution, the most critical aspect of film preservation. A videotape copy of a film is by definition an inferior copy (though some enhancements are technically feasible). NTSC (North American Standard) video has less than half the lines of resolution of 16mm film. Film's larger screen aspect ratio and the relative permanence of optical sound also give film an advantage over video. In screenings before large groups video cannot yet compete with film (though High Definition Video may eventually close the gap). Properly processed and stored, the original film will last longer than a videotape copy. The argument for preserving the original also assumes that in the constant state of electronic evolution in video technology there will always be a need to work from the film originals.

One also assumes that institutions will want to preserve the originals to protect the legal and historical integrity of the film's subject matter. In accepting responsibility for the historical materials entrusted to its care, the archive will be obliged to maintain continuous and permanent custody of the film copies until advanced deterioration makes it no longer feasible.

This chapter does not include consideration of nitro-cellulose motion picture film, which requires a different set of handling and storage techniques due to its chemical instability and extreme flammability. Nitrate motion picture raw stock was manufactured in the United States until 1951. It was manufactured in the 35mm gauge though some was split for use as 16mm film. Television news and documentary production employed 16mm safety acetate film and 16mm polyester film, so nitrate film remains outside the focus of this manual.

Newsfilm archives have enough concerns with safety films. We can be thankful that television stations didn't use nitrate film.

Storage Conditions

Providing proper storage conditions is undoubtedly the most important step an archive can take to ensure the long-term survival of its film. Black-and-white and color films have enough problems inherent in their composition without the harmful effects of polluted air and excessive temperature and humidity. Improper storage conditions can undo the most careful and painstaking restoration and have the opposite result of making preservation work more difficult than ever.

Rusted film can.

Air Quality

• To the maximum extent possible, store archival copies of film in a separate or compartmentalized vault. Designate the vault for storage and storage alone, and house reference or access copies in another location.

• Conduct as much staff work as possible outside the vault in designated work or office areas. Limit activities in the vaults to shelving, pulling and refiling, and to periodic inventories or surveys.

• Test the air in the vault for excessive dust and other particulate matter. Maintaining positive air pressure is an effective way of reducing particulate levels. Air filters in conjunction with the HVAC (heating, ventilation and air conditioning) system are also useful. Regular cleaning of shelving, storage containers, and floors will also help to reduce levels of soot and dust.

• Air content analysis is also necessary to measure the presence of harmful gases such as nitrous dioxide, sulfur dioxide, and chlorides, all of which should remain within archival tolerances for the long-term storage of film. Fumes from fresh paint are also harmful. "Cure" paint until the fumes are eliminated and exchange the air before placing archival film in storage. Chemical concentrations of any kind are best avoided. They can cause irreparable damage, such as silver migration, color dye fading, and deterioration of the film's acetate base. Archives located on university campuses may be able to obtain the assistance of science faculties to ascertain air content. Others should seek the services of environmental study vendors.

Humidity

Both black-and-white and color films require equally low relative humidity (RH) of about thirty percent for long-term storage.[2] If RH at this level is not available from the HVAC system, consider supplementary dehumidification units, particularly during the warm summer months in humid climates. Even moderate levels of about fifty percent will accelerate shrinkage and the fading of color dyes. Excessive humidity of sixty percent or higher encourages mold or fungus spores, high concentrations of which attack the film's base and gelatin which are made from organic materials. Rewash films infected with mold as soon as possible. Severe infestation may require rewashing whole parts of a collection. Proceed cautiously with a sufficient test period to ensure that the rewash does not cause any adverse chemical changes. Films stored in humid conditions for lack of other storage alternatives should be inspected more frequently than others.

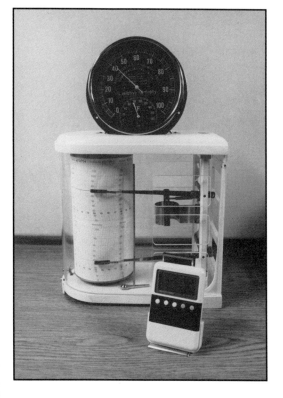

A variety of devices can measure temperature and humidity.

Very low relative humidity can dry out the film, making it become brittle and easily breakable. RH conditions lower than twenty percent are undesirable. Humidity is the most important factor in the process known as the "vinegar syndrome," a shorthand way of referring to the chemical deterioration of cellulose acetate motion picture film, a topic to which we will return.

A hygrothermograph. The advantage of this type of device is that it provides a record of temperature and humidity over a seven-day period.

Temperature

Recent investigations into the deterioration of safety film indicate that cool temperatures can increase film's longevity. Cool temperatures tend to moderate the aging process by slowing down the film's undesirable chemical reaction. An increase of $9°$ F ($5°$ C) doubles the rate of many chemical reactions. High temperatures accelerate chemical aging and cause dimensional and physical changes like shrinkage, curling, and breaking.

Store black-and-white safety film at less than room temperature. A setting of about $50°$ F ($10°$ C) is optimal. The maximum acceptable temperature is about $65-70°$ ($18-21°$ C) for long-term storage.

Store color film at even cooler temperatures, $35°$ F ($2°$ C) or below freezing. There are a number of different settings recommended by different groups, but generally the cooler, the better. Eastman Kodak and ANSI (American National Standards Institute) recom-

Cold storage vault (exterior) at the Chicago Historical Society.

Cold storage vault (interior) at the Chicago Historical Society.

74

mend a maximum of 36° F (2° C).[3] FIAF (International Federation of Film Archives/Fédération Internationale des Archives du Film) recommends 23° F (-5° C).[4]

Constant and consistent temperature and relative humidity conditions are essential elements of archival film storage and fluctuations are harmful. Record and measure storage conditions by using a hygrothermograph, which should be calibrated periodically for accuracy.

Cold temperatures in combination with low humidity raise problems of acclimatization. The best cold storage vaults have antechambers that help film reach equilibrium before being placed in the inner vault for long-term storage or before taking it out for use. The length of time for interim storage will depend upon local conditions, including temperature and humidity and dew point. It is important to prevent condensation from forming on the reel. Condensation can cause buckling and wavy edging. The process of taking an acetate reel from freezing temperatures and thawing it is not harmful if proper precautions are taken against condensation.[5]

Nonetheless, a proper storage environment is one that maintains fairly constant temperature and RH, with a minimum of cycling and avoidance of extremes.

Sealed Bags

Demoisturization and hermetic sealing in vapor barrier bags are necessary in storage conditions where the RH cannot be kept at low levels. Conditioning cabinets are effective in removing some of the film's moisture. Weighing the reel of film before and after conditioning is one way to measure demoisturization. The use of bags without demoisturization is counterproductive. It may even be harmful if the reel is deteriorating and exposed to warm temperatures as the result of a breakdown in the refrigeration system. Deteriorating film emits gases which act as catalysts. It is best to let them escape. Warm temperatures, deteriorating film, and hermetically sealed bags are a combination guaranteed to lead to catastrophic loss.

Two typical rusted metal cans received by the Wolfson Center against a backdrop of archival plastic cans. The Center has adopted the plastic archival can as its standard. All metal cans are replaced.

Storage Containers

Regrettably there is no ideal storage container. Metal ions found in aluminum and tin cans tend to promote deterioration of acetate bases in combination with excessive temperature and humidity. Acid-free cardboard boxes, benign in themselves, do not stack very well, offer little protection against water damage, and, in a fire emergency, cause fire spread in a vault of otherwise fire resistant and slow-burning safety film. Most plastic containers are unsuitable for archival film because they are made of compounds like polyvinyl chloride which emits off-gases that attack the emulsion and film base. Due to their relative stability, plastic containers made of polypropylene or polyethylene are most commonly used as archival storage containers, but even they breakdown over time and contribute to the film's degradation. Nonetheless, plastic containers made of polypropylene are used for archival storage since they offer a reasonable measure of protection. Polypropylene containers are also available with halogenated compounds used as flame retardants. The amount of halogen must be strictly controlled to protect silver emulsions and color dyes. But at low halogen levels and used in combination with cool temperatures, flame retardant plastic containers make a sensible compromise for long-term storage.

A buffered or coated polyethylene bag placed inside the container with the film reel inserted inside the bag offers an additional measure of protection against dust, dirt, excessive handling, and water damage. Remove the clear plastic bags that commercial laboratories supply.

Wind the film itself on a peroxide-free plastic film core and remove everything else from the container, including paper (except acid-free), rubber bands, paper clips, and other objects. Finally, store the film in the can horizontally in uniform size cans flat on the shelf, which will act to spread its weight evenly over a long period of time.

Secure Vaults in General

Film vaults should only contain film. Keep all extraneous materials, such as empty cartons, wooden pallets, brooms, dust mops, etc., out of the vaults. Place nothing in the

Store film horizontally. . .

. . .not vertically as some
shelving units allow.

vaults that is combustible or will serve as fuel in a fire or promote its spread. For this
reason metal shelves are preferred over wooden ones. Archival film should not be stored
with paper products. Paper records or manuscripts emit gases that are dangerous to film
emulsions and bases.

Archival film vaults require a minimum rating of six hours protection against burning.[6]
Sprinkler systems are frequently used as part of fire protection systems since they may
be part of the overall building requirements or mandatory under local codes, but in film

Off-site storage may be
another option to
consider.

77

vaults containing nothing but slow-burning safety film they may pose a potential hazard from water leaks more than from fire spread. Finally, the vault requires protection against theft or intrusion and against access by unauthorized persons.

Preservation Problems

There are two major preservation problems in the management of collections of 16mm safety film. One is the deterioration of film due to the "vinegar syndrome," and the other is the inexorable fading of color film.

Vinegar Syndrome

The 16mm films acquired from television organizations may not have been kept under the best of conditions. Cellulose triacetate film improperly stored for several decades has a limited life expectancy compared to newly-processed film placed in archival storage. The processing of newsfilm occurred years ago, probably under hasty conditions where archival wash was not a consideration. Years of poor storage conditions have likely taken their toll.

Moreover, the acetate base may also deteriorate from a process known as the "vinegar syndrome," first brought to the attention of film archives in 1987 by Karel Brems at a joint technical symposium. Dr. Brems described the hydrolysis of cellulose triacetate as a process in which film polymers react with moisture and heat, releasing acetic acid; hence the odor of vinegar.[7]

The damage from vinegar syndrome differs from the effects of excessive residual hypo which primarily discolors and stains the film and hastens the fading of color dyes. Vinegar syndrome attacks the film's base and image, causing shrinkage and other dimensional changes, releasing gases, emitting crystalline powder and leaving the film an odorous and unworkable mass. To make matters even worse, the escaping gases can attack nearby reels in good condition, initiating and accelerating deterioration. It is advisable to isolate deteriorating film in separate storage and to make arrangements for

Visually inspect film on rewinds.

copying while the film is still recoverable. Destroy film in advanced stages of decomposition, ones that have a powerful odor, show crystalline deposits, or stick or weld together.

The three major influences on the deterioration of acetate film are the usual suspects: temperature, humidity, and storage containers. William Lee and Charleton Bard described how high temperature and the moisture in humidity cause hydrolysis of plasticizers commonly used as flame retardants in the safety film base. "The hydrolysis of cellulose acetate," they wrote, "is acid catalyzed which means the rate of hydrolysis is accelerated as the level of acidity increases."

PH testing is a reliable means of measuring film's acidity and changes over time.[8] The process, unfortunately, is destructive to the film sample and the testing is somewhat impractical outside of a chemistry laboratory. A new product on the market designed for film cans changes colors in the presence of acidic off-gases. Nonetheless, the urgency of copying is directly proportional to the rate of acidification.

Studies conducted by the Image Permanence Institute (IPI) in Rochester, New York, illustrate that the deterioration of all cellulose ester films follows the same dismal pattern of degradation.[9] Cellulose triacetate is not necessarily more stable than nitrate (except of course in terms of flammability). Indeed, according to the IPI, both stored at lowered temperature and RH have about the same longevity. Since cellulose triacetate has played such an essential role in the preservation strategy of film archives over the last forty years, IPI's research is not easy to accept, and one can predict challenges to its methodology and conclusions. There is a consensus, however, that polyester film is far more durable than triacetate.

The Manchester Polytechnic Group, whose parallel research confirms the degradation pattern of cellulose triacetate, has also studied the effects of storage containers. The presence of metal ions accelerates the rate of deterioration because they also act as a catalyst to hasten undesirable chemical change. Metal cans as archival storage containers should be avoided. Among the metals, aluminum is the least damaging, and iron should be avoided under any circumstances as a storage container.[10] The iron oxides contained in magnetic sound tracks can also have the same unwanted effects, posing the same danger to the film base. Store magnetic tracks separately, never with the picture reels, and due to their impermanent adhesion, copy them to optical sound as early as possible.

Color Fading

Another sobering and unpleasant characteristic of archival film is that color images fade.[11] Derived essentially from organic materials, color dyes degrade from the effects of heat and humidity. Intensity of light can also influence fading, but it is more of a problem associated with color still photography due to the duration of exposure. Excessive residual hypo and the application of insufficient stabilizing agents used during processing also induce color fading. The yellow and cyan layers being the least stable among the three primary colors expose more and more of the magenta layer as they fade, which accounts for the pinkish-purplish hue of faded films. This is particularly true for prints, which fade much faster than color negatives. Antonioni's masterpiece of 1964, *Red Desert*, might appropriately be called the *Pink Desert* when suitably faded.

Some color correction is possible, although it depends on how much of the faded primary color remains. Significant loss in one dye layer can make the restoration of the original colors impossible to achieve. Filters are used in copying to restore the color balance. Color masking and black-and-white separation printing are other methods.[12] The Hollywood studios preserve many of their most commercially valuable color films on black-and-white separation masters, a technology not viable for 16mm documentary and newsfilm.

Reducing the storage temperature together with lowering the RH dramatically improves color dye stability. Charleton Bard, one-time supervisor of processing chemistry and image dye stability at Eastman Kodak, said in 1981: "If the temperature is reduced from 75° F to 45° F, the dark-keeping stability is predicted to improve by ten times. Reducing the temperature even further to 14° F yields a predicted 110-times improvement." Cold storage, therefore, is a practical way to retard the fading of color images.[13]

In addition to providing optimum storage conditions, an archive should plan to reproduce all of its critically important color film originals on modern film stock, specifically those with improved dark-keeping stability. Eastman Kodak began making LF or "low fade" series of color emulsions available in the early 1980s, following a spate of public criticism, and expression of concern by several leading Hollywood filmmakers over the fading of color film, including a number of Hollywood classics.[14] In response to this criticism Kodak introduced its LF series which had improved cyan stability. This allowed archives the opportunity, at additional expense, to recopy valuable color films onto modern stocks (acetate and polyester) with improved dark-keeping stability.

Recopying together with the use of cold storage will help ensure the survival of color film images in a quality form for several hundred years. In the next century, however, it is likely that the solution to the problem of preserving color motion pictures will be electronic instead of photochemical.

Archival Processing

Archival processing entails all the steps necessary to bring the holdings under archival control. Among the most immediate tasks are arrangement, proper identification, and inventory control. Preservation planning cannot take place without the completion of these steps. Indeed irreparable damage can occur if the holdings are not brought under archival control.

Arrangement

Archives follow rules of provenance and original order when arranging their film collections. It is difficult to exaggerate the importance of being able to document the origin and interrelationship of items within the holdings to facilitate historical research and to provide some legal basis for their custody. These principles govern the arrangement of most archival collections. On another level, it is also important to identify series within a collection. Common series are edited and unedited, news film inserts, outtakes, documentaries, and specials.

Nonetheless, modification of these rules may be necessary based upon technical considerations and common sense safety precautions that are somewhat unique to motion picture collections because of the multiplicity of copies needed for preservation and access.

First, separate collections or series into originals, intermediates, and prints with corresponding sound tracks, and arrange them into parallel files or sequences. Clearly label each container. Second, store these sets, preferably in separate vaults; or, if not available, in separate parts of the same vault. Such is the principle of "strategic dispersal" which offers a better chance of survival in the event of a disaster. Careful separation of copies will also reduce chances of staff errors in retrieval or use.

Further refinement of arrangement schemes is also warranted. Place color film in cold storage. Remove separate magnetic sound tracks and store them away from the film copies. Separate optical sound tracks, however, should always remain with the corresponding picture reels.

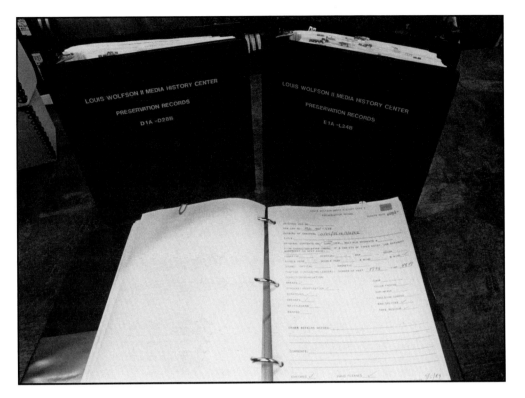

Preservation records.

Film Inventory/Identification

If it is the first obligation of every archive to separate its nitrate film from its safety film, surely the next most important is to compile an accurate inventory. Unfortunately this means more than just counting the numbers of cans. Rather, the inventory process begins to draw upon an understanding of motion picture technology, of basic film types and their generational relationship. If the preservation of motion pictures in archives were simply a matter of collecting prints, the rest of this discussion would probably be

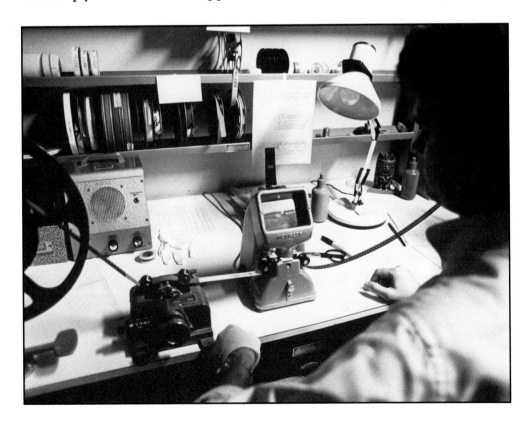

At work at the Wolfson Center.

81

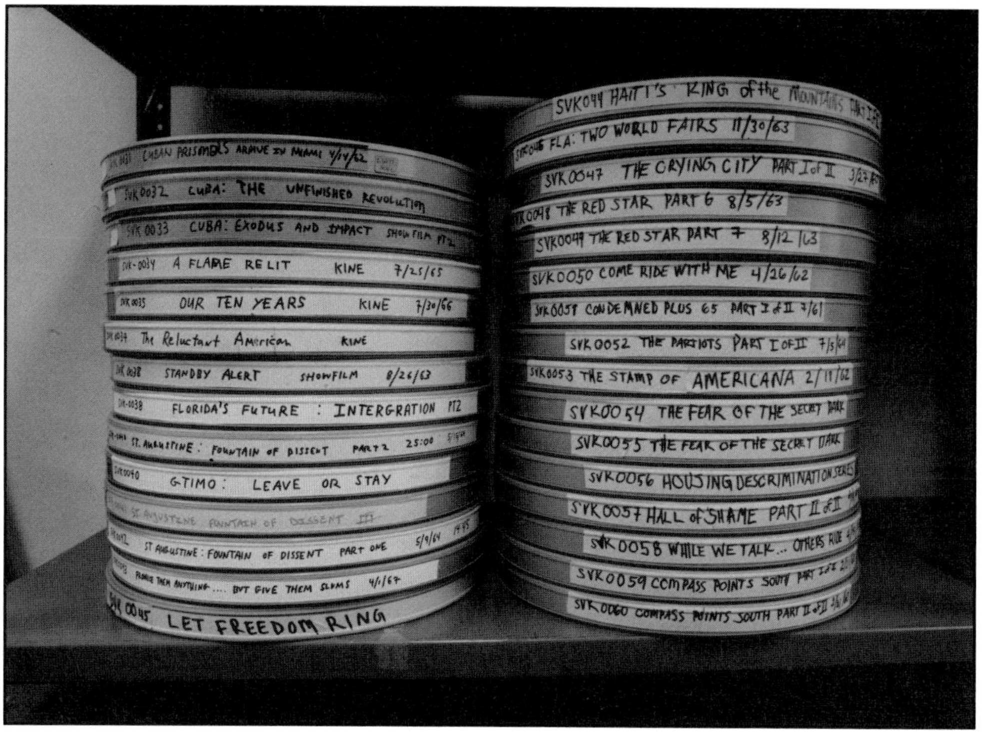

Kinescopes from the Wolfson Center's WSVN collection.

superfluous. Preservation, however, requires the acquisition of preprint elements, negatives, masters, etc., which should be carefully enumerated in the archive's inventories in order that subsequent stages of archival work can be planned and implemented.

Basic Film Stocks

In order to conduct an inventory, an archivist must first become familiar with generic 16mm film stocks. Some of the common black-and-white stocks are listed below:

Original negative
Original reversal
Fine grain master positive
Duplicate negative
Projection print

The original negative is the out-of-camera original. The master positive is used to make duplicate negatives, which are used in turn to make projection prints. Reversal film is a camera original, developed as a positive image. Subsequent copying of reversal film generates a projection print, thus saving a generation.

Kinescopes are also found in television film collections. Used mainly in the years before videocassettes when 2-inch videotapes were used only sparingly, kinescopes are 16mm films recorded from a cathode ray tube. They were made as direct negatives or positives and are characterized by a flat image with low contrast lighting.

Color film follows more or less the same pattern as that of black-and-white, except reversal printing is more common.

Original negative
Original reversal
Inter-positive
Inter-negative
Projection print

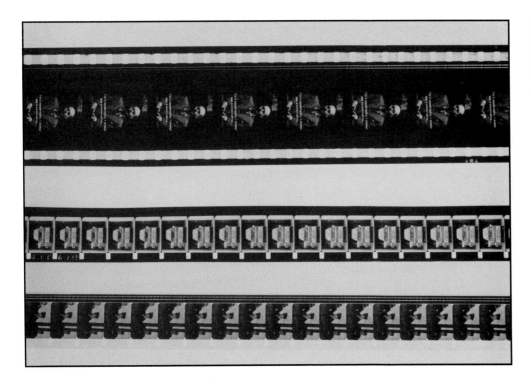

35mm film (top), 16mm film with magnetic soundtrack (middle), 16mm with optical soundtrack (bottom).

Here are some key dates in the introduction of 16mm color film stocks:

Kodachrome, 1935
Eastman Color, 1950
Ektachrome Commercial, 1958
Color Reversal Inter-negative, 1968

Large collections of newsfilm outtakes and unedited footage usually contain only original negative or original reversal with, hopefully, matching work prints. With featured news clips or documentary productions, any number of combinations are possible.

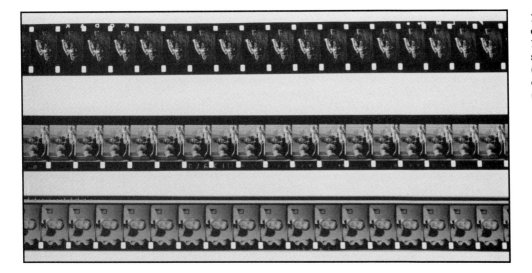

16mm silent double perf (top), 16mm magnetic soundtrack (middle), 16mm optical soundtrack (bottom).

Sound Film

While this breakdown may seem simple enough, sound film makes the identification of film types more complex. All 16mm sound film has a single row of perforations or sprocket holes. A sound track may be combined on the same reel with the picture frames to form "composite sound" or the track may be on a reel by itself to form "separate sound," also known in the parlance of film as "double system sound." "Double perf" film is categorically silent.

Film sound tracks can take either an optical or magnetic form. The optical soundtrack can be either positive or negative. It can be variable density, which looks like an endless track of barcodes. Or it can be variable area, where lines are modulated according to sound content. An optical sound head reads both optical forms. The optical sound track is printed on the unperforated edge of 16mm film.

16mm full-coat magnetic soundtrack.

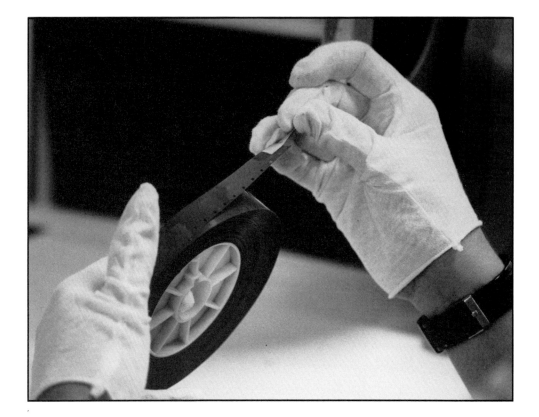

Magnetic sound takes the form of a stripe coated along the unperforated edge. A very thin oxide stripe running parallel to the magnetic sound track is a balance track which is used to render an even wind. Also, the film may have a separate "full-coat track", in which the iron oxide coating covers the entire reel forming the emulsion side. Magnetic stripe sound combined with the picture frames is composite sound. Magnetic stripe film on a reel by itself and full-coat magnetic reels are used in double system sound. A magnetic sound head reads magnetic sound and it is not compatible with optical sound. Many automatic viewers, however, are equipped with both types of sound readers.

A great deal of news sound originated on 1/4-inch open-reel recorders synchronized with the camera. Later the editors recopied the sound on to 16mm magnetic reels in order to work with sound and picture together. Ektachrome original with a magnetic stripe was also very popular for shooting news in the field due to the steps saved in processing and transferring sound.

Here is a summary, then, of the major sound elements typically found in news and documentary film collections:

Variable area, variable density
Composite
Separate optical track, negative or positive
Magnetic stripe
Full-coat magnetic
1/4-inch audiotape

In addition here are some helpful rules of thumb about 16mm sound film my boss never told me:

• Although camera originals are usually silent, many news film originals were made with composite optical and magnetic sound tracks.

• Fine grain master positives are usually silent.

• Black-and-white dupe negatives are sound or silent.

• Color preprint is always silent with the exception of an original reversal with magnetic stripe.

• Sound runs twenty-six frames ahead of the picture in optical sound; twenty-eight in magnetic.

A and B Wind

An understanding of a film's wind not only aids in the process of film identification but it is the key to communicating with the laboratory for specifying copying work and

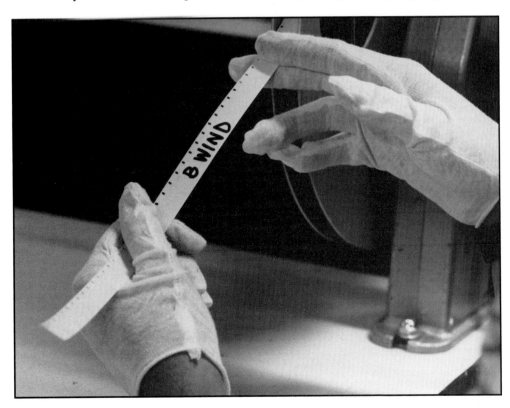

B-wind film.

A-wind film.

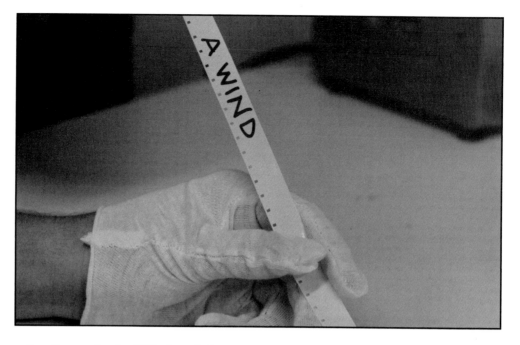

estimating costs. As difficult as it is to overstate its importance for 16mm film work, virtually none of the film preservation literature discusses wind.

A and B winds.

The wind of a film refers to the way a film is read. When raw film is exposed in a camera, the film's unexposed emulsion faces the lens and the camera's subject. The emulsion captures a mirror image of the subject. To read the picture correctly it is necessary to look through the base side. Therefore, all camera originals are "B-wind." Associating the letter B with base is an easy way to remember. Films read correctly through the emulsion side are "A-wind."

The winds, however, will change with copying. In contact printing films are copied emulsion to emulsion. Hence, B-wind becomes A-wind in the new copy, and, if copied to another generation, A-wind becomes B-wind.

86

Knowledge of the wind helps to determine a film's generation, such as distinguishing between an original negative and dupe negative. To assemble short reels for film printing, only like winds should be assembled on the same reel. To assemble short reels for film-to-video transfers, wind is less important, but make the short reels all read correctly in the same position. In furnishing a sale copy to a client researcher, the client may specify a wind that will be used to intercut with the client's footage, and optical printing may be needed. Unlike contact printing, optical printing does not require emulsion-to-emulsion exposure, so the rendered copy can be A or B-wind. Optical printing is usually twice the cost of contact printing, but may be worth the price to offset generational loss of resolution.

The Inventory

It is imperative to create a preservation inventory or shelflist early in the accessioning process. This serves as an accurate record of the holdings and provides the basis for space and preservation planning. It also provides for a limited level of research or reference

Accurate inventory and preservation records are imperative.

service. The key inventory descriptive fields vary from archive to archive, but they should include a file control number, title or caption, and date; and, above all, a precise description of the components. An example listing follows:

WKYJ-TV NEWS COLLECTION
    Series: Inserts

  1. Local elections coverage, May 1, 1968
     Original color negative
     Full-coat magnetic sound track
     Color work print, silent

As new copies are made, update the inventory to keep it as current as possible. Several database programs are available that archives can utilize to monitor their holdings in this manner.

It is important to understand that the inventory does not substitute for closer analysis, inspection, and repair. Preparing the inventory is just the first stage, one performed expeditiously by examining the container and labels, opening the container, looking at the reel as a whole, and unraveling a few feet. The immediate objective is to bring all of the holdings under archival control as soon as reasonably possible, deferring painstaking inspection and repairs to a subsequent stage.

Equipment

Archives require basic film equipment and related supplies to carry out their work in a professional manner. Equipment ranges from the simple to the complex, from modest costs to high costs. Practically speaking, few archives are in a position to purchase their own printers and processing equipment. Nevertheless, the basic tools can be acquired for a modest cost that will enable the archive to perform several critical tasks like inspection, repair, and cleaning. Even good, used film equipment can be acquired competitively due to the growth of the video industry.

Factors that have worked to the archives' advantage are the fundamental stability of film technology and the continuity of the 16mm gauge since 1923. Virtually all 16mm equipment is compatible.

Visualize film preservation equipment in the form of a work station that can be cloned one or more times commensurate with the resources of the archive. A typical work station consists of an inspection table with a built-in light box; a set of manual rewinds, with long shafts and split reels; a table-model hot splicer or tape splicer; and a synchronizer, used to measure and match picture and separate sound tracks. The approximate cost of this work station is $4,000.

To be able to view a moving image and listen to the sound requires another range of equipment. Several archives use a moviescope together with a separate optical or magnetic reader for detailed inspection and repair work. The scope and reader are used on the inspection table in conjunction with manual rewinds, a system that film editors have used for many years to edit and match work prints and conform negatives or masters.

Automatic inspection machines, though practical in circulating film collections, should be used in archives only with great caution. They can be used for larger reels in fairly good condition. Even so, operate them at the slowest speed since there may be a tendency to snap film at the higher settings. In addition, the operator must become very adept at the controls.

None of the above equipment is satisfactory for cataloging and research purposes. Automatic viewers are needed until video copies become available. Projectors are not suitable for everyday cataloging and research in archives due to risk of damage and the impracticality of their stop-and-go controls. Automatic viewers are available as table models and as stand-alones. For example, RTI's Cinescan, a table model, has a relatively large screen and will accept split reels. It is fairly easy to operate and has a good tolerance for shrunken film. It is moderately priced compared to others but is limited to single system sound.

Flatbed viewers or editors are stand-alone models, such as CTM, KEM, and Steenbeck, which are widely used in archives all over the world. They are available in several models that have two or more take-up plates. At least four plates are needed for double-system picture and sound tracks, and they are equipped with optical and magnetic sound readers. Although designed primarily for editing film productions, they have several features that make them suitable for archival work. The most important is a prism movement which enables the film to be transported with much less

Recommended setup: light table, hand rewinds, sound box, synchronizer, splicer, moviescope viewer, and sprocket repair unit.

tension than the intermittent movement in projectors, making the film less susceptible to damage. They also have variable speed and play, reverse, and pause mechanisms which are easy to operate. They will accept film on cores, have built-in footage counters, offer table work space, and have a large screen illuminated by low-intensity light sources or lamps. Flatbed viewers are essential equipment for quality control of new copies returned from the laboratories.

Cinescan with split reel.

A more basic setup requires only rewinds mounted on a table.

Automatic inspection machine. Fine for circulating collections, but not recommended for archival film.

Flatbed viewers can also be equipped with video cameras to give the archive the ability to view positives or negatives by reversing the camera's polarity. Second, this configuration provides a safe and inexpensive means of making video study copies of films, a feature that will certainly help to amortize the equipment's not inconsiderable cost, which, unhappily, is equivalent to buying an expensive automobile.

Several archives have used an Elmo film-to-video projector to convert their holdings to videocassettes, utilizing archive staff to perform the work. The process is generally safe

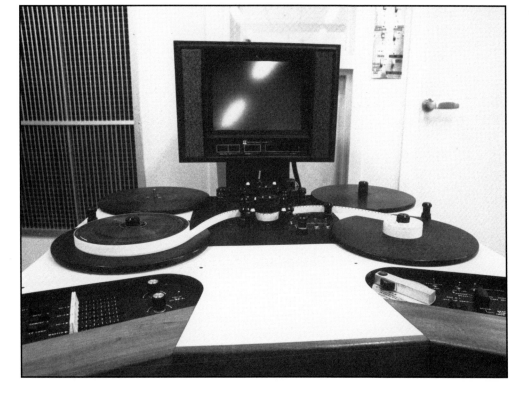

A four plate flatbed.

A more elaborate multi-plate flatbed.

and effective though it is not suitable for films with high shrinkage. The Elmo features optical or magnetic sound playback, and it can produce copies acceptable for broadcast use. Other equipment needed for film-to-video copies include a time-base corrector, a time-code generator, a character generator, and, of course, video recorders.

The Elmo TRV 16G film-to-tape transfer unit.

Keep equipment cleaned and properly maintained. Working with old and fragile film materials is difficult enough without adding more scratches and breakage due to dirt or poorly maintained equipment.

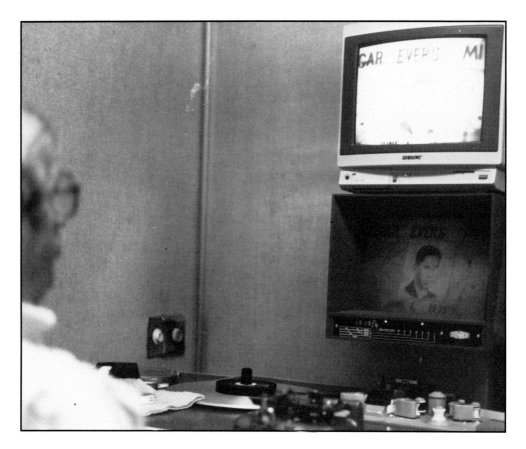

Modified flatbed viewer with a video monitor.

Wolfson Center set-up includes an Elmo film-to-tape transfer unit, time-base corrector/effects generator, black burst generator, edit control unit, two monitors and three decks.

In addition to major equipment, supplies and other relatively small items are needed to perform the daily tasks of working with archival film:

Brushes
Film leader and trailer
Hygrothermograph
Lint-free gloves

Supplies

The system in use.

Magnifier or jeweler's loupe
Marking pens for film
Plastic archival film containers
Plastic cores
Polyethylene film bags
Scissors
Scraping knives
Shrinkage gauge
Split reels

Some of the supplies needed to work with archival film.

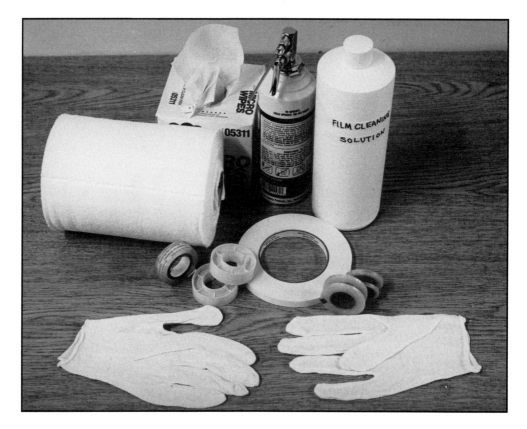

Inspection and Repair

Now that the whole collection is under archival control by means of an accurate inventory, the most painstaking work of inspection and repair can start. This does not, however, preclude singling out deteriorated film for immediate work identified during the inventory process.

To begin, it is helpful to distinguish between relatively large reels, for example, 1,200 and 1,600 feet of film, and smaller ones, 400 feet of film. Treat the larger ones as single items and plan to store them in their own containers. Treat the smaller reels as parts of larger ones. Indeed, one of the most time-consuming tasks is the assembly of the smaller reels into larger units, time well-invested that will promote efficient storage and handling and more cost-effective film and video reproduction.

Inspect each reel over a rewind table. Examine it for its general condition. Attach leader and trailer. Apply identification numbers. Measure the film's length from the synchronization mark or, if silent, from the first picture frame. Also measure the film's shrinkage at the beginning, middle, and end. Document this information in a parallel file.

Assess the film's damage and also document it for future reference. Look for scratches or abrasions and note if they are on the base or emulsion side. Judge the scratches; are

Synchronizer/footage counter and viewer on light table between rewinds.

they light, medium, or heavy? Check for brittleness, breakage, and curling. Check for stickiness, ferrotyping, stains, dirt, and mold. Check for edge damage and torn perforations. Look for breaks and test and count all splices.

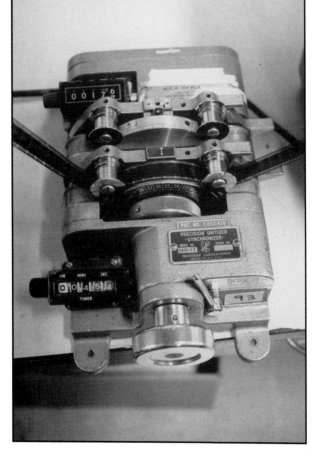

Synchronizer.

Assess the stability of the black-and-white image. Common problems are a softening of the image due to silver migration, fading away of the emulsion, and stains from excessive residual hypo. On color film, assess the degree of dye fading. Without densitometric measurements, only extreme fading to magenta may be noticeable.

Assess the stability of the base. Strong acidic odor or crystalline deposits indicate the advanced onset of decomposition due to "vinegar syndrome."

On sound tracks visually examine them in the same manner and test sound levels on readers. On magnetic film, check for peeling or other loosening of the oxide layer.

95

Densitometer.

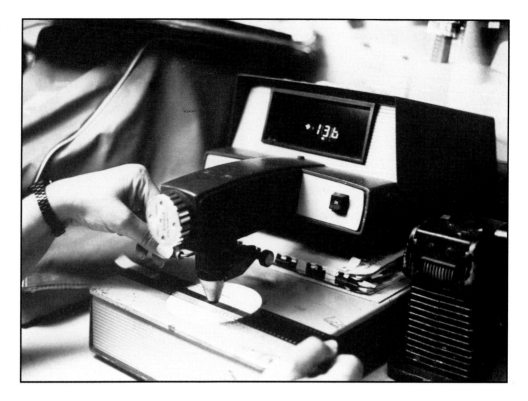

Film cleaning unit
between rewinds.

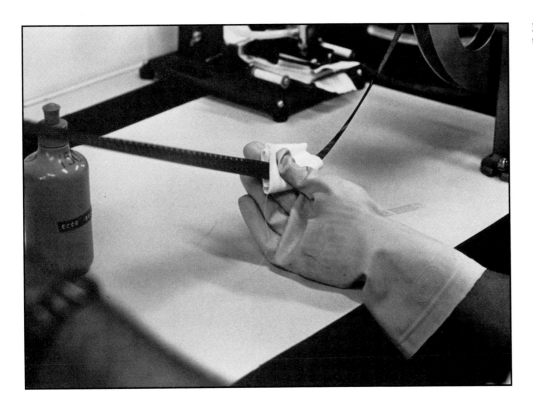

Removing masking tape residue.

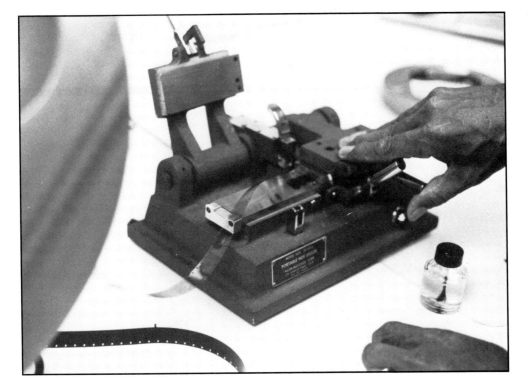

Cement splicer.

Tape splicer.

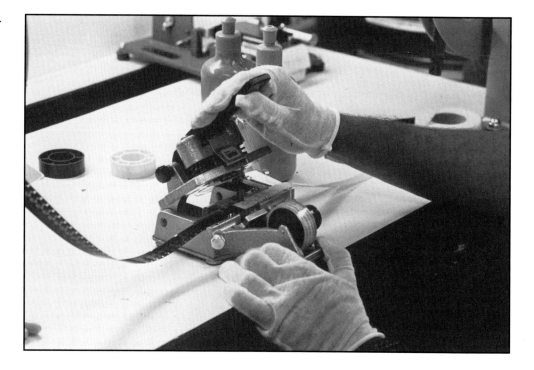

Repairs

Undertake some repairs during the initial inspection. Brush away dirt and identify areas that need spot cleaning. Use pads with an approved cleaning fluid and avoid using alcohol of any kind. Wipe dry with anti-static cloth. Rewinding wet film will cause blotching and staining. Remove tape, paper clips, staples, and any other foreign matter. Remove all plastic and metal reels, and wind the film onto a core.

Test and repair all splices, using a hot splicer and fresh cement or a tape splicer. Splicing is an exacting craft and technical staff should receive sufficient training and have experience before they attempt to splice archival film. A novice will destroy many frames before getting it right. Overly thick splices will impair film or video copies, while weak ones will separate during use, causing additional damage. Cutting and splicing out damage can be excessive; too many frames are lost and, if there is a separate track, synch problems occur. Above all, do not notch the broken perf because it will only weaken the film's strength.

Common defects and types of film damage which may be found in any newsfilm collection are illustrated in the following series of photographs (text continues following photographs):

Buckling.

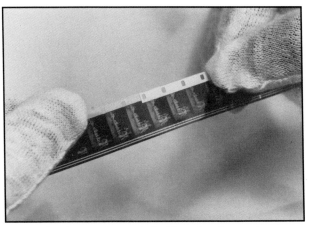
Torn perforations can be mended with perforation repair tape.

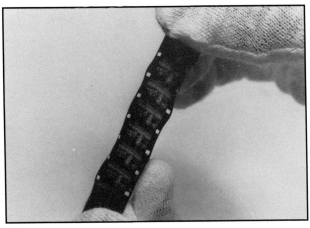
Shrinkage.

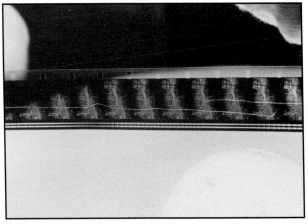
Emulsion scratches.

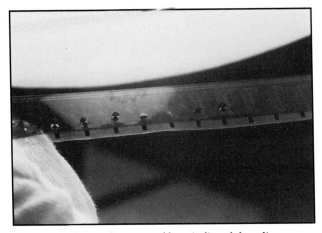
Sprocket marks—perhaps caused by misaligned threading or improper projection of film.

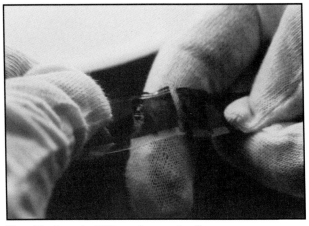
Newsfilm from the 1950s can be very fragile.

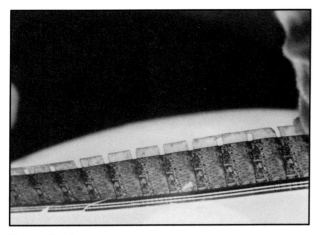

Torn perforations.

Crease or bend in the film.

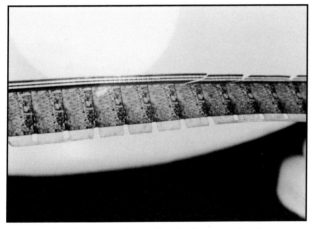

Tears and breaks in optical soundtrack; also note edge damage which enters the frame.

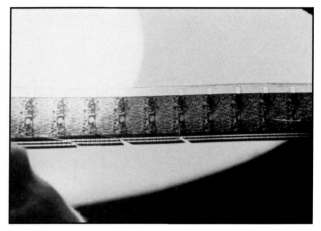

Four faded frames (left) in addition to tears and breaks in the sound track (bottom) and scratch mark (right).

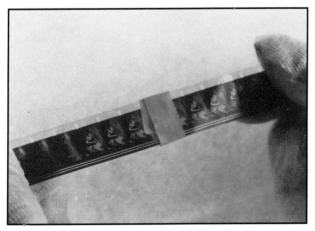

Masking tape splice.

TEXT CONTINUED ON NEXT PAGE

The Assembly

Tackling a large 2,000-foot can with numerous "rollettes" of film is a daunting task, because it requires not only inspection and repair but also organization and assembly. A good place to begin is to first ensure that there are guidelines for discarding the smallest reels and those whose subject matter have little or no research value in areas that relate to the archive's mission. Second, draw upon finding aids such as the notes of a cameraman or other documentation to determine the original order. Third, use the internal evidence in the film container such as file numbers, dates, and captions.

Can and date-card file from the WTVJ collection at the Wolfson Center.

Split reels come in various sizes.

•   In addition to these intellectual judgments, there are technical considerations that govern the assembly of small reels into more manageable units. Separate black-and-white from color. Separate negative from positive. Ensure that the winds agree, and that the emulsion position agrees.

•   Assemble the smaller reels into sizes of 400 feet or more, or to a more-or-less uniform size that is somewhat less than the intended can size. Strict uniformity of size is probably not possible. Between each segment insert a "slug" or blank leader and indicate the file or control number, title or caption.

A split reel separates to remove film wound on a core.

•   Rewind the inspected and assembled reel on a plastic core, rewinding at a tension that will not cinch the film. Aim for a tight even wind. Store the reel tails out. There is no decisive argument for storing emulsion in or out. Tape the film's trailer down, but do not tape the leader to the core; rather, insert the film in the core's slot.

•   Insert the reel of film in an opaque polyethylene bag to prevent the reel from sliding in the can. The bag will protect against excessive handling and possible water damage.

•   Store the bagged films in plastic archival film containers. They are available in polypropylene with safe levels of flame retardation. As budget permits, plan to replace all metal containers with plastic ones at the earliest opportunity. Plastic is not as conducive as metal to the development of vinegar syndrome.

•   Store the film can horizontally, which will evenly disperse the weight of the film over long periods of storage, and do not stack more than ten cans high.

•   Do not store magnetic film with picture reels since the off-gases from the magnetic oxide attack the film's base and emulsion. Magnetic film in fact is notoriously unstable and should be copied to optical tracks as part of the archive's preservation program.

An assembled reel ready to be shelved.

An assembled reel of film on a core requires a minimum of four hours work. The film leader marks different segments. In the background are rolls of film awaiting the technician.

During the inspection process some reels will be earmarked for laboratory work, including ultrasonic cleaning. Never place dirty film on the shelf for long-term storage. Also, single out deteriorating film and fading color film for the laboratory's immediate attention.

Make plans to reinspect the holdings and identify any changes taking place. Sight inspections are valid for general surveys. A carefully selected sampling inspected over a light table will also yield significant data. Proper documentation of inspection data is crucial to achieve any meaningful comparison from one round of inspections to

another. Poor storage conditions, mold infestation, and other problems will require more frequent periodic reinspections.

Quality Control

New film copies ordered by the archive should undergo a careful and timely quality control check before final acceptance. Evaluation criteria for quality control include: frame line, image stability and focus. Poorly copied shrunken film will have a frame line

An optical printer

and images that are unstable during projection. The focus may also "breathe" in and out, another sign of a poorly made copy. View the overall contrasts of blacks, whites, and grays and the amount of detail in each. In color film, skin tones are often a good measure of color accuracy and balance. For sound, check the audio level and its clarity; listen for background noise and distortion of voice and music. Check new lab copies for excessive residual hypo and, if necessary, return them for an extra archival wash.[15]

New preprint copies of archival originals ordered from a laboratory should be "fully timed" as opposed to "one lite" or "best lite." Full timing requires light density readings for each scene which the timer adjusts for the best light density during printing.

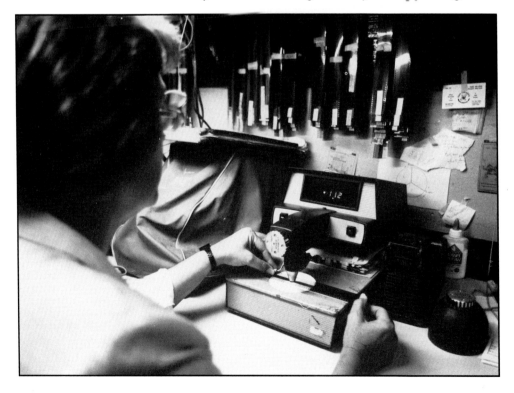

Lab technician checking film density on a densitometer.

Lab technician adjusts optical printer.

At the controls of a liquid gate printer.

Scratched or abraded film should be copied on a printer equipped with a liquid-gate chamber which helps to fill in the scratches and reduces their appearance by the refraction of light. Ensure that the laboratory cleans the film after liquid-gate printing to remove any residue.

Preservation Planning

Based on an inventory and inspection data, the archive can begin to define a preservation program composed of two primary stages: (1) film-to-film copying, and (2) film-to-video copying. For lack of funding and for reasons of accessibility, it is common for newsfilm archives to go directly to the second stage.

106

Film-to-Film Copying

To achieve long-term preservation, copy archival film to modern film stocks according to a systematic plan, commensurate with preservation needs, research priorities and interests, and available funding. New intermediate film copies are required as insurance for the future despite the glitz and seduction of modern video technology. Copy color film to modern low-fade emulsion stocks and place them in cold storage. Magnetic film is unstable and it too will have to be recopied as part of the preservation program. As a permanent record, polyester-based film is preferable to cellulose triacetate, although the availability of emulsions on polyester still continues to be a problem. Having no residual solvents or plasticizers, polyester is much less susceptible to moisture.[16] Stored properly, its life expectancy can be measured in centuries.

Film-to-Video Copying

Film-to-video copying is a very cost-effective way of providing access to motion picture holdings. The least expensive method is for the archive staff to make the transfer using a projector with a modified shutter movement. Elmo manufactures the TRV 16G, a unit used by many archives for film-to-tape transfers.

Video laboratories equipped with modern film-to-video scanners can make excellent videotapes of shrunken archival film. Some scanners are equipped with liquid-gate chambers for scratch reduction. Scene-to-scene correction is also available, at a much higher cost. Since the cost of the equipment and its operation is high, the rate for transfers per recorded hour is also high.

The reproduction needs of the archive are the foundation of its long range preservation plan, after the other requirements—such as archival storage conditions, capital equipment, inspection and repair, and archival containers—have been met. The task will take several years if millions of feet are involved. For funding and budgeting purposes it will be useful to categorize all the preservation activities, quantify them, and factor them against some established or known costs. In this manner, the archive can begin to

Good quality work can be done with an Elmo wired to any video deck or through a more elaborate system.

Film and video labs can provide high quality video transfers utilizing Rank Cintel equipment.

formulate a long-range plan that takes into account all of its principal objectives. Such a plan, needless to say, can serve as an important source of leverage in dealing with funding agencies or in negotiating with financial decision-makers.

Conclusion

At times the 16mm format may seem as obsolete as Sony's once touted Betamax. Its usefulness in broadcast news organizations has long expired. However, it is still used in documentary production and in some aspects of entertainment films by independent producers. Nonetheless, hundreds of millions of feet of 16mm film are still extant. As produced by television news groups, these films contain a systematic visual record of national, regional, and local history that the written word can never replace. The archive, using broad-based criteria, has a responsibility to identify the collections that possess enduring significance and research value.

After the films are determined to be archival, every decision concerning their storage, reproduction, and use should be carefully considered in view of their vulnerability and in the context of the policies of the archive. In addition, the archive has a special obligation to acquaint the staff with the knowledge and techniques that are essential for prolonging film's useful life, and to keep abreast of issues, trends, and problems that affect preservation decisions.

A newsfilm and video archive is an unusual enterprise because it brings together the humanist or social scientist and the technologist. The end result may be history-related, but getting there is completely dependent upon technology.

Footnotes

1. For detailed manuals, see Eastman Kodak, *The Book of Film Care* (Rochester, New York: Eastman Kodak Company, 1992 edition); Eileen Bowser and John Kuiper, editors, *A Handbook for Film Archives*, Second Edition (New York: Garland Publishing/International Federation of Film Archives, 1991); Herbert Volkmann with Henning Schou, editors,

Preservation and Restoration of Moving Images and Sound (Brussels, Belgium: International Federation of Film Archives, 1986).

2. Kodak, along with ANSI (American National Standards Institute), recommends a range of 20-30 percent relative humidity; Eastman Kodak, p. 17.

3. Ibid.

4. Volkmann and Schou, p. 37.

5. D. F. Kopperl and C. C. Bard, "Freeze/Thaw Cycling of Motion Picture Films," *SMPTE Journal*, August 1985, pp. 826-27; William T. Murphy, "Cold Storage for Color Film Materials," National Archives Technical Information Paper, No. 3, 1987.

6. Eastman Kodak, p. 28.

7. Karel Brems, "The Archival Quality of Film Bases," in Eva Orbanz, editor, et al., *Archiving the Audio-visual Heritage: A Joint Technical Symposium* (International Federation of Film Archives/International Federation of Television Archives/International Association of Sound Archives, 1988), pp. 31-36.

8. A measurement of 5.0 or less indicates that degradation is taking place; the film should be scheduled for copying. Eastman Kodak, p. 17.

9. James Reilly, "Current Research on the Stability of Acetate and Nitrate Motion Picture Film, " presentation at the Library of Congress in Washington, DC, January 5, 1991; P. Z. Adelstein, J. M. Reilly, et al., "Stability of Cellulose Ester Base Photographic Film: Laboratory Testing Procedures and Practical Storage Conditions," paper presented at the Society of Motion Picture and Television Engineers (SMPTE) annual conference in Los Angeles, October 28, 1991.

10. M. Edge, N. S. Allen, et al., "Fundamental Aspects of Degradation of Cellulose Triacetate Base Cinematographic Film," *Polymer Degradation and Stability* 25 (1989), pp. 345-62. See also their "Degradation of Historic Cellulose Triacetate Cinematographic Film: Influence of Various Film Parameters and Prediction of Archival Life," in *Journal of Photographic Science* vol. 36 (1988), pp 194-98.

11. Richard Patterson, "The Preservation of Color Films," *American Cinematographer*, July-August 1981.

12. C. Bradley Hunt, "Corrective Reproduction of Faded Motion Picture Prints," *SMPTE Journal*, July 1981, pp. 591-96.

13. Eastman Kodak, p. 38, table.

14. Harlan Jacobsen, "Scorsese Helms Industry Plea to Kodak," *Variety*, July 9, 1980, p.1.

15. For motion pictures the maximum permissible concentration of residual thiosulfate is 0.007 grams per square meter. Eastman Kodak, p. 16. See Methylene Blue Method in ANSI PH4.8-1985.

16. Eastman Kodak, p. 15.

Videotape Issues and Concerns

Steven Davidson
Louis Wolfson II Media History Center

When it comes to videotape, archivists find themselves in a dilemma. Based on technical specifications, we know that the best quality video recordings and film to tape transfers should be made using higher-end (read more expensive) equipment and broadcast quality tape. For reasons of space, institutional policy, staff or budget constraints many archives cannot achieve the ideal, but they are nonetheless actively collecting materials and making them accessible on videotape. This chapter provides an overview from the perspective of those institutions.

Steven Davidson has been the Director of the Louis Wolfson II Media History Center since its establishment in 1987. Before coming to Miami, he was the Director of Library Services at the Museum of Broadcasting and the Associate Director of the National Jewish Archive of Broadcasting in New York. Davidson has served on the Executive Board of the Association of Moving Image Archivists and Co-chairs its News and Documentary Collections Working Group. He actively works to promote the efforts of newsfilm and video archives to other groups around the country and has organized presentations at the Broadcast Educators Association, Radio-Television News Directors Association, the Society of American Archivists and the American Library Association. He is the editor, contributing photographer and co-project director of this manual.

Videotape Issues and Concerns

If an archive accepts a newsfilm collection, it's only a matter of time until video will come into play. Even if an institution has only decided to collect newsfilm, it is recommended that the film be transferred to videotape to make the collection accessible. So there is no escape – eventually newsfilm archives will be using, if not acquiring, video.

The good news is that some of the equipment components needed for film-to-tape transfer, playback, tape duplication and remastering can be utilized (in part) for all of those processes, and the cost of some equipment is dropping. For example, as recently as 1992 the cost of Betacam equipment was out of reach for most local news archives, in the $20,000 to $30,000 range. In 1994 playback-only models were available at around $5,000 and record models at $8,000. Sometimes there are advantages in waiting for the right time to buy equipment and letting technology come down in cost. But in general, the more expensive the equipment, the more features and capabilities it will offer, making better quality transfers possible and providing more control in the technical processes. The availability of professional staff that know how to operate the equipment is also a necessity.

The bad news is that it is generally agreed upon within the archival community that videotape and other magnetic recording media are a less-than-ideal preservation medium. In addition to the physical problems and tape defects to which all formats of videotape are prone, local news archives are also faced with a double dilemma: the multitude of formats which archives are likely to receive in donations from television stations, and the need to decide onto which format (or formats) to transfer newsfilm collections for access purposes. In both cases the dilemmas are never-ending.

Deciding on Formats

By means of a magnetic, mechanical, and/or electronic device, images and sounds can be recorded as electronic signals onto magnetic oxide particles which adhere via a binder to a polyester base. This is basically what happens when recordings are made onto videotape. There are many varieties of this medium, which came into existence in the 1950s. Since then, there have been numerous changes in tape technology both for hardware and tape itself. Some common reel-to-reel formats include two-inch Quadraplex, two-inch Helical, one-inch Helical, and 1/2-inch Helical. There are also cassette formats such as 3/4-inch U-matic, 1/2-inch Beta, 1/2-inch VHS, 8mm and Hi8.

112

Wolfson Center technician remastering a videotape. Top row of equipment (left to right): waveform monitor/vectorscope, black burst generator (on top), monitors, VHS deck. Bottom row: character generator, edit control unit and time-base corrector.

As long as archives will be receiving donations of programming from television stations, those materials will be in the format of favor at the time those recordings were made. It also seems that the period between the introduction of new formats is getting shorter and shorter, and archives need to be concerned, too, about acquiring and maintaining the equipment necessary to play and remaster (copy) those tapes. Similarly, the formats initially selected by an archive for film-to-tape transfer, whether for reasons of budget, staff abilities or institutional policies, may become obsolete or replaced by newer technologies. As noted by Dan Den Bleyker: "The Mississippi Department of Archives

Inside a 3/4-inch U-matic cassette.

Betacam SP deck.

and History decided on 8mm as our standard before the Hi8 format was introduced. If the timing were different, we might have chosen Hi8 instead of 8mm." John Lynch, Director of the Vanderbilt Television News Archive, notes that there will always be new formats on the horizon and "no matter what choices an archive makes today, given the same criteria, that same archive would certainly make a different choice or at least have more options to consider a few years down the line." Lynch recommends that "archives should not be on the cutting edge of technology...it's better to make a 'safer' choice rather than investing in a new format that may fall out of favor or has not reached mass saturation."

As with any other facet of archival operations, budget, staff and planning are critical in making equipment and format choices. However, if an archive has made the decision to collect materials on videotape – in addition to making materials accessible on video – it is safe to say that dealing with and/or considering the purchase of a variety of formats is inevitable. Even if an archive decided on a standard video format on which to transfer their newsfilm collection, it is likely that film and videomakers seeking to license footage will want it on Betacam SP. An archive may reach the point, as did the Chicago Historical Society and the Wolfson Center, where acquiring Betacam equipment – primarily for the purposes of providing footage to film/videomakers – becomes cost-effective and increases this aspect of collection use. While materials can be sent out for transfer and many film/videomakers will still accept 3/4-inch U-matic copies, having in-house Betacam capabilities is an asset, and nearing the time when it will be a necessity. After the transition from film to 3/4-inch U-matic tape, most television stations opted for Betacam (though other stations may be using MII, Hi8 and S/VHS) and those tapes will be coming to the archives.

Equipment Requirements

Whether an archive is collecting original television news and other programming on videotape, or is making materials accessible on tape, the following is a general overview of the types of equipment necessary. The list of equipment needed includes:

- Monitor: a television that receives its signal directly from the video source, such as a camera or a videocassette player/recorder.

VHS recorder/player.

3/4-inch U-matic videocassette recorder/player.

• Videocassette player/recorder, also known as a VCR: these machines are format specific, that is only VHS tapes can be played back on a VHS VCR; 3/4-inch U-matic tapes cannot be played on a VHS machine. Archives will need a VCR for every tape format in their collections. Remember that not all video players have record capabilities; some models only have playback features.

For some archives, the list of equipment ends here. The San Francisco State University Library made the decision to transfer their newsfilm collection to VHS.

A videotape head
inside a 3/4-inch
U-matic deck.

Though the 3/4-inch U-matic format was considered for mastering their collection, it was ruled out. SFSU collections librarian Helene Whitson says there were a variety of reasons for deciding on VHS, including the cost of equipment and videotape, space concerns and the fact that VHS was already the campus media standard. The Mississippi Department of Archives and History opted for the 8mm format as their standard,

The Mississippi
Department of
Archives and
History uses the
8mm videocas-
sette format.

116

primarily for space concerns and cost considerations. In addition, the Department's collection contains only original newsfilm and does not have a video news component.

A list of more technical equipment of use to news archives would include waveform monitors and vectorscopes, time-code generators, effects generators, time-base correctors and character generators. These equipment components are not format specific and can be utilized with any video format. This group of equipment enables technicians to check the level and quality of video signal, correct irregularities in a video signal, and add information to a video signal. The definitions are as follows:

Beyond the Basic Equipment

• Waveform monitor is an oscilloscope used to display a video waveform and its characteristics which allow for the checking of the integrity of the video signal.

• Vectorscopes are used to align the three video color levels – red, green, blue (RGB) – of the video signal.

• Time-base correctors (TBC) process a video signal and correct any irregularities that would prevent a stable video signal. In essence a TBC stabilizes and corrects a poor quality video signal so that tapes can be remastered or copied.

• Effects generators are used primarily in the realm of production and editing, but for newsfilm archives, certain models offer one very important function, sometimes referred to as reverse polarity or negative function. For those newsfilm archives that have negative film originals in their collections, this feature will provide the electronic capability of making a positive video image during the film-to-tape transfer process, thus avoiding the expense of a film laboratory.

• Character generator is like a video typewriter, enabling titles or credits to be superimposed on the screen and recorded on the videotape. Even basic character generators provide various type sizes and color text capabilities. Archives use this device to type a copyright notice or other information on screen.

117

Close up of time-base corrector and effects generator. Note negative "neg" function key in the center of the unit.

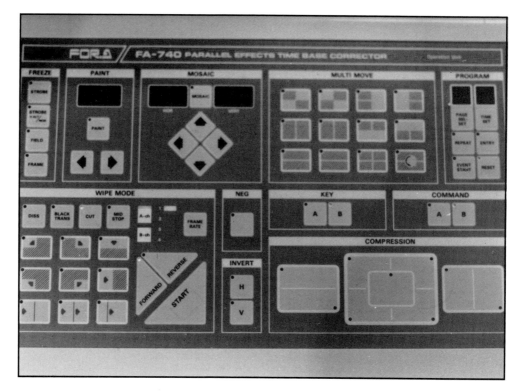

• Time-code generators insert on screen and/or on the videotape signal a sequential "time code" for each "frame" of video. Each frame will have its own time-code number which tells the time in hours, minutes, and seconds. In addition to making possible accurate editing of tapes, insertion of time code provides newsfilm archives a

Video typewriter/character generator.

Time-code
generator.

way of further protecting images, and a way for users of materials to cite reference points on the tape.

Keep in mind that adjusting the color or vertical control on video monitors doesn't compensate for defective or problematic videotapes. In some instances, video monitors are very forgiving, that is tapes may appear to look better than they really are. Problems occur when dubs (video copies) are made and the video signal doesn't always "lock up" (play back properly) and a time-base corrector is essential for remastering.

Is This Equipment Optional or Necessary?

While the above equipment may be viewed as optional, each component will enhance the operation of news archives, providing capabilities which make dubbing, transfers and other video activities more precise and of a higher quality. Additionally, each piece of equipment can be purchased individually and added to a system over time. The Wolfson Center began its film-to-tape transfer and video system with an Elmo TRV 16G, a basic 3/4-inch U-matic videocassette player/recorder and a VHS videocassette player/recorder. The Chicago Historical Society followed a similar path.

Unlike film, there are few physical tape problems which can be observed by the naked eye by examining a videocassette. Although some clues about potential problems may be derived from the condition in which the tapes were kept and how they were stored, those factors are not always a true indicator. Problems with tape playback or image and sound can only be determined with equipment – by playing the tape. Simply viewing a tape on a monitor can only tell part of the story. Because of this, the equipment components discussed above become important for remastering defective tapes and providing the ability to make better copies. But beware that older tapes can "clog" video heads and damage equipment. Additionally, older or problematic tapes may only provide "one more pass" in order to be remastered. Technical expertise is required and in some cases qualified outside labs should be considered if tapes are in very poor condition. In addition to this equipment, a few manufacturers offer video inspection equipment and these devices are format specific. They can be used to inspect and clean older tapes and spot check new ones before recording.

Video Inspection

Reference copy tape prepared for a researcher. Character generated text on top – time-code number on bottom.

Format Choices Affect Image Quality

Deciding on which format or formats to utilize is dependent on a variety of factors, and as long as newsfilm archives operate on modest budgets, there will be no single or correct answer. In selecting a format for film-to-tape transfer, there are several general guidelines to consider related to cost (budget), space, staff (technical capabilities) and institutional policies. But it is not just the cost of the equipment; transferring three million feet of film to videotape requires approximately 2,000 tapes, more if master and reference copies are made.

Film-to-tape transfers are necessary for ease of access and preventing wear and tear on

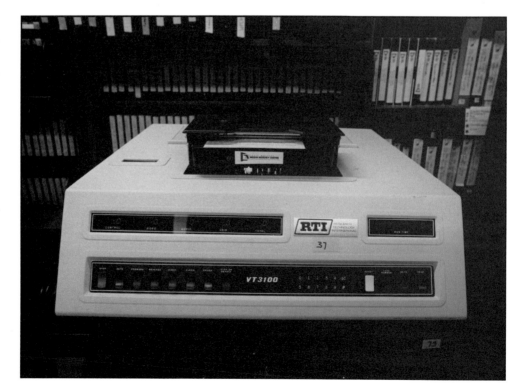

A 3/4-inch U-matic video inspection machine. This model cleans oxide particles and dirt off the videotape and provides a printout of tape defects. It can be used to inspect new tapes before recording and inspect older tapes before playing.

the original film. Any video format will accomplish these goals, but different formats will provide varying degrees of quality. Some archives, like the Mississippi Department of Archives and History and the San Francisco State University Library, transfer their collections to one format; other institutions, such as the State Historical Society of North Dakota and the Wolfson Center, make a 3/4-inch U-matic video master and a VHS reference copy. Having a 3/4-inch master provides for better quality reference copies and duplicates.

In terms of overall quality, VHS is on the lower end of the scale and Betacam SP on the higher end. Digital environments are still out of the budgetary reach for most local news archives and the standards and formats for these digital technologies are still evolving. Other current format possibilities include S/VHS, 8mm and Hi8, and 3/4-inch U-matic SP. If an institution has opted to collect video materials from local television stations, there is the possibility that, over time, those stations used a variety of formats, and the archive will need a range of equipment to playback those materials. In addition, many of these tapes will have to be remastered onto better quality if not different formats.

Images and sounds on videotape can be affected by a number of problems. There is, of course, the loss of information on a tape by accidental erasure. Economic, rather than archival, considerations can force the intentional erasure of information as a tape is re-used. Dropout – an impairment or loss of video information caused by a loss in the level of the recorded signal – normally results in a black or white horizontal line in the picture. Print-through can result from the magnetic field of one layer of oxide particles on a tape affecting the signal on an adjacent layer, and causes overlapping sound and sometimes picture. While these and other problems are inherent in the material itself, storage conditions – as with film – are a major factor in the long-term keeping characteristics of videotape.

Videotape Life Expectancy

Many archivists do not consider magnetic tape to be an archival medium because the information recorded on it is not permanent and can be altered or removed. While there is evidence that tapes produced in recent years may retain an acceptable signal for a least twenty to thirty years and possibly for as long as one-hundred years, there does not yet exist a means to guarantee a shelf life equal at least to that of safety film. Research in videodisc, laser, and holographic storage media, and digital mass storage may provide a means to preserve information on videotape sometime in the near future, but for now safeguarding appears to be the appropriate strategy.

The condition of a videotape depends on the quality of tape manufacture, and conditions of use and storage. Poor or uneven tape batches, overuse, hot and humid conditions, and dirty tape-player heads and transports all can severely shorten the life of a tape. As with safety film, making a copy of a tape for viewing while properly storing the original appears to be the best available means to safeguard a tape and still make the information it holds accessible. This arrangement also holds the promise that, when a truly archival means to preserve videotape is developed, the original material will still exist for preservation.

Tape Storage and Maintenance

Tape should be stored and used in a dust-free environment. Stability of the temperature and humidity levels is critical for proper storage of videotape. High temperature and humidity levels can disrupt not only the sound and image quality of videotape (the magnetic recording) but can also cause physical damage to the videotape itself. Magnetic recording tape consists of a metal oxide particle coating on a plastic backing material. Problems may occur with the particle coating, the backing or the playback equipment. Any type of disruption of the recorded signal or the videotape itself will eventually cause problems in playing back the videotape. Tape manufacturers say that tapes can lose a portion of their signal and not cause significant problems. For archives, its best not to take chances.

Most sources recommend storage at 65° F and 40%-50% relative humidity (RH). Some archivists have recommended storage at 50° F and 40%-50% RH. Recently, there has been evidence to suggest that a low humidity environment of 25%-30% RH may be best for long-term storage of videotape. In general, keep videotapes as cool and dry as possible.

Replace cardboard sleeves with hardshell cassette cases.

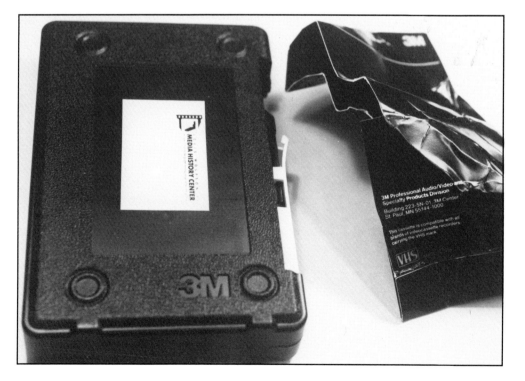

Videocassettes should be shelved upright.

If an archive does not have a climate-controlled facility, store tapes in an area with a constant temperature and humidity level, rather than one with fluctuations. Monitor the temperature with a recording thermometer/hygrometer.

Acclimate videotapes. If a tape is kept in cold storage, allow it to reach room temperature if you planning on moving it across campus, or across town, or even to another room in your facility. If tapes are not acclimated, condensation can form on the tape, causing problems for both the tape and the VCR during playback.

As with film, periodical checking, winding, and rewinding of tape is recommended for long-term storage. Reel to-reel-tape should be kept in its original box or replacement container, and cassettes stored in original boxes or cannisters which support the tape should be secured with an adhesive tab which leaves no residue after it is removed. Most sources recommend storing tapes – whether reel-to-reel or cassette – on end. Cassettes should be stored in an upright, "spine out" position in their cases. Cardboard cases should be replaced with plastic hardshell cases.

Tape should be fully wound with proper tension and uniformity before storage. There is no agreement on the type of direction of wind, however. Some recommend a real-time winding of a tape back to start without stopping before storage, while others suggest simply a full fast rewind. Another point of view suggests that a tape be stored "tails out," since there may be less of a chance for print-through to occur. Whichever recommendation is followed, it is clear that a tape must not be put back on a shelf after use without a uniform winding, since the starts and stops of normal play can result in wide variations in tension and wrap that may damage a stored tape.

Fast forward and rewind tapes periodically. For larger collections, this may be difficult; a typical video archive can contain thousands of tapes. Keep track of this activity with preservation records. Ideally tape should be exercised at least once a year. Never leave tapes in a VCR or remove tapes before rewinding. Always store tapes in their cases, and when purchasing tapes, always order with plastic sleeves or hardshell shipper cases, not cardboard.

There are two points of view on the need to keep tape away from anything which may generate a magnetic field. Recently, there has been discussion that the danger of a loss of signal from exposure to equipment which may generate a magnetic field has been overestimated. There has also been the more conservative view, however, that to be safe, tapes should be stored away from such things as motors, television sets, transformers, electrical fixtures, loudspeakers or other electro-magnetic signals. In addition, if a metal rack is used for storage, it should be grounded as a further safeguard against damage to the signal from voltage fluctuations or lightning.

With regard to transporting tapes, there is no evidence that passing videotape through x-ray machines at security checkpoints in airports is damaging. The handheld wands which may be passed around an individual, however, do generate a magnetic field; thus, tapes should be kept away.

Video Dubbing and Transfers

Never play an original tape after a copy is made. Make copies (dubs) as soon as possible, and store originals and copies in different locations. Always label the videocassette, the tape box, and if you have a character generator, label the tape "on screen." For remastering and for film-to-tape transfer, always use the best quality videotape of the format you have selected. These may be designated by the manufacturer as broadcast or professional grade tapes. Don't use recycled tapes, even those with only one pass (used only once) for remastering; always use new tape stock. Save the one pass or recycled tapes for exhibition or reference copies.

Maintain your equipment. Because of the rapid development of videotape technology and the variety of tape formats, it has become apparent that in long-term archival storage, equipment for playing tapes (as well as spares for parts and manuals for operation) also must be safeguarded. There already are formats, such as 1/2-inch reel-to-reel, which are no longer actively used and for which playback equipment is hard to find.

Keep service and operation manuals. Always make sure the video heads are clean. Dirty

Label both the videocassette and the cassette case.

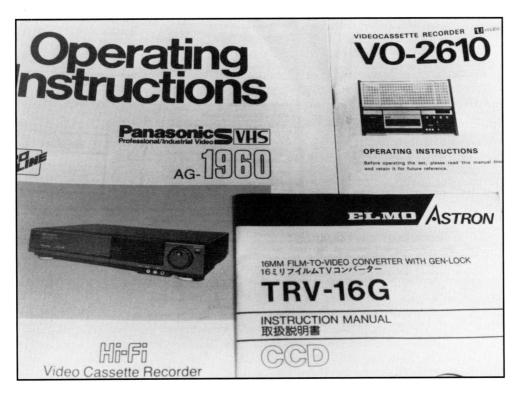

Always keep instruction and service manuals for all equipment.

heads can damage countless videotapes. Have test tapes on hand. If you don't have measuring equipment, several manufacturers offer test tapes, which provide color bars and gray scales to properly adjust monitors which will allow you to see the true quality of the videotape.

Remember that images and sound on videotape can be effected by a number of variables. One is accidental erasure, so always remove the tab on VHS tapes, and the button on 3/4-inch U-matic tapes to prevent erasure. Don't reuse videotapes for mastering. Video problems may occur as dropout, which is an impairment or loss of

Remove record lock-out button.

Remove cassette tab
to prevent
accidental erasure.

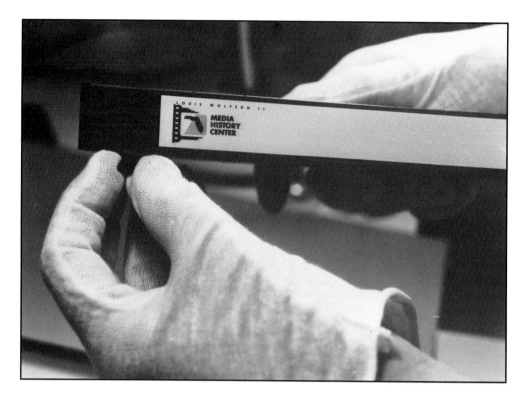

video caused by a loss in the level of the recorded signal; this may look like a black or white horizontal line in the video image.

Other tips:

- No smoking or eating in the work area, around equipment or videotapes.

- Regularly check video equipment and tape heads. Keep detailed service records.

- Leave several feet (at least one minute) of blank tape before starting to record.

- Do not manually forward or rewind tape in a videocassette.

- Record at standard speed with VHS.

- Older tapes often play back better on older equipment.

- Make master and reference copies simultaneously.

- Handle the videocassette by the casing; never touch the tape itself.

- Label tapes immediately.

Arrangement and Description

Helene Whitson

San Francisco Bay Area Television Archive

San Francisco State University

Gerry Yeager

Harford Community College

"Preservation or arrangement and description" may be the moving image counterpart to the chicken or the egg. Archives receive collections in a variety of conditions, sometimes with but often without accompanying documentation which aides both preservation and arrangement and description. The issues of which process comes first and how newsfilm/video collections should be organized are addressed in this chapter, which may solve both riddles.

Helene Whitson is the Special Collections Librarian/Archivist of the San Francisco Bay Area Television Archive at San Francisco State University. She is active in the Association of Moving Image Archivists, the Society of American Archivists, the Society of California Archivists, and was a member of the California Cooperative Preservation Program task force which drafted California's resource materials preservation plan. She has written *Strike! A Chronology, Bibliography, and List of Archival Materials Concerning the 1968-69 Strike at San Francisco State College* (1979); and *The California State University and College Trustees Almanac* (1981). Whitson also produced two videotapes, *KQED Film Archive Preservation Project* (1987) and *Unearthing the Past: Access To Local Television News* (1989).

Gerry Yeager is currently Head of Library and Information Services at Harford Community College, Harford County, Maryland. From 1976-1990, Yeager was Head of Special Collections at the University of Baltimore, where from 1985-1990 she was Project Director for an NHPRC-funded project to inventory, arrange, describe and preserve the WMAR-TV newsfilm collection.

Arrangement and Description

Arrangement and description are keys to local television news collection accessibility. The manner in which the archivist organizes and describes the collection has direct bearing upon the ease of collection management, knowledge of content, and retrieval of the desired footage. Consideration of collection organization should begin ideally before the collection is acquired and moved to a repository, so that the archival principle of *provenance* is maintained as nearly as possible. If the archivist is involved in negotiations with the station, s/he should ask for station records concerning the development of the News/Current Affairs Department and the methods by which its products were created. If the archivist is not directly involved in such negotiations, s/he should request that those who are involved obtain such information, which may include talking with camera crews who shot the footage, observing and documenting how and where the footage was kept at the station, discussing how it was used by producers and reporters, and reading scripts, indexes, and other finding aids produced by the station, if such records exist. Having complete records concerning the production of local television news footage and documentaries will aid the archivist greatly in the organization of the collection.

Local news collections are the products of the functioning of a particular department within the television station—the News and/or Current Affairs Department. That department exists to produce a product—The News—and incidentally other "special" or "documentary" programs. In order to create the product, many different decisions have to be made by the station, and those decisions should be documented in various policies, procedures, reports, etc. In the case of local television news archives, it is one product of the station which we find most interesting. That product embodies the station's philosophy, through what is covered and what is not. But, most important, that product records the history, events, activities and issues of our community, and as such, is a priceless record of local life.

The traditional archival repository holds records which document the origins and functions of organizations. Frank Evans' "A Basic Glossary for Archivists, Manuscript Curators, and Records Managers" provides a definition for archives as follows:

> Archives: The noncurrent records of an organization or institution preserved because of their continuing value...[1]

Between 1949 and the mid-1970s, local television stations sent reporters and camera crews out to film activities and events in the community, bring film back to the station,

develop it, and show it on the news. The film was usually used once, if at all, tossed back into a can or box, and then in some cases stored. Materials were not usually stored in any order, but simply put into available space. This process continued for the next 35-plus years, and stations began to accumulate thousands and thousands of feet of film in their storerooms. When stations switched to videotape for recording, they found that they had a more economical recording medium which could be erased and used several times. Stations still stored videotapes of important events.

With the station acceptance of videotape as a news-recording medium, station managers began to look at their storage space and the huge amounts of film taking up that space. Many of the recorded items were very local and/or very topical, and would never be used again. Station managers had several choices: (1) to discard their film, (2) to keep it, or (3) to give it away to other institutions. Many stations chose to discard their film, or at least to weed their collections, keeping only the most important items. Others kept their entire collections.

Local television stations created far more footage than what remains today. A station might have a complete list of all of its aired footage, as well as its outtakes and trims. Much of the footage, however, even though listed in station finding aids (if such exist), has been misplaced, misfiled, borrowed, or lost, so that what remains is in no way the entire representation of what the station actually produced.

In order to determine how a station's News/Current Affairs Department functioned, what it produced, how it produced it, and why it produced what it created, one must look at the records of the station and at the materials in their original, undisturbed order. The *provenance* of the collection at the station, i.e., the order in which it was organized and used, tells us something about how the station operated and how it viewed its own news and documentary products. Although the format of the collections differ from paper archival records, the principles of arrangement and description remain surprisingly similar, and one can apply the same terminology used with organizing paper records to organizing local television news collections. T.R. Schellenberg, one of the deans of modern American archival practice, describes the reasons for keeping materials in their original order:

> The principle of provenance has gained acceptance in the archival profession for a variety of reasons. (1) The principle protects the integrity of records in the sense that their origins and the processes by which they came into existence are reflected by their arrangement. (2) The principle helps to reveal the significance of records; for the subject matter of individual documents can be fully understood only in context with related documents. If records are arbitrarily torn from their context and reassembled according to a subjective or other arbitrary system, their real significance as documentary evidence may be obscured or lost. (3) The principle provides the archivist with a workable and economical guide in arranging, describing, and servicing records in his custody. To break up the existing natural units and substitute arbitrary new ones would consume a great deal of an archivist's time to no good purpose, and the complexity and diversity of the subject matter covered by the records would make the completion of any such undertaking impossible.[2]

Schellenberg goes on to reaffirm that the materials should be maintained in their original order as evidence of organization and function:

> While this arrangement will not bring records together by subjects that will meet all the research needs of scholars, it is the only workable way of placing records in order while preserving their evidential values... To rearrange according to some arbitrary plan records that are already in order or partly in order would be a prodigal waste of time, and to impose such an arbitrary plan of arrangement on the few records that are wholly without arrangement would serve no conceivable purpose.[3]

He does make two exceptions to the concept of original-order preservation, i.e., that the archivist may impose another order: (1) when the records have been reorganized by the originating agency after the primary purpose had been served, and (2) when the original order is unidentifiable or unworkable.[4]

Traditional archival records include such materials as administrative files, policies, minutes, reports, correspondence, manuals, photographs, publicity items, brochures, and objects, etc. Indeed, such materials also are created by local television station News/ Current Affairs departments as support materials for news and documentary production, and can be very important as background information for the news story and/or documentary. It is, however, the product of that department, and all the attendant records which surround the production of the material with which we are concerned.

Those who acquire local television news collections should be aware that the collections may include many types of materials, including differing formats, such as 16mm newsfilm, 1/2-inch, 3/4-inch U-matic, one-inch, and two-inch videotape, documentaries, kinescopes, scripts, finding aids (card catalogs, computer databases, logbooks, etc.), production records, photographs, organizational papers, papers of individuals connected with the station, and scrapbooks. Or, the collection can contain simply film and/or videotape, with no finding aids or other records at all. A local television news collection may include aired programs as well as outtakes and trims, the unedited footage often found as small, briefly labeled, or unlabeled rollettes. The collection may come in compiled reels, often of uniform size. Outtakes and trims may be of more historical value than the aired footage, since they are unedited. In addition, the collection may contain materials other than those produced by the station, such as national network materials, independent or government-produced film, commercials, and materials produced by other local stations or entities. All of the above elements (or the lack of some of them) tell us about how the department functioned.

Arrangement   Arrangement begins either before or at the point of collection transfer to the institution. If possible, archival staff should see to the packing of the material, unless station staff are

Checking rollettes (individual stories) against inventory record.

able to pack it in a useful order. *Provenance*, i.e., keeping the original order, is essential to later arrangement.

The process of organizing and making a collection accessible begins with the initial examination of the collection at the station or at your institution upon its arrival, taking notes on the various types of materials contained within. Materials should be kept in their original order as much as possible, maintaining the internal and external order of the collection, and documenting the methods used by the station to control the collec-

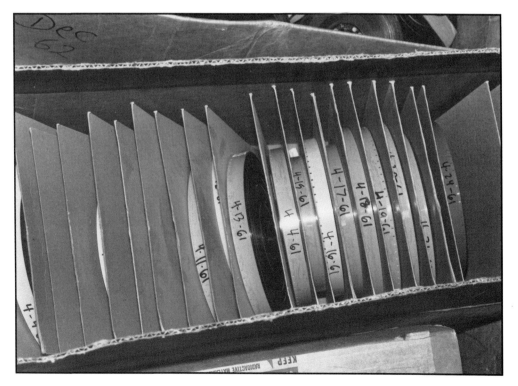

The leader indicates each reel's contents.

tion. During your initial examination of the collection, you might want to begin noting how the collection is organized into standard archival units, such as record groups and series. Internal order is defined as the contents of the can, box, or whatever holds the reel or reels. External order is defined as the arrangement of the entire collection, by date, subject, event, alphabetically, chronologically, etc. This original order then translates into record group, series, etc.

1. An accession record should be developed that includes:

   a. A description of the original order (chronological, alphabetical, numerical, etc.).

   b. The number of cans, boxes, reels, etc., their type (film, videotape, etc.) and general condition.

   c. An administrative history of the collection and the originating organization. (The information in sections a-c can be incorporated into a finding aid.)

   d. How the materials were transferred from the originating organization.

   e. Any other background information, including agreements, deed of gift, costs, restrictions, copyright ownership (and the attendant ability to license the footage or charge for use), reference service, insurance, etc.

2. Arrangement should be approached by keeping in mind that the collection must be preserved while making it accessible. If the footage is received in a state of disorder that renders it useless, then this is no order at all; however, more often than not, background information from the station can shed light on an order not easily identified. Markings outside the container can be very helpful:

   a. Alphabetical by titles.

   b. Chronological by dates.

   c. Numbering system.

Part of the KPIX collection at the San Francisco State University Archive.

d. Subject system.

e. A combination of the above.

The arrangement of the collection will have an effect on the identification of the intellectual unit, which is the definition of the item or the level of the item to be described or cataloged later. Initial examination is very important, and must be done with care. It is vital to develop a record of the collection's original condition and contents.

3. You will want access to your footage, and should know what you have and where it is. The following steps can aid you in organizing the collection for swift and accurate retrieval, as well as preparing it for future reproduction. Use of an inventory log sheet for each unit (reel) at this point will be invaluable through this whole process:

a. Arrange the film in the original order (intended order), as nearly as possible, and shelve horizontally with the can or box lip down. The order for each series can be different, depending on the use pattern. For example, the station might have arranged the news footage chronologically, while organizing documentaries by title and/or subject alphabetically.

Provenance decrees that a collection be kept in its original order, but how does one deal with the issue of *provenance* when the newsfilm collection comes in the format of thousands of tiny film rollettes (with or without cores), usually organized in a chronological system? What is "original order" in this context? Cans and boxes of these rollettes occupy much space, and would use much less space if they could be compiled into larger reels. Does such a process destroy *provenance*? By compiling the footage into uniform-size larger reels in accession number or chronological order, the archivist can save precious shelf space, money, and staff time, and place the film in a fixed position so that it will not fall out of the can/box each time the container is opened. If each one of the small rollettes has an identification number or code, the task is easy, because the collection can be arranged numerically. The numbers usually correspond to a chronological order. But, when the film has no individual identification number/code, and 15-20 rollettes are housed in a can or

Part of the collection at San Francisco State.

box, the only way to identify the exact order of shooting would be to see the angle of the light in the segment to determine the order of the day's filming! One then must look at the larger unit—the day's filming in a random order (unless a guide, log book, card catalog or other finding aid provides specific information concerning order)—and splice together all of the segments which constitute a day's filming. If this approach is chosen, the collection guide must note the original arrangement and why it was changed.

Arguments against splicing include wear and tear on all the film in a reel when searching for a specific segment, cost of duplicating an entire reel, and lack of flexibility due to placing the film in fixed order. Arguments for splicing include ease of transferring and uniform reel size, which saves space, time, and money. Is *provenance* destroyed? No, because the film is still in the same original order on the daily filming schedule. The film is simply in a fixed position.

Records can be divided and subdivided into four different areas, progressing from large to small: record groups, series, file unit, and document/item. These four standard and important archival definitions apply to the organization of local television collections.

(1) Record group. This category is defined as "a body of organizationally-related records established on the basis of *provenance* with particular regard for the administrative history, the complexity, and the volume of the records and archives of the institution or organization involved."[5]

In the case of local television news collections, one record group would describe all of the productions of a News/Current Affairs Department. Other record groups might be used to describe materials from the Public Affairs Department or station management.

(2) Series. Series are defined as "file units or documents arranged in accordance with a filing system or maintained as a unit because they relate to a particular

subject or function, result from the same activity, have a particular form, or because of some other relationship arising out of their creation, receipt, or use."[6] David Gracy comments that: "The series level is the most important one in arrangement, because here the archivist expresses the character of the group or collection by the divisions made of it."[7]

Series are distinctive groupings within record groups, such as daily news footage, documentaries, special programs, scripts, publicity materials, etc. Series include materials which have a likeness in common, and/or were created with a common purpose in mind. The format of a series may change, such as news footage changing from film to video, but the content remains the same. Therefore, all of that footage would remain in the same series.

(3) File unit. Gracy notes that: "A file unit is an aggregation of documents brought together, usually for convenience in filing, in such a way that they may be treated as a unit."[8] These smaller units are very specific, containing such information as correspondence for a particular period of time, different subjects, each in a separately-labeled folder, etc. The local television news equivalent of the file unit or file folder is the daily footage, i.e., all footage shot during a particular day. Although the subjects of the stories are different, the common factor is the date on which they were filmed.

(4) Document/item. This is the "atomic" level of archival hierarchy, the smallest division of materials, the individual item. David Gracy comments that: "A document is simply a 'single record or manuscript item.'"[9] The local television news equivalent of this unit is the segment, snippet, rollette—the individual story.

Describing all footage produced during a day, or indeed, the individual segment itself, while extremely desirable and useful, also is very time and labor consuming, as well as expensive.

Each roll must be
logged in, and its
physical condition
noted and repaired.

b. Verify any existing inventories or other finding aids.

c. Replace damaged or rusted cans, cassettes, or boxes, and transfer any markings to new containers.

d. Assign an internal inventory control number to each container/item.

Inventory control identifiers can be created as numbers, such as 1 to ?, or perhaps as letter/number combinations. If you are going to have more than one moving image

Segments in this can are on cores; note the masking tape splices and tape labels across the film segments.

collection, you might want to incorporate initial letters from the different collections, to differentiate between those collections. (For example, if the collection is entitled the Mary Jones Moving Image Collection, you might identify each can/ reel/box as MJ 1, MJ 2, etc. That would differentiate it from the next collection, the George Smith Collection, which could be listed as GS 1, GS 2, etc.) Remember that one of the major principles of archival arrangement is *respect des fonds*, i. e. that collections will not be intermingled.

The individual containers may be handled, examined, repaired, retrieved and transformed in later stages, so it is important to have an inventory number or code from the very beginning. Cotton gloves should always be worn when handling film.

e. Preparation of each reel for later copying and viewing:

(1) Examination, repair and cleaning of each segment/reel.

(a) Record findings for each reel on a log sheet. The log sheet should include space for the following types of information: call number; title; date; segment number/number of reels (if more than one for any item); videocassette number, if it has been transferred; type of film (reversal, negative, mixed, single perf, double perf, mixed); black and white/color; edited/ unedited; sound (optical, mag stripe, mag track, silent, mixed); footage per roll (including leader); time per roll (including leader); sync marks; condition (including surface contamination, rust, breaks, sprocket holes, scratches, color shifts, soundtrack damage, creases, brittleness, shrinkage, emulsion deterioration, twist, curl, abrasions, blistering, fluting, buckling, bad splices, and any other condition). Note repairs needed and repairs done. Also note if an individual segment has been compiled into a larger reel and/ or transferred to another medium.

(b) Examination of film on manually-operated rewinds.

(c) Removal of all masking tape, clips, glue, staples, etc.

Technician examines film using manual rewinds, viewing images on a moviescope viewer.

(d) Resplicing.

(e) Hand cleaning (with adequate ventilation).

(2) Verification of each container, i.e., is it what it is supposed to be? Sometimes labels on the outside have nothing to do with the inside.

(a) Check leader identification with container identification.

Technician writing identification number on film leader.

138

(b) Check against any existing finding aids or scripts.

(3) Preliminary subject inventory (broad identification by subject):

(a) Review each reel or tape or a sampling of reels or tapes for general subject areas.

(b) Prepare a preliminary subject inventory.

(4) Arrangement of other support materials in the collection, such as scripts, photographs, papers/correspondence, etc., as would be arranged in a standard archival collection.

The end result of collection arrangement is that your collection will have been examined, sorted, repaired, and organized into different record groups, subgroups, and series, thus providing both staff and patrons with an accessible collection.

Description

Arrangement permits the archivist to have physical control of the collection. Description provides the intellectual control. Concise, thorough, and accurate description is necessary to future access to the collection. The manner in which a collection is organized and described determines whether the user can locate desired footage, as well as the ease with which it can be retrieved. All of the information gathered during arrangement and description of the collection, along with background material about the collection, can be used to create finding aids.

As noted before, four major archival unit descriptions apply to local television news collection arrangement and description: record groups, series, file units, and documents/items. Arrangement and description of local television news archives is concerned mostly with the first two: record groups and series. T.R. Schellenberg notes that: "The term 'group' will be used to refer to units established on the basis of their *organizational* origins; the term 'series' to refer to units established on the basis of their *functional* origins."[10] Record groups and series descriptions should include the record

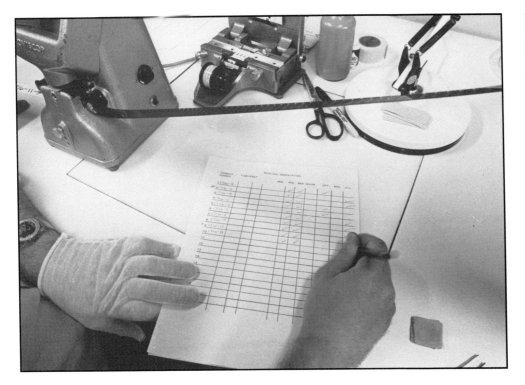

Noting technical information and physical condition on an inventory form.

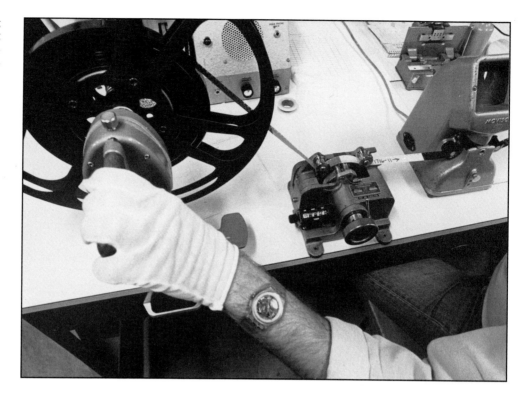

Carefully winding through film using hand rewinds, synchonizer (with footage counter) and moviescope.

group/series number, title, inclusive dates, size of series (e.g., 3,000 cans; 570 1/2-inch VHS videotapes), and a thorough, concise description of the contents.

Intellectual control is achieved on four levels: 1) the collection level, with a broad description of the context and history of the entire collection – the collection guide; 2) a series guide, which should be done for each series, describing each in greater detail; 3) the established unit within each series (e.g., the reel) is described by content, date, subject, geographic location, proper names; 4) within each reel it may be necessary to describe each segment in greater detail if the reel contains a variety of subjects.

A more basic setup with rewinds and a sprocket repair unit.

When planning for and beginning the description process, it is important to keep established standards and computerization in mind. Ultimately the collection may be entered on a nationwide database in MARC format. Additionally in-house computer software can be used for initial intellectual control. Therefore, providing uniformity in setting up record groups, series, file units, etc., from the beginning is essential, e.g.:

WMAR	0001	0001	0001
RG	SERIES	REEL	SEGMENT

Record Group Descriptions

Your description should begin with an overall description of your record group(s) which will evolve into the collection guide. One must remember that when we are dealing with materials from a local television station, we may have station records, but our primary collection(s) are the products of a department or departments. In the case of a local television news collection, the record group would be the product of the News/Current Affairs Department. Each record group should be clearly and concisely described, including a summary of contents, dates, and size of the record group. The following sample is the product of the News/Current Affairs Department of San Francisco's PBS station, KQED.

Record Group One. The Record Group in this case will be identified as the KQED Film Archive, and all the series within that group will be a division of the original group. The record group is the entire collection.

Record Group One: KQED Film Archive.

The KQED Film Archive is a collection of approximately 1.8 million feet of 16mm newsfilm taken by San Francisco's PBS station, KQED, between 1967-1980, as well as selected documentary footage produced by the station. The collection was acquired in 1981, and offers a broad variety of unique materials for those interested in studying the history and culture of the Bay Area, including creative arts, humanities, social sciences, and science. Segments and programs include interviews with creative artists, local literary figures, politicians and labor leaders, as well as documentation of social/political events, including the San Francisco State College strike, 1968-1969, and the assassination of Mayor George Moscone and Supervisor Harvey Milk. The science programs include series on viruses, on youth and drugs, and lectures on the elements.

Each new accession, of materials from a different station would be a different record group. Following is a record group description of another local television news collection:

Each can contains several days of news shows.

Record Group Two: KPIX Film Library

KPIX, a CBS affiliate, is Northern California's oldest TV station, beginning in 1948. Its approximately seven million feet of 16mm film documents the life, history, culture, and development of the San Francisco Bay Area, one of America's major metropolitan areas, from 1948, the post-war years, to 1980, the years of Silicon Valley and high technology. In between are the beatnik years of the 1950s-1960s, the rise of the hippie and psychedelic culture, the emergence of the gay movement, and the area's development as an important multicultural community. The collection was acquired in 1986.

Series Descriptions

Series can be defined as units which make up the record and are divided according to their function. News footage is one such grouping:

• Daily News (news film/video) which may be in different formats, or a combination of film and video produced in several different gauges.

Other typical series which come with local television news collections include:

• Documentaries.

• Special programs, such as a weekly news wrap-ups.

• Compilation programs, usually by subject, such as "sports" or "events."

• Scripts.

• Finding aids produced by the station.

• Other series, segregated by format, such as kinescopes, two-inch videotape.

• Still photographs of news events.

• Departmental publicity materials.

• Papers of department personnel, such as producers, reporters, camera people.

• Off-air taped footage, which is different from the department-produced news footage, since this footage was copied by the repository or another party.

Other items of interest in the local television news collection record group might include:

• Reference materials.

• Scrapbooks.

• Organizational papers.

The aforementioned series might have been produced by the News/Current Affairs Department, or another unit. Or they may cover more than just the activities of the News/Current Affairs Department. The archivist will have to determine the correct placement of these materials in the organizational scheme.

When doing initial series descriptions, it is helpful to have a worksheet. Elements to be looking for and described on a series description worksheet include:

Record Group:

Series number:

Series name:

Identifier:

Medium: film (gauge)   video (size)   other

Color: black/white   color

Sound: silent   optical   magnetic stripe   magnetic

Type of film: negative   positive

Editing: edited   outtakes/trims

Arrangement: chronological   alphabetical by title   alphabetical by subject   other

Inclusive dates:

Number of items:

Condition:

Related series:

Notes:

The information compiled on the worksheet can be used for developing indexes and for cataloging the collection. Much of the information also can be used for indexing/ cataloging individual segments and/or reels.

Often local television news collections will provide scripts with the texts of the local news footage. The scripts can be arranged chronologically or by subject, depending how

Newscripts from the Wolfson Center's WTVJ collection.

the station organized its news footage. Scripts should be given the same identifier code as the news segments they report. Other common categories include still photographs of news events, and special programs. The series subject may be different, but the principles of description remain the same.

Finding aids are the guides to your collections and the materials contained within. Frank Evans, et al, describes them as follows:

> The descriptive media, published and unpublished, created by an originating office, an archival agency, or manuscript repository, to establish control over records and other holdings. Basic finding aids include guides (general or repository and subject or topical), inventories or registers, location registers, card catalogs, special lists, shelf and box lists, indexes, calendars, and, for machine-readable records, software documentation.[11]

Finding aids are crucial access tools to local television news collections. You and your patrons cannot use your collection(s) if you have no access to what is contained within. If a local television news collection comes to an archive without such aids, the archivist may create them cursorily during the examination and organization of the collection, and in detail later.

Simply put, the finding aid allows for the retrieval of needed information from the collection. Finding aids, either manual or automated, are created at all levels of control: Collection, Series, File Unit, and Item. Some of these finding aids evolve as part of the arrangement and description stages. For example, the initial log or inventory sheet becomes the framework for a finding aid on the file unit (reel) level because it describes the reel. This manual log sheet can become an automated and searchable finding aid for each reel.

Ultimately, the finding aid must provide subject access to the collection, and this access must begin with a controlled vocabulary. Whether it be the *Library of Congress Subject Headings*, the *Library of Congress Graphics Thesaurus*, or a vocabulary created specifically for the collection, a base from which to build must be made. From this base, place and proper names, geographic descriptions, time, etc., can be added.

Finding Aids

Log book, card catalog and printed finding aid from San Francisco State University.

The term finding aid also applies to a collection guide created by the archive specifically for the user. These thorough guides contain the following parts:

1. Title page, e.g., *A Guide To Emmy Award-Winning Programs, 1974-1986, Submitted to the Northern California Chapter, National Academy of Television Arts And Sciences,* by Meredith Eliassen.

2. Nature and type of material. Describes what it is, e.g., one-inch daily outs; 3/4-inch U-matic documentaries, etc.

3. Acquisition. This section describes how you got it.

4. Administrative history. This section presents a brief, concise biography of the creating organization.

5. Scope and content notes. This section describes exactly what is and is not in the collection, giving the size, inclusive dates, number of items, arrangement order, format, significant contents and omissions, etc. It is very much like the Record Group definition.

6. Series descriptions. This section lists all of the series. It is usually the area where the public collection description ends.

7. File Units/Documents/Items. For many researchers, these levels of descriptions are the most useful. If they are available and not too extensive, they may be included. In terms of local television news collections, they may contain subject, date, and identifier.

8. Restrictions. This section, which includes restrictions imposed by the donor, might state copyright and licensing information.

9. Institutional archives rules and regulations. This section might describe who can use the collection, how materials can be reproduced, etc.

Patrons who use local television news archives seem to ask for certain elements of the collection. The most often requested access point is for subject material, whether stock footage, such as cows eating buttercups in a meadow, or a particular prize-winning cow who received a 4-H award in Smithville on July 12, 1962. Patrons will ask secondly for information by date, either a specific day, such as July 12, 1962, or month, or even year. Format also is important. Many researchers assume that local television news collections are on video, when the bulk of the collection may be on film. You may indeed have video tape, but it might be two-inch video for which neither you nor any laboratory within 1,000 miles has the equipment to view or reproduce. Your call number/footage identifier also is important, for it allows the patron to request a specific item, and the archive to retrieve it quickly.

The finding aid you prepare is a critical access tool for the patron. It should be concise, thorough, and full of information. For further information, see David B. Gracy II, *Archives and Manuscripts: Arrangement And Description*, pp. 21-30; and the Society of American Archivists, Committee on Finding Aids, *Inventories and Registers: A Handbook of Techniques and Examples*, Chicago, 1976.

Conclusion

One of the most difficult tasks in the administration of local television news archives is in organizing the collection, both physically and intellectually. Paper archives have been examined and processed for many years, and standardized processes have been developed for arranging and describing the collection. One of the challenges of the local television news archives is to use the established theory and practices of archival arrangement and description and apply them to moving image collections. The framework exists! By our work in arranging and describing our local television news collections, we will be adding a new dimension to these crucial archival processes.

Footnotes

1. Frank Evans, et al., "A Basic Glossary for Archivists, Manuscript Curators, and Record Managers," in *The American Archivist* 37 (July 1974), pp. 415-33.

2. T. R. Schellenberg, *Modern Archives: Principles and Techniques*. Chicago: University of Chicago Press, 1975.

3. Ibid, p. 188.

4. Ibid, p. 190, 193.

5. David B. Gracy II, *Archives and Manuscripts: Arrangement and Description*. Chicago: Society of American Archivists, Basic Manual Series, 1977, p. 5.

6. Ibid, pp. 7-8.

7. Ibid, p. 7.

8. Ibid, p. 12.

9. Ibid, p. 13.

10. T. R. Schellenberg. *The Management of Archives*. New York: Columbia University Press, 1965, p. 161.

11. Evans, et al., p. 422.

9

Cataloging

Jane Dunbar Johnson
UCLA Film and Television Archive

*Just as there are standard practices for organizing
and preserving newsfilm and video collections, so
too are there standards for cataloging. However,
when it comes to cataloging issues relevant to
newsfilm/video materials, all the rules for cataloging
have yet to be written and there is discussion about
how much information should be included in
cataloging records. This chapter provides an
overview of the cataloging issues facing newsfilm
and video archives whose collections contain unique
materials comprised of millions of feet of film and
thousands of hours of videotape.*

Jane Dunbar Johnson is Cataloger for the UCLA Film and Television Archive, where she catalogs news and documentary
footage, theatrical films, and television programs. Working with Archive curatorial staff, she developed online inventory
procedures for the Archive's KTLA newsfilm collection, some 14,000 rolls of news footage shot between 1958-1981.
Previously, she cataloged documentary photographs and political posters for the Library of Congress as part of its Optical
Disk Pilot Program. She received an MLS from UCLA in 1984. She is a member of the Association of Moving Image
Archivists, and Online Audiovisual Catalogers, Inc.

Cataloging

The following chapter is intended to familiarize newsfilm archivists with national standard cataloging practice. It outlines the basic cataloging processes, sets forth fundamental cataloging principles which have developed over the last hundred years or so, and includes an annotated bibliography of the cataloging tools required to create national standard cataloging records for newsfilm.

The Complexities of Newsfilm Cataloging

Newsfilm cataloging is a very labor intensive process. It is not unusual for a single film can to contain twenty or thirty segments of news footage, each with different physical attributes and unrelated to the others in content. Secondary source material received with the collection, such as scripts, inventory lists, or subject index card files, must be compared and evaluated for accuracy and suitability for inclusion in the cataloging records. Samples, at least, of the newsfilm itself may have to be viewed in order to verify

Providing intellectual access to these materials will be problematic and labor intensive.

content and relationships to secondary sources; frequently though, the film is received unprocessed, so that it cannot even be viewed without hours of preparation. Providing intellectual access to the collection can also be problematic; undoubtedly the most salient access point for users accessing newsfilm is the subject heading. Subject headings should be assigned from an authoritative standard list; those not found there by the cataloger must be formulated according to established policies and fully cross-referenced in order to optimize retrieval. This process of establishing, assigning, and maintaining a controlled vocabulary is known as authority control, and is probably the most time-consuming part of the cataloging process.

Why National Standards?

Until recently, most institutions have cataloged their newsfilm collections according to local policies quite outside the realm of national standard practice. In so doing, they have in effect been reinventing the wheel, establishing, ad hoc, cataloging procedures and subject heading lists which were, in fact, already in wide use for library and archival print materials, and ready for adaptation to newsfilm cataloging. (Other institutions, with larger collections and more severe staff shortages, lacked the resources required to reinvent the wheel, and instead left these invaluable collections languishing on the shelves, unused.)

By following national standard practices, newsfilm archivists can avoid such unnecessary duplication of efforts, and at the same time provide a means for distributing more widely their information-rich cataloging records.

One of the national standard tools which has been successfully used to provide access to newsfilm is the MARC (MAchine-Readable Cataloging) Format, a system which facilitates the exchange of cataloging data in large part by organizing the data into precisely defined fields and subfields. Archives creating records in the MARC format expand the number of online catalog systems available to them, since many off-the-shelf software packages are designed for use with these records. Some archives may find that they can load their MARC records into the library catalog of their parent institution; others can contribute records to a bibliographic utility such as OCLC or RLIN. In any case, the use of standard cataloging rules and the MARC Format provides the potential for national, and even international, distribution of records.

A typical collection can include 16mm film and any number of video formats.

Cataloging according to national standard practice does require substantial investment and commitment on the part of the archive. Staff with the expertise necessary to evaluate available online systems and create MARC records according to standard cataloging rules generally hold a Masters of Library Science (MLS) degree or its equivalent, or have considerable experience in a traditional library environment. Library and information science is in itself a complex field of study; experienced practitioners are crucial to the successful adaptation of its principles to archival newsfilm.

Levels of Description and Fullness of the Records

The term "item" in this chapter refers to the individual newsfilm segment, i.e., the intellectual entity; this will not always correspond to the physical item, since many newsfilm segments (items) may be spliced together onto a single physical piece—the reel. The sheer volume of most newsfilm collections, together with the staff shortages typical in archives, renders full item-by-item cataloging of entire newsfilm collections virtually impossible for most institutions. Although it is not necessary to fully catalog each individual item in a collection, everything must be described at some level in order to obtain full bibliographic control (or filmographic control, if you will) over the institution's holdings.

The previous chapter described four basic levels of archival description: the record group, the series, the file unit, and the item. For any one of these record types, the cataloger may create a full record, a minimal-level record, or an "enriched" minimal-level record as defined locally by the institution. A minimal record at the item level might include leader title, shot date, and physical description only. A full record at the item level might also include the exact footage count, a summary and/or shot analysis, camera operator (if known), reporter, subject headings, etc. Any of these record types, at any level of fullness, can be created using standard cataloging rules and the MARC Format. The level(s) of archival description employed, and the fullness of each record, should be decided on a collection-by-collection basis by each individual institution in accordance with local needs.

Cataloging entry for one of the programs within the documentary series *Eyes on the Prize.*

It is important to remember that online cataloging records are flexible, unlike their print or card catalog counterparts. This inherent flexibility allows the cataloger the option of creating minimal records now, and building upon those records as information becomes available in the future. The "right way" to describe newsfilm will vary from collection to collection, and may change over time, depending upon how much is known about each item, how much is likely to become known, what other secondary sources exist to provide access to the material, how much cataloging time is available, and user demand.

The newsfilm cataloger, in consultation with the archive's public service staff (sometimes one and the same!), should evaluate user needs, the nature of the collection itself, and institutional resources to determine the most effective means of providing access to the materials.

In any case, the cataloger must always bear in mind that the most important point of access for most newsfilm researchers is the subject matter of the individual news segment. Unfortunately, the segments are not usually physically arranged according to subject. (Typically, they are arranged chronologically, with many segments spliced together on a reel, or many small rolls residing together in a can.) Therefore, to create a record describing a single reel (or can full of rolls) may hinder rather than help access, because the record would contain a listing of the reel's contents in one area of the record, and a listing of authorized subject and name headings (access points) in another area of the record. The user then is faced with trying to match up the relevant access point(s) with one of the many segments described in the contents note.

If each record describes a single item, the user can readily determine the subject matter of each individual segment. By examining the subject and name headings which have been assigned to a particular segment, the user can then retrieve similar items by searching those same headings. Access points might include the date of the event, headings for persons or places depicted or discussed, the television station, the topical subject matter, and form of material (broadcast news, unedited footage, documentaries, etc.).

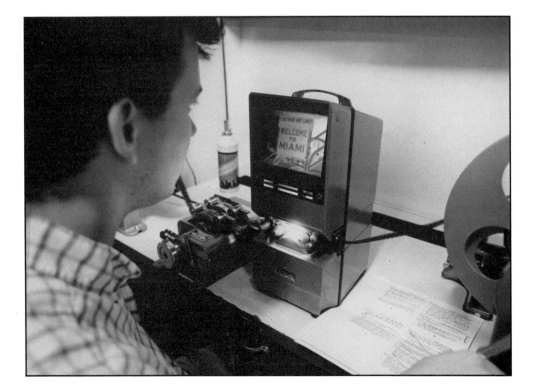

Checking film segments against an inventory record during inspection.

To prevent wear and tear on original film and for easier access, most newsfilm/video archives work from video transfers.

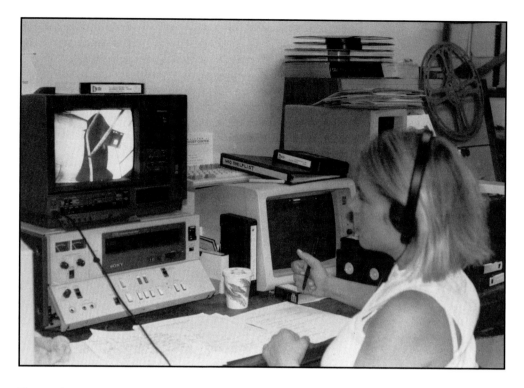

Even when it is not possible at first to provide all these access points for each item, it is often best nonetheless to create records initially at the item level, even if the only information available for the item is leader title, shot date, station name, physical description, and form.

Using this method, information which pertains to a particular segment, but which is obtained sometime after initial input (sometimes years after!), can readily be added to the record describing that individual segment. In general, it is far more difficult to add item-specific information to a record describing the file unit, series, or collection as a whole.

Item-level cataloging also ensures that all information of interest to the general public is easily accessible to the greatest possible number of researchers in a single place—the catalog itself. The problem with printed finding aids is that users are, in most cases, required to visit the archive in order to study them. It is often wiser to incorporate this finding aid data into the catalog record; unlike printed finding aids, machine-readable catalog records have the potential of reaching vast numbers of researchers as they work at home, in their office, or at a local library.

Although at first glance it would seem to be more cost-effective to create a few group-level records rather than a great many item-level records, one should not presume that this is the case. The extent to which it is the case depends in large part upon the editing capabilities of the system used for inputting the records. Indirect, long-term cost savings may also be effected by eliminating the need to create and maintain manual finding aids. When cataloging data is centralized and straightforward, it is more easily accessed and interpreted by researchers; this allows the intermediary (the reference librarian, curator, or archivist) more time to pursue other important activities.

Creating the Cataloging Records

Cataloging consists of a series of processes. The first is the description, in which the cataloger records information sufficient to identify the item (or group of items): title, statements of responsibility (where available), place and date of publication or distribution (if applicable), physical description, etc.

The *Anglo-American Cataloging Rules* (Second edition, revised; referred to hereafter as *AACR2R*) and *Archival Moving Image Materials: A Cataloging Manual* (*AMIM*), together with the *Library of Congress Rule Interpretations*, provide instructions as to how this information should be determined, in what format it should be recorded, to what level of detail, and so on.

Also part of the description are the added entries, or additional access points under which the user will find the identifying data, or body of the description. Added entries are typically made for persons or bodies responsible for the creative and/or intellectual content of the work, such as the production company, broadcasting company, anchor,

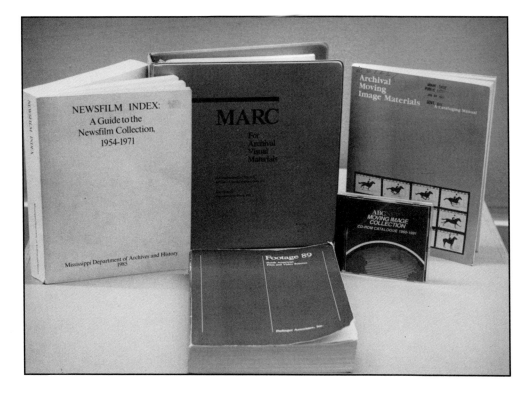

etc. *AACR2R* rules instruct the cataloger as to which names and titles should be indexed, and in what form.

The next process is subject analysis, in which the cataloger adds topical subject headings to the record, as well as headings for persons, geographic names, and/or corporate bodies as subjects.

The form of headings for personal, corporate, and most geographic names are determined using rules in *AACR2R*. In many or most cases, depending upon the collection, names to be used as access points have already been established by the Library of Congress and can be drawn from their authority list, *Name Authorities*. Topical headings and certain types of geographic headings are determined using rules in *Subject Cataloging Manual: Subject Headings*. Usually, topical headings of these types have already been established by the Library of Congress and can be drawn from their authority list, *Library of Congress Subject Headings*.

Also included in the general category of subject headings are genre and form headings; the national standard for newsfilm (or any moving image) cataloging is *Moving Image Materials: Genre Terms*.

A major component of the cataloging process, which is closely related to the assignment of entries and subject headings, is authority work, the process by which a heading is established and cross references made. Authority work should be done for any heading established for the first time. The end product of the authority work is the authority record, which indicates the authorized form of the heading, see and see also references, the cataloged work which generated the heading, and in some cases, scope notes which help to define the term and distinguish it from others which are similar. *AACR2R* and *Subject Cataloging Manual: Subject Headings* provide instructions on determining the correct form of heading, and types and forms of references.

Institutions creating national standard, machine-readable records for inclusion in an online catalog will require an additional cataloging tool, the *USMARC Format for Bibliographic Data* and its associated code lists. Within the framework of an *AACR2R*-formatted record, the *USMARC Format* dictates a more detailed structuring of the record

Required reading
for cataloging.

156

to allow machine processing of the data and sharing of records. Data elements, roughly corresponding to the organization of an *AACR2R* description, are separated into fields; each field is identified by a tag, or numerical label, which tells the machine what data follows, and so how to process and display it. Each field contains subfields (identified by codes) and two indicators which interpret or supplement the data found in the field. In addition, the *USMARC Format* stores certain pieces of data in coded fields to facilitate machine processing.

The *USMARC Format for Authority Data* is the national standard format for authority records.

In conclusion, it should be emphasized that newsfilm cataloging is not a simple process, nor is it a quick one. Unedited newsfilm in particular, lacking as it may be in written documentation, presents new challenges to the cataloger on a daily basis. An informal survey of the nation's leading news archives, conducted for the UCLA Film and Television Archive, showed that 10 hours of cataloging (using various local practices) are usually required to process a single hour of news footage. Cataloging to national standard might be expected to take somewhat longer. Archives committed to providing access to these invaluable visual documents will consider it time well spent.

Principles

When librarians and archivists first began describing their collections, it was with the needs of their own, local, public in mind. Over time, it was realized that the sharing of cataloging records would benefit both users and catalogers. To facilitate such sharing, cataloging practices were codified, the most recent cataloging code being *AACR2R*. *AACR2R*, like many of its predecessors, is based on certain cataloging principles. Most of the principles (understandably, given their age) have been stated in terms of book cataloging, but can be readily applied to many types of material, including newsfilm. The most fundamental principles, and their sources, are stated below.

Objects of the Catalog

The objects of the catalog are 1) to enable a person to find a book of which either the author, title, or subject is known; 2) to show what the library has by a given author, on a given subject, and in a given kind of literature; and 3) to assist in the choice of a book as to its edition (bibliographically), and as to its character (literary or topical).[1]

Translated into newsfilm cataloging parlance, this might read: The objects of the catalog are 1) to enable a person to find footage of which the subject, title, or persons or companies responsible are known; 2) to show what the archive has by a particular person or company, on a given subject, and in a given form or language; and 3) to assist in the selection of footage as to its version, and as to its genre, form, or subject.

Pending a user study on newsfilm researchers' needs, it can probably be assumed that subject access is the most important form of access to these materials. Titles for news broadcasts vary, on title frames and in secondary sources; titles for unedited news footage are elusive or non-existent. "Authorship" for broadcasts is diffuse, split as it is between writers, reporters, anchors, cameramen, and producers; for raw footage, it is often not determinable. However, company names such as television stations can be quite important.

Convenience of the User

The convenience of the public is always to be set before the ease of the cataloger.[2]

Universal Bibliographic Control

Have each document cataloged only once, as near to the source of publication as possible, and make basic bibliographic data on all publications issued in all countries universally and promptly available, in a form which is internationally acceptable.[3]

Restated for application to newsfilm, this might read: Catalog each item only once, as near to the source of production as possible, and make basic filmographic data on all footage created in all countries universally and promptly available, in a form which is internationally acceptable.

In the case of unedited newsfilm, it is unlikely that a given item would be available to several archives to catalog; it should be fairly obvious, however, that broadcast news programs likely to be held by several institutions need not be cataloged by each individual institution. Rather, one institution (ideally the one nearest the source of production) could catalog the broadcast, then distribute the cataloging record (via a network, for example) to other institutions, thereby saving the other archives unnecessary duplication of effort. The use of national standard cataloging tools facilitates the sharing of records in this way.

Structure of the Catalog

The catalog should contain at least one entry for each item cataloged, and more than one when necessary to meet users' needs.[4]

Kinds of Entries

Entries should be of three kinds: main entries, added entries, and references. "The main entry must be a full entry, giving all the particulars necessary for identifying the item"; added entries are additional entries, based on the main entry and repeating under other headings information given in it.[5] The main entry for newsfilm would typically be the title, with additional entry points for such things as topical subjects, persons depicted or discussed, and persons or bodies responsible for the content, such as reporter, producer, etc. References direct the user to another place in the catalog.

Uniform Heading

When variant forms of a name or title occur, all works for which a particular person or body is responsible are found under a single heading. The uniform heading chosen "should normally be the most frequently used name (or form of name) or title appearing in the works cataloged or in references to them by accepted authorities."[6]

Specific Entry

The heading should be as specific as the topic it is intended to cover. As a corollary, the heading should not be broader than the topic; rather than use a broader heading, the cataloger should use two specific headings which will approximately cover it.[7]

This is the rule of specific entry originally stated by Charles Cutter.[8] It dictates, for example, that newsfilm about AIDS should be assigned the heading for AIDS and not the broader heading DISEASES. Like most of the principles included here, this one was written with books in mind. It has been suggested that visual materials, being more difficult than books to browse, warrant more extensive subject cataloging. This might include for example, assigning a general as well as a specific heading in some instances (e.g., YELLOWSTONE NATIONAL PARK and NATIONAL PARKS).

Another aspect of visual materials which distinguishes them from printed materials is that their subject matter can be expressed in terms of both its "of-ness" (explicit content) and its "aboutness" (implicit content). For example, a story about the illicit drug PCP may be illustrated by extensive footage of some of its effects (homelessness, traffic accidents, etc.). The footage is about drug abuse, but it is of people living on the street. It is important when cataloging newsfilm (or any visual document) to provide access to both the implicit and explicit subjects. The question the cataloger must always ask is: Would a user interested in a particular topic be satisfied if s/he retrieved this particular item? If the answer is yes, the heading for that subject should be assigned.

Bibliography

Following is a bibliography of the minimum list of tools necessary to catalog according to national standard. As with the principles, no standards have been written for newsfilm per se; the titles below were designed to cover either 1) all moving image materials, or 2) all physical formats which might be found in libraries, archives, and museums.

Anglo-American Cataloguing Rules. Second edition, 1988 revision. Chicago: American Library Association, 1988.

The standard cataloging rules for the U.S., Great Britain, and Canada; often referred to as *AACR2R*. Part One, entitled Description, consists of thirteen chapters, including a chapter on general rules (Chapter One) and rules for analysis, i.e., the process of preparing a bibliographic record describing a part or parts of an item for which a comprehensive entry, or collective record, has been made, such as a newsfilm segment which forms part of a reel (Chapter Thirteen). Each of the remaining chapters in *AACR2R*'s Part One provides rules for the description of a particular form of material, such as "Books, pamphlets, and printed sheets," Manuscripts, Music, Sound Recordings, etc. Moving image materials are covered in Chapter Seven. Within Chapter Seven, rules are organized according to "areas" of the record: Area 1 is Title and Statements of Responsibility; Area 2 is the edition area; Area 4 is the publication, distribution area, etc.

Part Two (Headings, Uniform Titles, and References) provides instruction in the choice and form of headings (personal, geographic, and corporate names, including conference headings, and uniform titles). The final chapter instructs the cataloger as to the provision of references in authority records.

Appendices provide guidelines on the use of capitalization, abbreviations, and numerals in records, and a glossary.

AACR2R conforms with the International Standard for Bibliographic Description (ISBD). It was designed for use in manual or automated systems, but does not refer to the MARC Format or include examples of MARC records.

Many individual *AACR2R* rules are clarified or modified in U.S. institutions by *Library of Congress Rule Interpretations* (*LCRIs*; see below). Where *AACR2R* provides an optional rule, to be heeded or ignored at the discretion of the individual institution, the *LCRIs* will often indicate LC practice, which has become a defacto standard.

Wendy White-Hensen's *Archival Moving Image Materials: A Cataloging Manual* can be viewed as a gloss for *AACR2R*'s Chapter 7. (See below.)

Library of Congress Rule Interpretations. Base text plus updates. Washington, DC: Cataloging Distribution Service, Library of Congress, 1991.

A defacto standard established by the Office of Descriptive Cataloging Policy at the Library of Congress. In addition to interpreting *AACR2R* (clarifying, or in some cases modifying, individual *AACR2R* rules which have been deemed vague, ineffectual, or unnecessarily labor-intensive), the *Rule Interpretations* record official rule changes (as determined by the Joint Steering Committee for the Revision of *AACR2R*), LC decisions on optional and alternative rules, and LC cataloging routines related to the rules. Arranged by rule number; indexed. An update subscription provides quarterly additions and changes.

Individual rule interpretations are also published in *Cataloging Service Bulletin* (see below).

White-Hensen, Wendy. *Archival Moving Image Materials: A Cataloging Manual*. Washington, DC: Motion Picture, Broadcasting, and Recorded Sound Division, Library of Congress, 1984.

Detailed cataloging rules which are based upon and elaborate upon rules in *AACR2R*'s Chapter 7, which were found lacking in detail by archival moving image catalogers. Makes a fundamental break with *AACR2R* practice in its recommendation that several versions of a particular moving image work be included on a single record. (Standard library and archival document practice would be to make a separate record for each version and bring together all the versions in the catalog by means of a single "uniform title.") *AMIM* also departs from traditional library cataloging by relying far less on transcription as the basis for the cataloging record. In a record created using *AMIM*, data transcribed (copied) from title frames is often indistinguishable from data obtained from reference sources.

Chapters in *AMIM* correspond, for the most part, with chapter sections in *AACR2R*; for example, *AMIM* Chapter 1 corresponds with *AACR2R* Rule 7.1 (Title and Statement of Responsibility).

Does not include rules for choice and form of headings, methods of analysis, creation of authority records, or guidelines for use of capitalization, abbreviations, and numerals.

Appendices include examples of cataloging records, and a glossary. Designed for use with manual or machine-readable records, but does not include examples of MARC records.

ALA-LC Romanization Tables: Transliteration Schemes for Non-Roman Scripts. 1991 edition. Washington, DC: Cataloging Distribution Service, Library of Congress, 1991.

Tables for over 140 languages, including special characters, character modifiers, and guidelines for capitalization and word division where applicable. Useful when transcribing title frames appearing in non-Roman scripts.

Library of Congress. *Name Authorities*. Washington, DC: Cataloging Distribution Service, Library of Congress.

A comprehensive listing of all name, uniform title, and series headings established by the Library of Congress and other participating institutions in accordance with *AACR2R* rules for establishing names. Includes personal names, corporate names, conference headings, uniform titles, series, and names of political and civil jurisdictions. Does not include non-jurisdictional geographic headings, such as mountain ranges, city sections, etc. (Cf. *Library of Congress Subject Headings*.) For guidance on which types of headings are found in *Name Authorities* and which types are in *Library of Congress Subject Headings*, refer to *Library of Congress Subject Cataloging Manual: Subject Headings*.

Available from LC's Cataloging Distribution Service in a cumulative microform edition or CD-ROM (both updated quarterly), on magnetic tape (new tapes issued weekly), and online through bibliographic utilities such as OCLC and RLIN.

Library of Congress. Office for Subject Cataloging Policy. *Library of Congress Subject Headings*. Washington, DC : Cataloging Distribution Service, Library of Congress, 1991.

A comprehensive listing of subject headings, including non-jurisdictional geographic headings, established by the Library of Congress based on literary warrant and according to rules set forth in its *Subject Cataloging Manual: Subject Headings* (see below). Includes tens of thousands of fully cross-referenced headings, ranging from very general terms, such as "War," to specific headings such as "Iran-Contra Affair, 1985-1990."

Available from LC's Cataloging Distribution Service in book form, with annually published new editions; in cumulative microform edition or CD-ROM (each updated quarterly), on magnetic tape (new tapes issued weekly), and online through bibliographic utilities such as OCLC and RLIN. The book edition includes an introduction on use and nomenclature of subject headings. All editions should be used in conjunction with *Subject Cataloging Manual: Subject Headings* and with *Name Authorities* (see below). Some topics are expressed in the form of a name heading followed by a topical subdivision, so that half of the heading is derived from *Name Authorities*, and half from the subject list; *Subject Cataloging Manual* clarifies how distinctions between heading types are drawn.

Library of Congress. Subject Cataloging Division. *Subject Cataloging Manual: Subject Headings*. Fourth edition. Washington, DC: Cataloging Distribution Service, Library of Congress, 1991.

Instructions for establishing and assigning Library of Congress and Library of Congress-style subject headings. Includes general guidelines, such as the number and specificity of headings to assign, and the point at which a new heading should be established. For catalogers establishing a new heading, gives guidance on research, including a list of commonly used reference sources, instructions on formulating the heading and establishing scope notes and references for it. Enumerates which types of headings are found in *Name Authorities* (above) and which in *Library of Congress Subject Headings* (above). Includes lists of subdivisions which can be appended to name and subject headings in order to bring out a more specific topic. Appendices provide instructions on abbreviations, capitalization, diacritics, and punctuation. Indexed.

Yee, Martha M. , compiler *Moving Image Materials: Genre Terms*. First edition. Compiled for the National Moving Image Database Standards Committee, National Center for Film and Video Preservation at The American Film Institute. Washington, DC: Cataloging Distribution Service, Library of Congress, 1988.

A list of genre and form headings to be used as index terms. In USMARC Format records, these headings appear in the 655 field. Includes about a dozen terms which would occur with some frequency in newsfilm collections.

USMARC Format for Bibliographic Data. Washington, DC: Cataloging Distribution Service, Library of Congress, 1988.

The USMARC Format provides a structure for the exchange of records in machine-readable form. It defines the labels (field tags, subfield codes, etc.) which identify individual data elements in the bibliographic or filmographic record. The newsfilm cataloger uses *AACR2R* and *AMIM* to determine the content of the record (e.g., the form of the title, name headings, etc.); in an automated environment, s/he then uses the MARC Format to label the data so that it can be loaded into an online system and, if desired, exchanged with other institutions via networks or bibliographic utilities such as OCLC or RLIN. In addition to the variable fields in which the standard filmographic data is found, the USMARC Format consists of a leader (coded information required by the machine for the processing of the record), and a directory, which contains the tag, length, and starting location of each variable field within the record. The USMARC Format includes an appendix which gives the Minimal Level Record Requirements for a National Level Record.

USMARC Code List for Countries. Washington, DC: Cataloging Distribution Service, Library of Congress, 1988.

Within the USMARC Format are several fields which store, in coded form, the name of a country or countries associated with the work. For example, field 044 contains a "Country of Producer" code. Country codes are listed here, along with instructions for their application.

USMARC Code List for Geographic Areas. Washington, DC: Cataloging Distribution Service, Library of Congress, 1988.

Within the USMARC Bibliographic and Authority Formats is a field (043) which stores, in coded form, place names associated with the work. Codes for geographic areas are listed here, along with instructions for their application.

USMARC Code List for Languages. 1989 edition. Washington, DC: Cataloging Distribution Service, Library of Congress, 1989.

Within the USMARC Bibliographic and Authority Formats are several fields in which language codes are used. For example, field 041 in the bibliographic format contains language codes for multilingual items, such as subtitled films. Language codes are listed here, along with instructions for application.

USMARC Code List for Relators, Sources, Description Conventions. 1990 edition. Washington, DC: Cataloging Distribution Service, Library of Congress, 1990.

Divided into six parts, not all of which will be used by newsfilm catalogers. Part 1 contains a list of relator terms for use with name headings; the terms were not designed for use with moving image materials; for codes applicable to newsfilm, refer to *Cataloging Service Bulletin*, no. 31 (Winter 1986), p. 71-75, and *Cataloging Service Bulletin*, no. 50 (Fall 1990), p. 51. Parts 2 through 4 list codes indicating the source of the subject category code, classification scheme, subject index term (e.g. *Moving Image Materials*; see above), respectively. Part 5 is a list of non-USMARC Formats with their associated codes; Part 6 is the code list of descriptive cataloging rules, such as *Archival Moving Image Materials* (see above).

USMARC Format for Authority Data: Including Guidelines for Content Designation. Washington, DC: Library of Congress, 1989.

The USMARC Authority Format provides a structure for authority records in machine-readable form, similar to the one used in the USMARC Bibliographic Format. It is designed to carry "authoritative information concerning the standard forms of names and subjects to be used as access points on bibliographic records, the forms of these names and subjects that should be used as references to the standard forms, and the interrelationships among these forms." In short, it contains a record of the cataloger's authority work. Like the Bibliographic format, it defines the labels (field tags, subfield codes, etc.) which identify individual data elements in the record. Having researched the heading as necessary to determine usage, the cataloger then determines the form of both headings and cross references using *AACR2R*, then tags the data as specified by the Format. This enables the data to be loaded into any online catalog which accepts USMARC authority records, and if desired, shared.

Cataloging Service Bulletin. Washington, DC: Library of Congress, Processing Services.

A quarterly publication providing current information on Library of Congress cataloging practices. Includes lists of revised subject headings, changed Library of Congress Rule Interpretations, and occasional articles of particular interest to newsfilm catalogers, such as "Guidelines for Subject Cataloging of Visual Materials"[9] and "Relator Terms for Archival Moving Image Cataloging."[10]

Footnotes

1. Charles A. Cutter, *Rules for a Dictionary Catalog*, fourth edition, rewritten. Washington, DC: U.S. Government Printing Office, 1904. Cited in Michael Carpenter and Elaine Svenonius, *Foundations of Cataloging: A Sourcebook*. Littleton, CO: Libraries Unlimited, 1985, p. 67. [The third principle is of lesser significance for newsfilm, since a given title (or segment of footage) doesn't generally exist in more than one version.]

2. Ibid, p. 66.

3. Dorothy Anderson, *Universal Bibliographic Control: A Long-Term Policy – A Plan for Action*. Munich: Verlag Dokumentation, Pullach, 1974, p. 11. Cited in Lois Mai Chan, *Cataloging and Classification: An Introduction*. New York: McGraw-Hill, 1981, p. 22.

4. International Conference on Cataloguing Principles, *Report: International Conference on Cataloguing Principles, Paris, 9th-18th October, 1961*. London: Organizing Committee of the International Conference on Cataloguing Principles, 1963. Cited in Carpenter and Svenonius, *Foundations of Cataloging: A Sourcebook*, p. 179.

5. Ibid, p. 180.

6. Ibid, p. 181.

7. David Judson Haykin, *Subject Headings: A Practical Guide*. Washington, DC: U.S. Government Printing Office, 1951. Cited in Lois Mai Chan, Phyliss A. Richmond, and Elaine Svenonius, *Theory of Subject Analysis: A Sourcebook*. Littleton, CO: Libraries Unlimited, 1985, p. 109.

8. Cutter, *Rules for a Dictionary Catalog*. Cited in Chan, *Cataloging and Classification: An Introduction*, p. 22.

9. "Guidelines for Subject Cataloging of Visual Materials," *Cataloging Service Bulletin* 48 (Spring 1990), pp. 42-45.

10. "Relator Terms for Archival Moving Image Cataloging," *Cataloging Service Bulletin* 31 (Winter 1986), pp. 71-75.

Research and Reference Service

Dan Den Bleyker

Mississippi Department of Archives and History

This chapter provides the archive's perspective of providing access and reference services to moving image materials. It addresses all areas of concern including access policies, equipment needs, license fees, copyright, processing and handling of requests, and working with researchers and other users.

Dan Den Bleyker has been the Audio-Visual Records Curator with the Mississippi Department of Archives and History since September 1985. He received a BA from the University of Southern Mississippi and completed course work for an MA in History and a Masters in Library Science. He was a member of the Film/Television Archives Advisory Committee and a charter member of the Association of Moving Image Archivists.

Research and Reference Service

One of the most important reasons for supplying high quality reference service for local television newsfilm and video collections is the encouragement it provides to interested parties to make productive use of the collections, and this, after all, is the reason for preserving the material. There is little reason for carrying out the basic archival collection techniques on film and video material if archivists and curators are not going to promote the use of the collections, and quality will encourage this.

On an ever-increasing basis local television moving image materials continue to be used in a variety of ways, from historical and cultural, to media and communications analysis, to use in the classroom.

Perhaps the single largest use of local film and video material is in television documentaries such as the *Eyes on the Prize*, and *The American Experience* series. Local newsfilm collections are also used by the three major U.S. networks, independent local stations,

Footage from the Mississippi Department of Archives and History is incorporated into this Civil Rights exhibit at the State Historical Museum in Jackson.

foreign news broadcasters, independent production companies, and others. While the material is sometimes incorporated in theatrically-released films, such as Oliver Stone's *JFK* and *The Doors*, or Ron Mann's *Twist*, it is also used for research purposes by the motion picture industry to get ideas for set and costume design for films, dialogue and location.

Local newsfilm and video is also being incorporated into museum exhibits such as the Civil Rights exhibit at the Mississippi State Historical Museum in Jackson, Mississippi, the Civil Rights Museum in Memphis, Tennessee, and the Historical Museum of South Florida. Increasingly museums and cultural organizations are seeking to incorporate images from local television collections as an integral part of their exhibitions. Another interesting way for using moving image material is in tributes for local dignitaries. During the past year, local television news film from the Mississippi Department of Archives and History was used at a banquet for a retiring superintendent of schools in a short documentary piece about the superintendent's career. The Wolfson Center in Miami held a very successful seminar featuring archival images tracing the career of Dante Fascell, who ended his term in Congress after serving 30 years.

Now, the largest group of researchers utilizing the collections are film and documentary researchers or producers, followed by news broadcasters and academic researchers. In the future archivists can expect their materials to be utilized by an ever-increasing variety of users and purposes, ranging from incorporation in new productions, to primary source information for academic researchers, to use by the general public. This will happen as historians and social scientists become more visually aware, and archives promote access of all kinds.

For convenience, local newsfilm and video will be termed local newsfilm throughout the rest of this chapter. Reference services for local newsfilm collections may be broken down into two categories: (1) making the materials available for research use; (2) making copies of material available for inclusion in productions. There is a cost to the institution in providing these services, but this can also be a great source of revenue.

Generally, policies vary from archive to archive as do fees. Some institutions have minimal charges or none at all, in keeping with institutional policy of supplying reference for other types of collections. Generally archives charge research fees, which also vary. However, it can be said that with tightening budgets, public archives are reviewing policies and fee schedules for use of moving image material for research purposes. Like commercial archives, most newsfilm archives charge fees if materials are to be used in new productions and these charges also vary.

Contact with Researchers

The first contact with researchers may be by telephone, mail, or in person at the archive. It is at this time that the researcher should be made aware of what may be available and the procedures for using the material. A printed user policy and fee schedule should be presented to the patron to familiarize them with the institutional guidelines and fees. It is important that patrons are aware of the fees and policies and understand them before a reference interview is conducted. This can save many headaches from occurring later, such as patrons accusing a curator of not informing them of an important point about the use of the collection. There always seem to be questions or attempted negotiations over the cost of licensing fees.

User Policy

The user policy should clearly state what patrons can expect from the archive, such as time constraints placed on the use of collection, how much the reference services will cost, if exemptions may be made to the policy, how to request an exemption, and the amount of time the user can expect before receiving an answer to a reference request. The purpose of the user policy is not to discourage usage, but to provide the rules for an orderly method of accessing and using the collections.

Fee schedules should clearly state what the costs will be for using material from the collections. The uniqueness and demand for the material in the collection must be considered when determining fee schedules. Other factors are the time it will take to provide user copies, the quality and format of the copies which can be provided, and the amount of staff time necessary for filling a request.

After patrons are given time to read the user policy and fees schedule, they should be encouraged to ask any question they may have about either. It is best to resolve any difficulties which might occur between the archive and the patrons at this time rather than waiting until hours or days have been spent on research. A clearly written and followed user policy can eliminate many of the problems which can and sometimes do occur between film users and the archive. If your institution does charge fees for research, consider the policy of payment of fees prior to your commencing the research.

Reference Interviews

Once patrons understand the polices of the archive, an in-depth reference interview should be conducted. It is at this point that reference archivists should determine exactly what is needed. Many times, as with other types of reference requests, patrons have not narrowed their requests. This means wasted time for reference staff and researchers. Be wary of patrons who state they wish to see everything about a subject without expressing a clear focus. Many times, in the end, it will become evident that they are only interested in the events of one particular day or a very specific part of the story.

There are cases, however, when there are very broad queries, and archivists should be prepared to assist in such a request. For example, researchers for major documentary productions should be given an overview of the collection directed by what they stated in the reference interview. First, archivists should give a general introduction to the collection including the dates, areas of strengths and weaknesses of the collection and the formats of the original material. Researchers should be informed about viewing procedures and also be made aware of any restrictions on collections whether donor initiated or by archive policy. They should be informed of any copyright restrictions or clearances which they have to obtain in order to use the material in productions.

Finding Aids

At this point, patrons should be given information about the repository's finding aids and encouraged to use them. The aids may consist of printed indexes, card catalogs, computer-based catalogs and databases, national database utilities, or the staff's expertise with the collection. In all likelihood, the finding aids will consist of a combination of the above.

Requests

In order to access local newsfilm collections, it is not always necessary to do research at the archive. Copies of both film and video material can be made available for shipment to researchers around the world. Charging a fee for these outside (mail-in and phone-in) reference requests for use of material may be necessary because conducting research and processing film/video requests is labor intensive. The materials must be viewed, repaired, and described at the very minimum before reference copies can be made. In-house reference services tend to be less expensive, because researchers can handle much more of the research. As the cataloging information about collections is entered into more nationwide utilities, it will become easier for researchers to conduct their research before they even contact the archive.

A sample request from the Mississippi Department of Archives and History will illustrate how quickly material can be supplied to a user. An urgent call was received from a producer requesting footage for use that day. The film was taken to a local television station where it was transferred to videotape, sent to the producer via satellite and put on the air that evening. Agreements were faxed and payment was made electronically. The Wolfson Center has used air couriers when requested by clients because overnight delivery was not quick enough.

One of the most difficult and expensive aspects of supplying reference service for newsfilm is making the material available for viewing. The equipment for preparing film for reference can be as inexpensive as a pair of rewinds, a sound box, a splicer and a moviescope. The films should then be transferred to videotape for access. Never "project" archival film; use only a moviescope or a flatbed film viewing table. The most practical solution is to make videotape transfers of all or part of the material in the collection for reference viewing.

It is possible to allow patrons to view original material under strict supervision, but this should be done only if an archive staff member handles the material and should be done only in special situations. Under no circumstances should patrons handle original material because even experienced film handlers can damage film. Never send original material to a researcher; it can be damaged, misused or lost in shipment.

Fortunately, today there are reasonably-priced methods for making film-to-video transfers in house. The most basic system is a film-to-tape transfer unit (such as the Elmo TRV16) which connects directly to a video recorder of any format and a monitor for playback. Prices range from about $5,000 for a bare-bones system to over $50,000 for a variety of formats and other types of equipment. Institutions can add equipment components gradually over time depending on their needs, the level of requests and the amount of money they have to spend. There is also the possibility of obtaining equipment from television stations along with the film collection. The best transfers are made using a telecine, such as a Rank Cintel, but the cost of acquiring and maintaining this type of equipment may be prohibitive for most archives. A word of warning: when accepting any donated equipment with collections, be prepared to spend time and

Part of the Wolfson Center system.

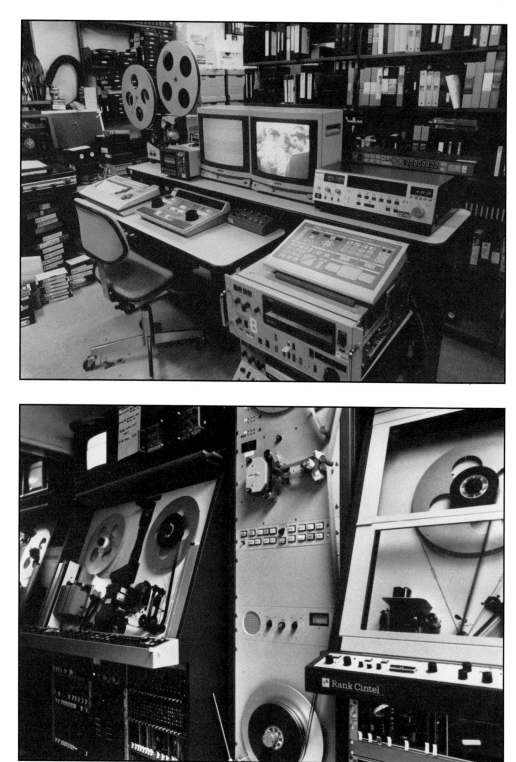

Rank Cintel transfer equipment is on the wish list for archives, but available at film and video labs when high quality transfers are needed.

money on maintaining it. If taped reference copies are available, patrons can view the material at their convenience. A time code "burned" (superimposed) into the reference copy serves as identification by viewers and speeds up the process of making copies for patron use. The biggest factor preventing most repositories from preparing reference copies is the cost, but it is justified when compared to the possible damage which may be done to the film if its mishandled. The costs, if done on demand, will be charged to the researcher making the request.

Reference tapes can be produced on any video format: from 8mm video to Betacam. Some of the factors to be considered when deciding on which format to use are the following: the quality of the reference copy, the cost of equipment to make the reference copy, the expertise to produce the copy, the expertise to maintain equipment for producing and viewing reference copies, and the amount of storage space available for the reference tapes. The researcher may also request a particular format. Under ideal circumstances, a high-quality master tape should be produced before or at the same time as the reference tape. If this is done the high quality master tape can be used for making reference tapes as needed and for making use copies. An important factor to be considered when selecting a recording medium is, will the technology used for making the reference copies be available in the future? Will the recording and playback equipment be available in five, ten or twenty years?

Viewing Stations for In-house Reference

Once the material has been transferred to reference videotapes, one or more viewing stations will have to be set up. The most convenient viewing stations consist of combination VCRs and monitors, available in 8mm and VHS formats. The number of viewing stations required depends on the number of reference users and the amount of money available for purchasing equipment. These stations can also be used by staff for cataloging.

Out-of-Town Requests

The same factors apply to out-of-town requests, except after the researcher decides what they want, the tapes are shipped (at researcher's expense). When you send any copy of your materials out-of-house, archives take certain risks if not careful.

Once a copy leaves the archive, it is difficult to maintain control over its use. The archive should have users sign a reference agreement stating they will not make further copies and they will return the copy by a certain date (ninety days, for example) or when their research is finished, whichever is first. This will keep the honest user honest.

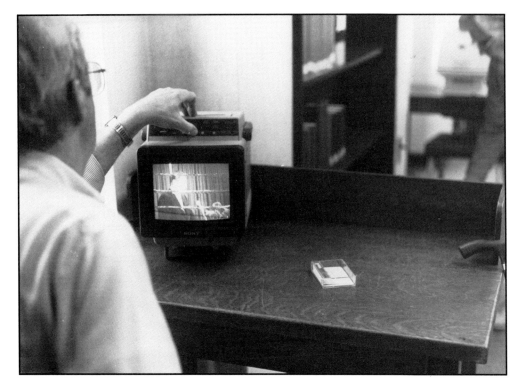

An 8mm viewing station at the Mississippi Department of Archives and History.

Basic VHS viewing stations. These combination VHS decks and monitors are portable and require no setup time.

Unfortunately, unscrupulous users can easily take advantage of the situation, so archives have to be on the alert for misuse and do everything in their power to stop it. The misuse of copyrighted material can be legally pursued, and not only can the distribution of a product which contains unlicensed material be stopped, but there is also the possibility of collecting damages. Even though there is a chance of losing some control over the collection, supplying reference copies is one of the best ways to promote the use of the collection, and that makes the hazard worthwhile. Legal issues concerning the protection of film collections should be discussed with legal counsel before the first reference copy leaves the institution.

There are two practical methods of maintaining some control over the unscrupulous use of information sent out as reference copies. First, send a minimum amount of reference material. The best way to keep the copy amount to a minimum is to conduct a thorough reference interview and only send what is requested. The other way to discourage illegal use of reference material in actual productions is to burn in time code and to transfer the image to VHS tape. Every repository will not have the time-code generator for burning in time code; in this case, as poor a quality VHS copy as is possible should be sent. The quality of VHS tape usually is too poor for use in productions. Unfortunately, even with these precautions, there is never a guarantee that the material will not be used illegally. Whatever archives decide in the case of misuse, they should always maintain the authority to deny access to material if misuse is suspected. For example, if a user is planning to purchase the rights to footage for one purpose but is suspected of planning to use the material in one or more additional productions without paying, use of the material should be denied.

If patrons decide to use material from a collection in a production, archives should be prepared to have broadcast quality copies of the material. Of course, patrons should be expected to pay for reproduction costs for the copies and for the use of the material in their production. Each user should sign a license agreement with the archive agreeing to pay the fees and to follow the conditions for use. Users should also be expected to pay for any other expenses incurred in making the copies. Fees are a matter to be calculated by the institution and there are many variables to consider in setting fee schedules.

Recommended
equipment needed
to provide
protected preview
tapes includes a
character generator
(bottom left) and a
time-code generator
(top right) with
other components

Time-code
generator.

Window dub with
time code and
Wolfson copyright
notice.

The license agreement should contain an exact list of the material to be copied, the title of the production the material will be used in, the inclusive dates for the showing of the production, and a listing of all charges to be assessed for use of the material.

The next step is to decide where to have the film-to-tape transfer made. Both parties will have to decide where the copy can be made. Factors which will determine how the copy can be made are the quality of the copy required, the amount of money the patron is willing to spend, the companies who will produce the transfer, the speed with which the patron wants the copy, and the manpower available at the archive to have the copy made.

The best possible choice for the transfer is to do it in-house. This will ensure that the film is not damaged by an outside vendor. However, archives may not have the capability to produce broadcast quality copies, and an outside vendor will be selected. Although some patrons will be satisfied with the quality of copies produced in-house, others will want a better quality copy or a different format.

A 3/4-inch videocassette containing footage requested from the Wolfson Center for a production. "Clean" footage without time code is provided to the reseacher only after time-code numbers and payment are received by the Center.

When the material to be transferred or copied has to go out-of-house, it is up to the archive to make the final decisions on who will make the transfers and how the material will reach the vendor. Remember that it is the archive's responsibility to protect the collection, and they make the final decisions about the collections, not the user. Resource lists of vendors with notations about their dependability and trustworthiness are very helpful. When in doubt about the lab's quality of work, call other institutions to get their opinions. Even making a preliminary visit to the lab to inspect the operation should be considered. The responsibility for the safety and preservation of the film lies with each archive and this should be taken into consideration when deciding who may handle the materials.

If an off-site vendor is chosen to make the transfers, it is recommended that archive personnel hand-carry original material to the vendor. There is a documented case of a national delivery service losing some rare early newsreel film of Albert Einstein which was being shipped to a film laboratory (*Memphis Commercial Appeal,* March 9, 1990, p. B5). The film was later recovered, but what if it had not been? Copies can be sent by courier service or the Postal Service, but never the original. Time usually has to be reserved for the copy or transfer equipment at the vendor, so the material will be off-site for as short a period as possible. It is the user's responsibility to pay for archive staff time for transporting the material as well as mileage and all other related expenses, including room and meals for the person escorting the film. If users do not wish to pay for the services, they should be told their requests cannot be met.

As with reference copies, only as little film as needed should be copied. The reason for this is to maintain control of the film wherever possible.

The curatorial responsibilities related to moving image collections are large; however, it must also be remembered that simply protecting and preserving the collections is not enough. Newsfilm curators are responsible for the preservation of a large segment of mid-twentieth century American history. This responsibility extends to making the film and video available for use. If repositories fail in their reference responsibilities and the collections are not made available for use, there is little sense in maintaining them. If the collections are merely locked away and never seen by anyone again, there is little reason for preserving and maintaining the collections. It is the archive's responsibility to reach a balance protecting the collections while at the same time making them as accessible as possible to a wide variety of users.

11

Licensing Footage: A Researcher's Perspective

Kenn Rabin

Fulcrum Media Services

Many newsfilm/video archivists find themselves explaining to researchers that they are "not stock footage agencies," operate with small staffs, and are engaged in a variety of activities in addition to licensing materials. Researchers, perhaps more accustomed to the ways of commercial agencies, often don't understand. This chapter provides insights looking across this chasm from the perspective of an informed researcher.

Kenn Rabin has been a consultant and film researcher on most of the major PBS historical documentaries of the last decade, including: *Vietnam: A Television History, Eyes on the Prize, The Philippines: In Our Image, Making Sense of the Sixties* and *The American Experience*. As founder of Fulcrum Media Services, he has also worked on network documentaries, TV and cable miniseries, and features. He served as Archival Manager on Kevin Costner's *500 Nations* and film researcher on ABC News' *20th Century Project*, and developed archival database systems for the Rock and Roll Hall of Fame. In 1988 he was nominated for an Emmy for his work on *Eyes on the Prize*, and in 1992 shared an Emmy nomination for his work on the late Marlin Riggs' *Color Adjustment*. He has worked on a multimedia project for teaching World and American History to high school students, as well as a project to reform music rights clearances for documentary producers.

Licensing Footage:
A Researcher's Perspective

A good archive has an ambiguous mission at best: to preserve and protect its holdings and their market value, as well as to make those holdings available to the public, or some segment of the public, for study and/or duplication and dissemination. This almost contradictory charter is not unlike that of the National Park Service: the parklands remain pristine when people are barred from them, yet the whole idea of national parks is to give us the opportunity to enjoy the natural landscape. How can we develop a scenario that accommodates both sides of this paradoxical situation?

An archivist once told me that, when starting out in her business, she had believed the historical film footage she managed should be available to anyone who wanted it, free of charge or encumbrance, simply because it contained our shared history, to which we are entitled to have access. She has since revised her attitude, needless to say. Yet her sentiments strike a fairly universal chord among users: deep down, most people who use moving image archives (particularly, historically oriented archives, as opposed to

Entitlement to this material has a cost in both time and money.

stockshot libraries) believe they are entitled to avail themselves of relics of their own history—if not without any encumbrances, at least without undue obstacles. And the more experience a person has in dealing with historical archives, the more this attitude is tempered with the understanding of the mitigating realities.

This sense of entitlement is an important psychological notion with which to begin. I myself have been known to share it, even while acknowledging such issues as copyright, intellectual property, the origination and ownership of materials, and the costs of maintaining a collection. In fact, I believe that this very attitude about availability without undue obstacle actually can be shared by archivists and their clients, and that such a consensus could provide the foundation for a good working relationship between them. This would make history more accessible to the masses, as well as help archivists maintain their collections. For whether a collection is commercial or public, funds for preservation and for purchases (such as additional collections, screening equipment, vault space and other necessities), are directly related to the visibility and usability of the archive. An archive that serves no one gets no funding.

The question, of course, is: what constitutes a reasonable encumbrance, based on ownership either of the intellectual property represented by an article in the collection, or of the physical article itself—or of both? And what can archives do to make users feel those encumbrances are reasonable?

What follows is a "wish list," presented to archives on behalf of the end user, or at least by a certain end user, in the hope of answering these questions:

Have some idea of what policies and pricing strategies your colleagues invoke. Every experienced user can tell a story about some private collector, or in some cases a larger archive, whose pricing or licensing policies were so out of line with the rest of the industry that the user couldn't possibly navigate these incongruous waters.

Archives are entitled to set prices for the material they hold—and rarity can certainly be a factor. However, to ask $25,000 for a thirty-second clip, for example, or to ask a client producer to assign rights to the finished product back to the archive is unreasonable, and will result in no use at all.

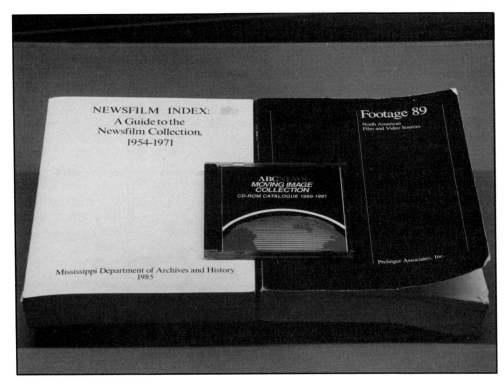

The Mississippi Department of Archives and History published an index to its newsfilm collection, ABC News issued a CD-ROM, and *Footage 89* provides a directory of archives and their holdings.

179

The Wolfson Center is in the process of computerizing its card-catalog subject file for easier access.

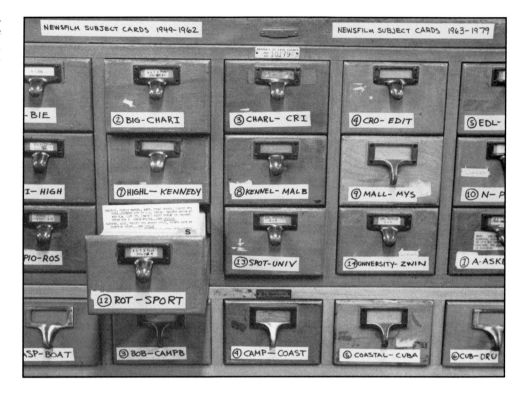

Make information about you holdings, prices, and policies accessible. Simply, the greater the accessibility to information, the more likely you are to make sales. Some archives freely distribute rate sheets, policy statements, printed and illustrated catalogs, or CD-ROMs of their holdings. These aids make is easy for potential clients to budget for use of your material, search through your holdings in the comfort of their own offices, or even order material blind, without having to travel to your archive to do basic card and computer research. Interactive CD-ROM archival lists are a tremendous boon to researchers: I am able to sit at my desk and do a full-text retrieval search through all the holdings of ABC News, for example. Then, I can call in can numbers from San Francisco, and get material duplicated and shipped in a day or two, all without having to travel to New York. I can't tell you how many clients have opted to get material from ABC rather than other sources, just because of that instantaneous availability. Other archives make nothing public, not even their rate sheets, preferring to develop prices and policies on a case-by-case basis. This is less desirable, since filmmakers have a hard time knowing if they are in for a bad surprise when doing business under these circumstances. I'm not saying that you shouldn't negotiate on a case-by-case basis (this is often a saving grace for a client with limited funds or an unusual distribution scheme); I'm just suggesting that you publish a "list price" for each market, so potential users know the worst-case scenario. Then, you can negotiate with them based on individual needs, markets, and amount of material. Don't keep users totally in the dark at the outset.

Make rough viewing materials reasonably accessible. In addition to making information available, try to develop a policy of offering access to nonmaster viewing materials, without undue restrictions, time delays, or up-front costs. Since many film and television producers cannot easily travel to your archive to screen materials, you might want to consider developing a strategy for making materials available on VHS cassettes for quick screening (including an on-screen burn-in or other impediment to piracy, of course). In exchange for this service many archives charge a research fee for their staff to pull the material, as well as a small dubbing fee. These can be structured per item, per hour, or per cassette. In general, the more you can practice "outreach" to your clients, the more clients you'll get.

Let the price reflect the rights you are selling. If you sell public domain material, you

180

have a right to charge a usage fee, since you are supplying the actual materials, even if you don't own the underlying copyright on the intellectual property. But your usage fee should be just that: a fee that represents use of the materials. It should not be as high as a fee for material whose copyright you own. This issue often causes confusion among users, and perhaps a change in nomenclature would help alleviate the confusion. Consider using the terms "license fee" or "rights fee" to represent materials for which you own the copyright, and "use fee" or "materials fee" to represent a lower price for physical materials (either public domain, or owned by another entity from which the user will have to obtain clearance or pay rights) for which you do not own copyright. Having to pay for material twice—to the owner of copyright, and the holder of material—puts a financial strain on the would-be user. I recommend setting materials fees that reflect the user's need to purchase some rights elsewhere.

Don't "just say no" if rights are complicated. Relative to the question of material for which one archive does not have all rights, some archives don't want to be bothered with licensing a piece of film or tape if the copyright is unclear, or if underlying rights (such as appearance releases, music, or union payments for talent) are at issue. As a result, they refuse to make the material—which is sometimes precious or monumentally important—available at all. Instead of closing the door completely, see if you can explain the situation to the users. Tell them they will be required to sign a contract indemnifying your archive. Require users to be responsible for getting all appropriate clearances and presenting copies for your review. The point is: give users the option to do the legwork to your satisfaction, rather than completely cutting off the possibility of their using the footage.

Structure your pricing by markets, with options to more markets later on. Most archives charge per-second or per-foot fees (with overall minimum guarantees) based on the proposed distribution of the finished product into which their material is being incorporated. It would be extremely helpful for you to confer with your colleagues in order to standardize how markets are broken down and what they are called. For example, most archives have one fee for home video, others differentiate between home video on laserdisc and one VHS cassette, and still others split out U.S. home and world home video. Most license home video in perpetuity; some put a time frame on the license. Producers and distributors encounter untold frustration keeping track of what

Film and video makers are not the only ones to license materials. Here, a producer for National Public Radio selects audio from television news programs for a radio broadcast.

markets they have purchased from each archive, and for how long! Also, consider building in option periods during which clients can return and purchase additional markets for a discount. Most archives encourage this bundled purchasing by routinely offering fifty-percent discounts on additional markets purchased at the same time footage use is reported. This usually occurs at the picture-lock or postproduction stage, by which time producers have not even finished their films, let alone determined the potential for home-video distribution, overseas broadcast, theatrical sales, or any other markets. If you build in a standard six-month or one-year window from the date of first broadcast, during which they can buy additional markets at a sizeable discount, you'll see more clients come back to do just that and all you'll have to do is issue the new contract or addendum and collect the additional fee.

Sell rights in perpetuity in order to avoid additional paperwork and follow-up. Most users would rather pay a little more for rights in perpetuity that have to keep track of material from several different archives, each of which has its own licensing term. I've worked with labyrinth spreadsheets and timelines for the purpose of alerting producers as to when they had to contact each archive to extend the license for each market. To help users avoid this nightmare, base your rate sheet on perpetuity. Then, for users who have finite, short-term uses (such as a film to be shown at a single conference, or a one-time-ever broadcast), negotiate a lower rate, if the amount of material involved is significant enough to warrant it.

Reserve per-cut minimums for small orders. Many archives have a standing policy of invoking per-cut minimums, that is, when filmmakers use shots cut shorter than the minimum, they must pay as if they have used the minimum. This policy was originally established to protect against users who, for instance, would turn the archives upside down to have a hundred original reels duplicated, then create a fifty-second montage of a hundred half-second shots—and pay for only fifty second usage! For such labor-intensive projects, the minimum makes sense, and archives would take a heavy loss if they didn't invoke it. However, outside of the worlds of television commercials and MTV, most clients don't tend to cut this way, so rather than having a standing per-cut minimum, a fairer policy would be a per-cut minimum for orders totaling less than, say three minutes, or for whatever market limits make sense, such as a standing per-cut minimum only for TV commercials and certain other special uses. (Note, however, that most users expect and accept the idea of an overall project minimum averaging between fifteen and thirty seconds of use.)

Begin to develop rates and categories for new media and distribution schemes. Multimedia CD-ROM and interactive laserdiscs are just two of the emerging technologies, and Direct Broadcast Satellite (DBS) and fiber-optic digital downloading are on the horizon. It's too early to collect the necessary data about sales potential and market size in order to develop the best practices for these new media, but it's advisable to stay in touch with the markets, your clients, and other archivists to see how things are shaping up—and to begin determining a breakdown of categories and fair rate for these uses, as well as devising consistent nomenclature.

The obvious message behind all these suggestions is: be sensitive to the needs of your clients in general, and on a case-by-case basis, and help them understand what your needs are as guardians of this precious material. Understand that you've been appointed to safeguard a part of our shared history and culture, and that, with such cooperation, the material can be both well-maintained and used to its maximum potential. Beginning with this century, we have had the unique opportunity to revisit decades gone by in sight and sound. This increased ability to see and study our own past may contribute to a future in which we learn from and repeat our best efforts, and avoid our worst mistakes. Preservation and accessibility comprise the delicate balance that must be maintained for this to happen, and it is the responsibility of us all.

12

Shopping In Film Archives: A Producer's View

James A. DeVinney

Documentary Writer/Producer

This chapter title aptly describes the perspective of filmmakers in finding footage for their productions, and as archives and filmmakers know, shopping doesn't always mean buying.

James A. DeVinney has been involved in documentaries since 1985, when he joined Blackside Inc. to work on the civil rights series *Eyes On The Prize.* One of his films for that series, "Bridge to Freedom," was nominated for an Academy Award in Documentary Features and also won an Emmy for Outstanding Individual Achievement in Writing. DeVinney won a second Emmy for writing the opening program of *Eyes on the Prize II,* "The Time Has Come." In 1992, DeVinney was part of a team of producers and writers at WGBH-TV in Boston who created the four-hour film *The Kennedys,* shown on *The American Experience,* for which he earned his third Emmy. He recently completed "Silicon Vision" for the *Discovering Women* series. DeVinney is currently producing and writing two documentaries for *People's Century,* a WGBH/BBC co-production recalling the history of the twentieth century, and he is also a lecturer in the College of Communication at Boston University, where he teaches writing.

Shopping in Film Archives: A Producer's View

There's a lot of talk in the world today, but there's very little communicating going on. I'm not talking about leaders of state or husbands and wives. No, I'm talking about film archivists and film producers. Conversation between these two combatants usually breaks down by the third sentence:

Filmmaker: "Hi. I need to find some film."

Archivist: "What do you need?"

Filmmaker: "Well, what do you have?"

The battle lines are drawn. The archivist, looking for specific information to fill the request, concludes that the film maker is vague, indecisive, a "flake." The filmmaker, "trying to keep his options open," doesn't want to be too restricted and concludes that the archivist just doesn't understand the creative process.

No doubt this same filmmaker, when he goes out to dinner, wants to know what everyone else in the restaurant is eating before placing his order because he just knows the guy next to him is going to be served something that looks better than what he's getting.

But this guy is the consumer. Without him, a lot of film reels are going to sit on the shelf until Judgement Day, i.e., until the grants necessary to sustain the collection are cancelled for lack of need. So if the filmmaker is the justification for maintaining the archive, maybe it would be a good idea to try to understand this "flake." What does he want anyway? I'm one of those "flakes" and I'd like to open my filmmaking soul to the archivists of the world in hopes that they may come to better understand others of my ilk.

My first experience with archive footage began in 1985 when I was hired to produce a couple of films for *Eyes on the Prize*, a PBS television series depicting events in the Civil Rights Movement of the fifties and sixties. The series was recognized for its journalistic integrity, but also because it demonstrated that history is composed of dramatic stories. It was, I believe, the drama of those films which contributed so much to their universal acclaim.

I then worked on the sequel series *Eyes on the Prize II* and most recently completed work on a film, *The Kennedys*, for the PBS series *The American Experience*. After researching so much archive film, I noticed that my use of such material fell into three main categories.

1. Exposition

This is basic to every film and storytelling technique and it takes various forms.

a. Scene Setting

In the fouth episode of *Eyes on the Prize*, I had to take the viewer from Birmingham, Alabama (large industrial city), to Albany, Georgia (rural Southern community). I needed to establish each of those locations to see what they looked like and give a sense of the people, how they lived, where they shopped, where they worked.

In Birmingham we settled on a distant view of the city from Red Top Mountain which showed high rise buildings towering over a grid of intersecting streets, then we cut to a downtown street with shoppers and workers crossing heavily-trafficked streets or ducking into one of the local department stores. We were careful to show the store names because they would later figure into the story.

In Albany, we showed people gathered outside a simple clapboard storefront shaded by large trees while a few cars and bicycles drove down unpaved streets. The light filtering through the trees gave a dreamy, almost romantic view of this community in contrast to the glaring light of the city.

All of these scenes were black and white, set in the early sixties with recognizable styles of clothing and automobiles. It only took a few shots in each location to quickly establish the mood and tone for each location without excessive narration. In each case the footage was found through local television archives. WSB-TV in Atlanta had the Albany material. The Birmingham scenes had been thrown away by a local television station but were rescued from the trash heap by a staff person who got the station to sign the rights over to him.

b. Introducing Characters

How to introduce a character is not as obvious as showing a new location. Just having a shot of the person may not say as much as the filmmaker wants to say. This is one of those times when a filmmaker may be vague in stating his request. He really doesn't know what he wants until he sees it.

In the opening program of *Eyes on the Prize II*, we had to introduce Malcolm X. Many films establish him in opening shots as angry, accusatory, denouncing white people. We wanted to offer a softer, milder more youthful Malcolm X at the start to make him more accessible for all audiences and then to show him change and grow so that his later anger would have a righteous foundation. We found just the right shot in a CBS documentary about Harlem. Malcolm X was not only approachable, he was smiling. There is precious little film of Malcolm X smiling.

Usually I prefer to introduce my character by having them speak, especially if they are saying something which establishes their character, their philosophy, their role in the film. In that film set in Albany, Georgia, I was able to introduce the leader of a local movement by allowing him to speak for himself. As the man addressed a church congregation, he said: "You want to know what the Negro in Albany is going to do? He's going to do whatever is necessary to insure his freedom." His statement was followed by applause which gave us the opportunity to add narration which further identified the speaker's importance to the story.

But the right silent shot can be just as effective. In *The American Experience: The Kennedys*, an editor found a beautiful shot with a surprise in it. Over a shot of Joseph P. Kennedy stepping out of an airplane, the narrator talked about Kennedy's ambition for presidency. When his hopes were thwarted, he decided that his son Joseph Jr. would one day become president. At the mention of the son, Joseph P. Kennedy, Jr. stood up, popping into the shot quite unexpectedly. The scene vividly portrayed the smiling, ambitious figures of the father and his handsome son at start of the film setting events in motion.

c. Theme Setting

Sometimes I like to establish program themes even as I'm introducing my character. In that *Eyes* show number four, I introduced Dr. Martin Luther King, Jr. as he was speaking to churchgoers in Albany, Georgia. In his speech, Dr. King spoke of the need for "nonviolence" as a means of securing people's rights. "Nonviolence" was a major theme of that program—it wouldn't work in Albany, it would in Birmingham—and I had a wonderful opportunity to introduce a major character in my film and a major theme at the same time.

2. Illustration

An important part of the documentary is illustrating the events which make a moment worthy of historical notice. Illustration, for the most part, is the easiest part of the film-buying process with less chance of misunderstanding between filmmaker and archivist. "Do you have film of such-and-such event on such-and-such date at such-and-such location. Good! Send me fifty feet." Archivists and film makers have an absolute love fest at a time like this.

In the final program of *Eyes II*, we interviewed Frank Legree in Miami who described his experience as the first black man to buy a house in the all-white neighborhood of Liberty City back in the mid-1950s. The neighbors picketed his house for days and someone once threw rocks through his front windows. Returning to my office in Boston, I called Steve Davidson at the Louis Wolfson II Media History Center in Miami to see if he had any footage of Frank Legree. I was happy when the answer was yes but I became ecstatic when the film arrived. There was Mr. Legree standing in front of his house, broken windows behind him, and marching in front of him were lines of white women carrying signs which read "We want this nigger moved." That shot never fails to get a gasp from the audience whenever I show it and combined with the interview, it conveys more power than I could ever have gotten from a line of narration.

Not every interview or line of narration can be illustrated so perfectly and there may still be awkward moments between archivist and filmmaker. The difficulty comes when the filmmaker wants a piece of footage so much he can taste it, but it eludes him. An ugly question rears its head: "Did anybody cover it?"

Archivists don't worry about that question. They have what they have and they're there to protect it. They're not there to worry about what they don't have. The filmmaker always worries about what he doesn't have and he knows there are three possible scenarios that address his question—"Did anybody cover it"—and he frets about which scenario applies to each problem shot.

1) Quite often, events are staged in such a way to attract news crews and reporters and there's a lot of coverage.

2) Sometimes the significance of an event is not appreciated until after the fact so no film crews were present to document it.

3) Other times, an event of casual interest to a news crew becomes a major story and the crew scores a real scoop since no one else covered it. In this last case, the coverage exists, but I can't find it if I don't know about it or don't know who covered it. I can drive everyone around crazy wondering if a shot is a 1), a 2), or a 3).

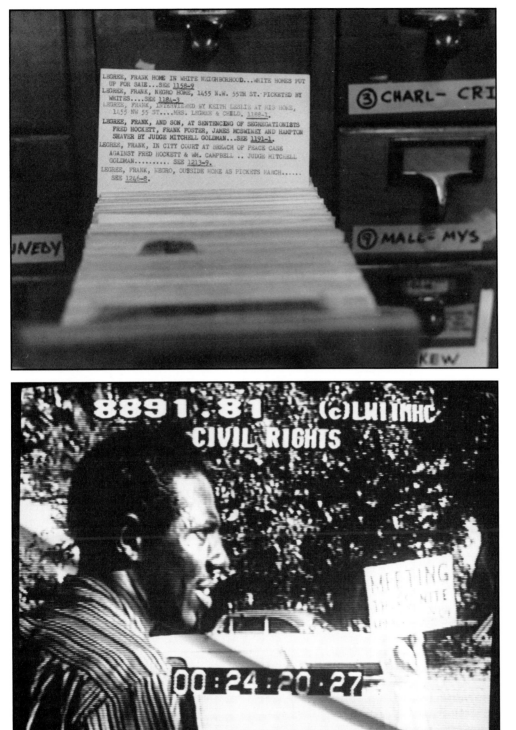

I built a whole show around Stokely Carmichael's Black Power speech in Greenwood, Mississippi. And then I couldn't find the speech on film. I read about it in books, I had newspaper accounts of it, I interviewed people who were there about their reactions to it, but none of the archives I researched had the speech. I knew everything there was to know about that moment, I even had photographs of him making the speech, but I didn't have the speech. Finally an entry in Dan Einstein's book, *Special Edition: A Guide to Network Television Documentary Series and Special News Reports, 1955-1979*, made reference to a CBS documentary about Black Power and the date of the broadcast occurred a week after Carmichael's speech. That documentary, we soon discovered, contained a thirty second fragment of the speech—enough to make my film.

In the making of *The Kennedys*, I had similar difficulty finding a Robert Kennedy speech in Indianapolis, Indiana, following the assassination of Dr. Martin Luther King, Jr. One of the network archives had coverage, but the angle was weak and the sound was poor. We finally found a better angle with excellent sound at WISH-TV in Indianapolis. In the film, I used both versions, cutting to the WISH version as quickly as I could.

3. Dramatic Scenes

It is not unusual for me to buy more than one version of a story. The film quality is only one consideration. Often a scene is long enough to go beyond mere illustration. It becomes a dramatic moment in itself. Robert Kennedy's speech in Indianapolis is an example. Not only was Kennedy talking to a racially mixed crowd about Dr. King's death, he was unknowingly foreshadowing his own death two months later. At a time like this, I may need to buy a story or two to set the scene (exposition) and to visualize a line of narration or an interviewee's sound bit (illustration). But there's more to it than that. I am now opening the film to allow the characters to speak, to take the viewer inside the scene to experience what happened on this particular occasion.

Every film needs a number of dramatic moments. They can be small but poignant: If John Kennedy had lived and been re-elected, he would have been inaugurated for his second term in January of 1965. But he died and Lyndon Johnson was elected and sworn in on that date instead. The purchase of a single story gave me a dramatic moment in *The Kennedys* because one shot showed Robert and Edward Kennedy standing in the cold listening to LBJ take the oath of office. You can see their pain in facial expressions. Were they remembering their brother's inauguration four years earlier? Were they thinking of what might have been? The shot carried enough ambivalence to allow each viewer his own interpretation.

Other dramatic scenes are bigger and I will sometimes buy ten to fifteen stories, allowing my editor to cut the scene like a feature film: John Kennedy's funeral, the beating of civil rights marchers by the Alabama State Troopers near the Pettus Bridge in Selma, the assassination of Robert Kennedy.

I am not merely seeking volume when I buy a lot of stories for a scene, I am trying to get the work of several cameramen who were in different locations to get a variety of shots and angles. I also come to know and buy the work of specific cameramen who have demonstrated a good eye and consistent technical quality.

Overall, I am very stingy when I buy film for exposition and illustration, often starting with a single story unless a researcher or a film archivist tells me there's some good material in a second story and I shouldn't miss it. I'll take a chance on those one or two stories and only go back for more if I or my editor feel the coverage is thin. Since my early assemblies may include a number of events which may drop out of the film, I don't want to buy a lot of film I'll never use. Once my film starts to come down to size, then I may go back to strengthen those scenes which are still in the cut or buy scenes that I may have skipped over during my earlier buys. For dramatic scenes, I'm much greedier, but these are scenes so important to the film that I know they won't drop out.

Other Considerations

Once the sought-for film is found, the hardest part must be done, right? Wrong! The filmmaker can still aggravate the hell out of the archivist. Why? What could he possibly want now? Only great shots and perfect audio with world-wide rights, in perpetuity, for very little money.

188

At work on *The Kennedys*: Elizabeth Deane, Chuck Scott (seated) and Jim DeVinney at WGBH.

The rate an archive should charge for their material is dependent on so many things that no one standard can realistically be set. Quite frankly, I wait for the archive to tell me what its rates are and then I argue. Even if I like the rate, I'll probably argue. It's my job.

What am I willing to pay? Naturally I expect to pay all reasonable costs for research and duplication. But what about rights fees? WGBH in Boston has a rate card that ranges from five dollars per second to forty-five dollars per second. The rates are dependent on how the material is going to be used: for audiovisual or for broadcast, local or international, one-time use or in perpetuity? And the choice that is near and dear to me: non-profit or commercial? I am not willing to pay the same rate for a piece of film as Oliver Stone would pay for use in his theatrical film *JFK*.

There are considerations which might make a piece of film more expensive and I am willing to consider those factors. For instance, a film may have additional costs because there are union fees associated—AFTRA or the Writers Guild might have to be paid if one of their members had a role in the original material. This may effect how I use the material. If I can't use a reporter because of a union restriction, I may still be interested in the "B" roll that doesn't show his face or use his voice.

The fee I eventually pay is based on how much material I actually use. I may order fifteen minutes of material from an archive and only use ten seconds in my film. I expect to pay for ten seconds. Occasionally an archive will require a minimum order because the fee for ten seconds may not make bothering with me worthwhile. (WGBH charges a minimum fee of thirty seconds.) I, of course, must decide whether the material is good enough to agree to the minimum. If the answer is no then I won't use that material at all.

I may want a discount if I'm going to use a lot of material from an archive—say 15 minutes or more. If I'm making a one-hour film, this is not a realistic expectation. But if I'm doing a series of films, this could be an important issue. I have had discounts as high as fifty percent.

A rate card is very helpful. I like knowing what costs I'm getting into now and later. In my first contact, I often just buy rights for PBS and audiovisual use. (PBS rights include four releases in three years with each release containing the right to broadcast the program repeatedly within a seven-day period.) Then I go back to the archive when I have my deal for home video or foreign broadcast rights to buy the additional rights (step-up fees). Ideally, these fees should be part of the original agreement or it can become difficult later. Just because I paid for the film the first time doesn't mean I'm going to pay an exorbitant step-up fee if the deal turns sour. I can re-open a film (and I have) to take shots out if I can't get the rights I need. Similarly, the archivist may not be able to track the film and negotiate in all of its sales, so the clearer the first contract is about these fees, the more likely the payments will be made. Often the producer isn't even around when subsequent sales are made. Producers rarely make any money from these sales and therefore are not likely to keep up with who's being paid and who isn't. But a contract on file can guide the distributor back to the basic commitment.

Other services are also worthy of consideration: How fast can an order be turned around? What is the policy on screening copies? How high a quality can the archive provide: 3/4-inch U-matic, Beta SP? Is the material an original or a copy? Who owns the rights and what rights are available?

I often like some technical information about film: black and white or color, positive or negative, optical or mag stripe. I am always concerned about film with a negative, optical sound track. It never transfers well to video—the sound is often muffled or distorted. In these cases, I like to order a positive print made of the film before the transfer to video is made. Most archivists don't understand this, but they shouldn't feel bad—many filmmakers don't understand this either. If the film is badly scratched, I may ask that it be run through a liquid gate during the transfer process.

Sound is very important to me. I believe that the picture satisfies us intellectually, but the sound satisfies us emotionally. That's why a musical score is such a major part of every feature film. But natural sound is also important. Silent scenes never play with as much power as scenes with sound. I will sometimes buy a story that has good audio even thought the shots may be a little weak.

Another big question that's always on my mind—does the archive have cut stories or does it have outtakes? Sometimes I only want cut stories, especially if I'm looking for a

"Can I get that film tomorrow...what about the video?"

famous sound bite or a famous shot, the icons of our culture. But a cut story limits me to the choices made by the original reporter and the original editor. I may have a different perspective and need slightly different material. I often look into outtakes to find the set up for the story, the principal character entering the room or the question which prompted the response. Or I may need cutaways of the reporter, or audience shots.

I have based most of my comments on film stories in archives. My hopes are the same if I am looking for video, but sad to say, my expectations are reduced. Video research is never as satisfying. For example, rarely do outtakes get saved on video. Too often the sound is mixed with a reporters voice making it unusable. And most of the time, stories which get saved are "clip reels," reels made up of shots deemed most worthy of saving for future use. These shots are usually too short, the sound bites are clipped or they have character-generated text recorded over them, and they are often several generations old so the quality is poor.

These are a few remarks from a consumer of film and video archives. I'm really a very friendly guy but must admit that now and then I am inclined toward obsession trying to make the best, most historically accurate film possible. Occasionally in that quest I am afraid I am too impatient or too abrupt on the phone. I know this because it is not uncommon for me to hear the gnashing of teeth in the archives of America as I conclude my order with: "Oh, and can you get that to me by tomorrow? Here's my Federal Express number."

13

Television Archives and the Academic

Dr. Brian Rose

Fordham University

While filmmakers tend to be the most visible users of newsfilm/video collections, there is a growing interest by the academic, educational and scholarly community. This chapter provides a perspective on the educational use of film and television news material and how archivists and academics can cooperate for mutual benefit.

Dr. Brian Rose is a Professor in the Department of Communication and Media Studies at Fordham University. He is the author of *Television and the Performing Arts, Televising the Performing Arts,* and the editor of *TV Genres* (all published by Greenwood Press).

Television Archives and the Academic

Until recently, scholars of local television have faced a unique problem—the material they hope to study has often vanished into the airwaves. Television stations are notoriously cavalier about what they produce, rarely saving their original productions, especially when videotapes can be easily recycled for new programming. Even stations that try to maintain a strong local news archive tend to discard outtakes and raw footage, holding on to just the edited broadcast story.

There are a number of reasons why television outlets are so reckless with their past— after all, many produce four or more hours a day of newscasts, with a couple of hours more a week of local talk shows and features. Keeping a record of all this demands a sizeable commitment for videotape and proper storage facilities, which is often difficult for stations to justify. Add to this the fact that many broadcasters fail to see the historical value of what they air. Television is, for them, a twenty-four hours a day electronic delivery system, and they have little time, interest, or money in preserving what they transmit for the benefit of future generations.

Fortunately, researchers interested in local television news and programming are not forced to rely on the whims of station owners in their search for this most ephemeral of material. Local television newsfilm/video archives have begun to appear throughout the country, bent on collecting as much of their community's moving image past as they can. The task has not been easy, but thanks to the concerted efforts of dedicated and persistent archivists, more and more television stations are willing to donate whatever programming material they have, happy to take advantage of the kind of controlled storage conditions they are unwilling to provide on their own. To supplement their collections, some archives, following Vanderbilt University's lead regarding network news, now tape local newscasts to provide an ongoing record of television coverage. Though they may receive cut-story tapes years down the line from the television stations, local archives off-air record because those tapes will provide researchers access to the entire broadcast in context.

For scholars and for the public at large, the commitment of television archives to acquire and preserve the local airwaves has been of enormous value. My own experiences at the Louis Wolfson II Media Center in Miami may serve as an example. Founded by an initial donation by the former CBS-affiliate WTVJ consisting of millions of feet of news footage stretching back to 1949, the Wolfson Center maintains a formidable collection of film and videotape covering the last five decades of South Florida television history. WTVJ (now an NBC owned and operated station) continues to donate materials, as do other local stations. I was drawn not only by the Center's extensive material on the early days of local broadcast journalism, but also by its willingness to use its holdings as part of an ongoing dialogue with the community it serves. Public seminars are regularly held to look at the way television covers historical and contemporary issues, with screenings from the Center's collection used as a point of reference and discussion. Academics and journalists are featured guests in these presentations to share their viewpoints and exchange ideas from a diverse and active audience.

The Wolfson Center provides an important model for how a television archive can function both as a source of historical preservation as a well as a vital community resource. These dual roles, however, are admittedly difficult at the present for many television archives. Because of the priority of preservation needs, material may not be easily available for scholarly or general use. There are additional problems in determining just what should be collected and how best to achieve these goals. Academics and archivists must also come to terms with what an archive means—is it just a cold storage locker to keep the past frozen? Should its use be restricted only for the most serious research? What should the archives' relationship be to the public and to future students of history and the media?

Resolving these issues is of great importance, but for broadcast historians, the more immediate concerns are centered on how to effectively utilize local television archives

Wolfson Center seminar participants Gregory Lukow (American Film Institute), Barry Sherman (Peabody Awards), Jim Gaffey (CBS News), Ernest Dick (Canadian Broadcasting Corporation), Dan Den Bleyker (Mississippi Department of Archives and History), Brian Rose (Fordham University), and Ron Simon (Museum of Television and Radio).

in their own work. For scholars used to dealing primarily with printed records, the ability to study television news and feature reports first-hand is often like uncovering buried treasure. The sheer power of the visual image and the nuances of voice and facial expression open entirely new areas for analysis. So too does the careful scrutiny of editing techniques and other aspects of television news production.

It is also useful to compare story coverage between network and local television news. Major local or regional events that assume national importance are usually reported in very different ways by stations with a direct community connection. Stories are invariably examined in greater detail with intriguing shifts in focus and attention. Several television archives make things easier for the researcher by having copies of both the national and local newscasts for stories concerning their region. Otherwise, researchers and scholars must seek out these material from a variety of archives.

Similarly, the growing number of local television archives around the country can provide scholars with the rare opportunity to trace the evolution and coverage of major historical events from city to city. The struggle for civil rights, for example, was reported differently in every broadcast market; by studying local television newsfilm from the 1960s in say, Jackson, Mississippi, and Miami, Florida, researchers can gain a fascinating perspective on the varying ways race relations were covered and discussed in two key states. What can also be gained is a feeling for the distinctive textures and atmospheres of specific cities at specific times—qualities which can rarely be found in newspaper accounts but come across with tremendous immediacy on film or videotape.

The great advantages of local television archives are offset, at least initially, by some problems of adjustment for scholars and students used to conventional document research. The enormous quantity of material housed at many television archives makes it difficult for institutions to properly note and index every bit of information in a news report or documentary. Dozens of people may appear in a single local television story as well as different themes and issues—how to make a thorough and available record of all of this is a topic of continuing concern in the archival community, where resources are often stretched to the limit. As a result, researchers may have to rely a bit more on serendipity. Tracing a story on local government responses to the Watts riots in Los Angeles may mean looking at every southern California newscast for months in order to find the appropriate information. But such a broad scan can also lead to previously unconsidered aspects of the story, such as a small feature on community activists buried inside a much larger report (which itself may not have been indexed). A smaller problem confronting television historians involves the issue of citations. Unlike print, video and film contain no page numbers. Most researchers are content to simply note the date of broadcast, though in an hour-long program, this may lack a certain degree of precision. Fortunately, some archives store their material with the television time codes "burned" (superimposed) on the tape, making it possible to note details to the twentieth of a second.

For academics constrained by tight travel budgets but linked to the world by their computers, the information highway promises to be a valuable tool for television archival research. Many archives are planning to put their catalogs online, making it

Wolfson Center off-air recordings are utilized frequently by researchers.

Dr. Paul George (Miami-Dade Community College, right) and students from his history class at a Wolfson Center seminar, with guest lecturer Dan Den Bleyker (Mississippi Department of Archives and History).

easier to see what's currently available and who has what. The real excitement in archival circles, however, concerns the ability to put their actual holdings of film and video on the Internet. Obviously, this would involve a hefty commitment of staffing, money, and new technological interfaces. Still, the potential for an easily-available electronic archive of our television past is nothing less than exhilarating. Whether this comes to pass and in what shape depends a great deal on how academics and archivists help to plan their mutually-beneficial future now.

Outreach

Karan Sheldon
Northeast Historic Film

While the **Field of Dreams** *approach to outreach – if you have it, they will come – may be appropriate for some institutions, there are other ways to promote access. Moving image archives can plan and maintain a variety of programs and activities based on their collections – such as screenings, seminars, and exhibitions – even with small staff and limited budgets. This chapter provides some examples.*

Karan Sheldon is co-founder of Northeast Historic Film, an independent, nonprofit moving image archive established in 1986 and located in Bucksport, Maine. Northeast Historic Film's mission is to collect and preserve northern New England's moving images. Sheldon was formerly at WGBH-TV, Boston, where she worked in The Caption Center and on the documentary series *Vietnam: A Television History*.

Outreach

What is Outreach?

Having built your collections and established procedures for maintaining them, your institution might wish to plan and pursue a program of outreach in order to inform people about your organization, collections and programs.

Outreach can be any activity directed toward enhancing understanding and use of your collections such as public programs and academic uses. Types of outreach include screenings; public exhibitions of audiovisual materials along with other interpretive objects; distribution on film, videotape or disc by loan or sale; publications (print or electronic) relating to your collections; papers given at professional meetings; workshops and seminars for teachers and archival professionals; facilities tours; and publicity relating to these activities. This chapter addresses some specific instances of outreach which have been used by newsfilm archives and various kinds of moving image collections.

"Trends in Broadcasting and Documentary Filmmaking" with Barry Sherman (Peabody Awards) and Jim DeVinney (WGBH) at the Wolfson Media Center. (Note technician recording seminar for inclusion in the Wolfson Center's collection).

200

Outreach, in some senses, helps to justify the resources committed to your collections. Outreach activities give people an opportunity to know about your work, and offer them the opportunity to use and benefit from your materials. Successful programs may help your staff, your board, and other members of your organization's "family" to better understand your collections and their significance.

Increased use of the collections by different groups of people—an enlarged audience— can be useful in increasing the dollars available to the collections. In times of competition for budget dollars successful outreach may be essential to your operation's future.

The Wolfson Center offers tours of its facility on a regular basis.

Outreach activities may be, as they are for a great number of nonprofit archives, an integral part of your organization's mission. Some corporate and state archives may differ in not having a specifically defined public outreach mission, but there may be, as described below, other senses in which outreach may be beneficial.

Why Do Outreach?

Some reasons for doing outreach activities:

- To foster enhanced public perception of the value of the materials in which you've invested so much time and effort to preserve.

- To increase understanding of twentieth-century history and culture.

- To serve and build constituencies (public, academic, professional).

- To further involve people, including your board and volunteers, in your organization.

- To get feedback on your preservation work and the meaning of your collections.

- To gain recognition for your unit or institution.

- To help build collections and gain financial support.

The more people see and use your collections, the more they will understand the importance of helping your preservation efforts. As Alan Lewis noted at the Madison Conference on Local Television News Archives:

> One goal of outreach might be to sensitize your superiors in your parent corporation or your governmental structure to the value of your collection, to your needs, and the impact that your collection can have to the community and to the parent organization. Remember, your first goal is to survive, and one way to survive is to tell your story and tell it where it counts.

Why Not do Outreach?

Given the list of reasons for undertaking an energetic outreach program, is there any logic behind a "go slow" position? Yes, there is. Before hurtling into an ambitious outreach program there are at least three questions to consider:

- Will adding public programs strain your institutional resources? Do not promote activities that exceed your ability to deliver them. Planning and step-by-step action are essential.

- Do the activities fit comfortably within the definition of your organization? It is unwise to contort your organization's mission with ill-conceived or irrelevant public activities.

- Do you have adequate policies and procedures for the protection of your collections? Never undertake public programs that put your archival materials at risk.

Three Parts to Outreach

Should your collections and archival procedures be in order for an outreach effort to go forward, you might conceive of your task as having three parts:

- STRATEGIC: Marketing to promote your materials and services.

- PHYSICAL: Preparing and distributing materials for public use such as videotapes, printed guides and brochures.

- INTELLECTUAL: Preparation of "software" such as staff training, speech writing, and groundwork for offering consulting services.

This chapter does not cover general marketing issues that should be kept in mind when developing your strategies and outlook. There are many resources—marketing professionals, workshops and books—to be tapped. Among the latter, *Guerilla Marketing Attack*, by Jay Conrad Levinson, contains a bibliography on promotion including brochure preparation, etc. Levinson hammers home, in the commercial context, important marketing concepts: commitment, quality and patience. Whatever your outreach program, it will take time to see results.

Strategic Marketing: Research, Planning and Evaluation

When contemplating a new or expanded outreach program, carefully examine your archive's mission statement or statement of purpose. Your institution may have well-defined constituencies. You might wish to evaluate your relationship with these constituencies. Do your clients (e.g., students, film researchers, television news personnel) know what services you provide? Have you surveyed them recently to find out what you might offer in the way of enhanced (or streamlined) services?

A well thought-out, professional survey of your users is an excellent initial form of outreach. Don't survey idly, though. You're asking your partners, those people who use and support you, to take time and thought to share their opinions. Employ professional assistance in preparing the survey and evaluating the results. Make the results known to survey participants as a matter of courtesy and outreach. Report up and down the line in your own organization and then set objectives that reflect the results.

Suppose your institution, with a mission to serve the general public, wishes to expand in a particular area. For example, you're a historical society and want to reach a broader selection of secondary schools. You envision a series of teacher workshops. Wait! Make sure you have a plan first. It may sound obvious, but involve members of the group you want to serve in your planning.

Be certain—particularly when you're adding expenses and staff responsibilities—that you have the support of your board and staff. Your unit will have to ensure a commitment to adequate personnel and financial resources to undertake the plan. Commit at the outset to evaluating your efforts as they progress. Continued growth and funding should be dependent on objective evaluation.

Large institutions have departments devoted to outreach functions. For example, The Museum of Television and Radio in New York has an Exhibitions and Seminars Department. The department's decisions are made in association with other museum departments. Seminar ideas come from a variety of sources including the Curatorial Department and the president's office. Speakers are proposed at a policy committee meeting, and once the decision is made to hold a seminar, the Exhibitions and Seminars department undertakes the implementation, coordinating with other relevant offices.

Staffing

Seminars are often planned in conjunction with exhibits and screening series. For example, an exhibit on *Star Trek* will have an associated seminar with members of the series creative team. Other seminars are organized around the oeuvre of an individual, e.g., Caroll O'Connor talking about his career, or a thematically-based exhibit cosponsored with the Writers Guild of America.

Once a program decision is made, the coordinator of Exhibitions and Seminars is in charge of contacting and coordinating with the guest, scheduling the evening, selling tickets, and coordinating with the PR and publications departments to advertise the event. The department also coordinates with Visitors Services staff for personnel for the event; with the Technical Department, which works the theaters and tapes the seminars; and with the Membership Department, which provides information to members.

Ideally there are at least six months of planning time between the time a name comes up and the actual event. Calendars are computerized and the department is networked within the museum so it is easy to keep other people and departments informed.

In many of the archival outreach projects mentioned in this chapter, the objectives are met without benefit of staff exclusively assigned to outreach duties. DeSoto Brown at the Bishop Museum Archives, Honolulu, administered and carried out an extensive tour of "Hawaii on Film" without additional staff assistance—along with his other archival duties. Dan Den Bleyker at the Mississippi Department of Archives and History, Jackson, is the sole staff member curating and performing outreach activities for his collections.

Funding Sources

The budgeting process is an important part of the strategy. Perhaps outreach activities are already part of your institutional budget. More likely, the expenses of new activities will have to be met by revenues created through the outreach. Some examples include admission charges for events; subscription fees or dues; sales or rental fees for use of products; or grants, gifts and bequests earmarked for outreach.

Admissions

Weigh whether charging admission for an event or series is worthwhile. If your out-of-pocket costs can be covered in some other way, free admission may bring you a larger audience. However, it has been said that if there is no charge for an event, the public might suspect that it's not worth paying for. Know your market. It may be worthwhile testing free admission against a range of ticket prices, although it is hard to control the many variables such as weather and competing events in order to determine objectively what draws best.

Project Funding/Grants

It is often easier to obtain funding for outreach than for other archival activities because funders like to know that their support is reaching people directly. Options for funding include broadcast companies; for example, the British Broadcasting Corporation under-wrote a retrospective on director Dennis Potter for The Museum of Television and Radio. Broadcast industry associations, advertising agencies and regional advertising associations may be able to underwrite programs.

Corporate Special Event

An event with food can be surprisingly effective at attracting people. Consider having a reception funded by a corporate sponsor. Cindy Martin of the Southwest Collection at Texas Tech University, Lubbock, participated in the Texas Historical Association's annual meeting. Martin asked Exxon to pay for a reception and screening from the Southwest Collection's materials. Don't forget in-kind support in the form of goods and services from corporations.

Government and private funds may be available for outreach activities.

204

Humanities Council Funding

When the outreach involves history and other humanities content, consider involving historians and scholars in relevant disciplines in planning, interpretation and speaking, with funding from your state's humanities council. For a directory of state councils, contact the National Endowment for the Humanities division of state programs. Likewise, arts commissions may have grants for outreach projects.

In-Kind Services

Many businesses may not be able to afford cash donations but could consider donating goods and services for your outreach effort—that they may be able to write off. One example of this is broadcast PSA time; others are videotape stock, editing facilities, or space.

A production house in Portland, Maine, donated their studio to Northeast Historic Film for a premiere of a TV news compilation videotape which would be used for outreach. Invitations were sent to the production and broadcast community, to the archive's members, and clients of the production house. The production company provided the facilities and refreshments and in return received favorable publicity, and some new contacts—potential future clients—who otherwise might not have walked through the door.

Consider outreach as "three dimensional." You can develop:

- Deeper commitment from a small number of people.

- Wider exposure among a larger number of people.

- Strive for both...over time.

Scale, Scope and Schedule

The outreach formats you select will determine the shape of the audience you cultivate. A regular series requires regular commitment. If you're in a small community it may not be possible to have a large audience every week. But perhaps you want an ongoing relationship with "regulars" committed to your cause. If so, an informal lunchtime screening series, for example, may fill the bill.

If, on the other hand, your organization wants to cultivate a major corporate donor, fill a press book with stories about your organization, and reach the society set, a splashy once-a-year gala may be just the thing. The Louis Wolfson II Media History Center, Miami, initiated an annual media awards ceremony that draws attention to the organization and features material that will end up in the collection. The event is also self supporting.

An established organization with staff available to undertake curatorial and administrative tasks related to outreach may have a regular weekly screening and lecture series as well as annual special events and other programs, while a small or start-up organization might want to test the waters with just one or two events a year—and do these cooperatively. From a modest beginning of several screening and seminars a year in 1987 (the year of its founding) the Wolfson Center now presents public access programs, screenings, seminars, exhibitions and workshops year round.

Cooperative Events

"Piggy backing" is a key concept for beginning outreach activities. Many nonprofit organizations regularly seek programs, and you may be able to easily provide them or components for them.

Cindy Martin of the Southwest Collection, Texas Tech, recalls quickly assembling a program for the Popular Culture Association. "We showed the *New Home Show* at the State Fair of Texas in the 1950s, which put us to sleep after we'd seen it 50 times, and it was just what they wanted to see....they loved it."

Note that the material Texas Tech provided seemed old hat to those familiar with it, but it was new to this audience. Can you look at your collections in new ways? Note also that the Popular Culture Association was responsible for the program, facilities, the publicity and arranging for a room full of interested people.

The Louis Wolfson II Media History Center has done seminars in conjunction with the Miami Film Festival, the Fort Lauderdale Film Festival and the Jewish Film Festival. Cooperative events broaden everyone's audience and allow for sharing of resources and public relations activities.

Finally, make use of your calendar. If Popular Culture called you once before, keep a calendar so that you know when their program committee will be planning the next event. If you want to continue a relationship, call them.

Firm understanding of the calendar is essential to outreach. It's not easy to declare a "first annual" event when you're just testing the water. Evaluate the event and if it worked the first year—or if with a little tweaking it could be a real hit next time—start right away preparing for the second annual. Initiating and sustaining an annual event requires institutional commitment and resources. It has to be planned and put on the calendar so everyone involved knows what the preparation time-line will be.

If you're coordinating with other groups, many annual meetings have programs planned six months or more in advance. Special events can take more than a year to pull off. It's never too early to block out the coming year's events and to try to determine what

Documentary filmmakers Robert Stone (*Radio Bikini* and *Satellite Sky*) and Ron Mann (*Comic Book Confidential* and *Twist*) at a Wolfson Center seminar on documentary filmmaking and archival images.

else is happening on the dates you select. If your target audience is busy, you're out of luck. Conversely, if the American Historical Association calls you but you're already booked for the Odd Fellows, don't hold up either party's decision-making process.

Many groups may never have considered your resources. Cindy Martin describes how the Southwest Collection launched a campaign to make their resources better known in the region, "to let people know what materials we had, bring them in, and help them use the materials we had. We hit every lady's club, organization and Rotary for miles around."

Use your primary resource, moving images and sound, for spreading the word.

Physical Materials

A Sample Reel is one of the first things a small institution should consider producing for launching outreach. It needn't be highly produced, or have added narration. In fact a staff person providing the introduction live is often better for several reasons. If you can afford the staff time or can field appropriate volunteers or board members it is a good idea to conceive of your outreach as a person-to-person activity, introducing your organization and its mission through its people. Also, live mediation allows you to customize the presentation for each audience, answer questions, and gauge the audience's reaction.

Changing technologies are providing new media for the dissemination of sample reels. The Image Bank produced a sample disc from its stock footage collections on CD—with digital moving images—using a collection of Quick Time clips recorded at 10 frames per second. Three hundred clips are available in categories such as "People and Industry." The CD is distributed with a user's guide and other printed material—and a certificate for a free pint of Ben & Jerry's ice cream.

For awareness and fundraising the Oregon Historical Society produced *Picking up the Pieces*, a videotape on conservation efforts at the society, including books, printing, and film. The eight-minute tape was produced at low cost on the institution's 3/4-inch U-matic editing system and has been used one-on-one with prospective donors, and with staff. A follow-up mailing brought donations. For widespread cultural outreach at low cost, the society spent $1,500 on a videotape to accompany a touring show on the North Pacific. *Cross Currents* (22 minutes) uses archival footage from the Oregon Historical Society's collections on logging, fishing and shipping. The show went on tour to Russia and China. Because of the foreign distribution, the soundtrack is a music track only; story identifications are provided with a printed key in various languages.

PSAs and Regular Spots on TV may be possible if you have broadcast connections. The Louis Wolfson II Media History Center runs a regular cable program called *Rewind* on Miami's public access station. Twice daily, the archive presents a re-broadcast of newscasts and documentaries from the 1950s and 1960s. The programs are preceded by a brief introduction by individuals who were involved in creating the programs, including broadcasters and historians, and are followed by a short overview of the Center and its activities.

The Southwest Collection, Lubbock, Texas, cooperates with a local PBS affiliate on re-broadcast of *Texas in Review*, a 16mm television series originally sponsored by Humble Oil between 1952 and 1958. Staff of the Southwest Collection tapes two-minute studio introductions putting the material into historical context. Each episode concludes with a slide at the end of the broadcast with information on the Southwest Collection and availability of the series to researchers at the archive. Six to eight weeks of introductions are taped at one time. The series is in its second season of prime-time broadcast. About two-hundred episodes of the series exist and as the two seasons already broadcast on KTXT have been popular the re-broadcasts are likely to continue.

Visual Materials for Schools. The National Jewish Archive of Broadcasting, New York, is piloting the Jewish Heritage Video Collection, an educational package including half a dozen videotapes with printed curricular material for schools, community centers and libraries.

The Canadian Broadcasting Corporation is making some past CBC programs available for educational use in schools. Many of them include teachers' guides to facilitate their use in the classroom. The CBC is also marketing *News in Review*, a series of videotapes on current news issues, specially compiled and edited from stories in CBC News Libraries. They are sold through a subscription to schools and come with a media guide to help students and teachers make the best use of them.

Pending funding, the Mississippi Department of Archives and History hopes to put together some twenty-minute videocassettes from television newsfilm from Jackson, Mississippi, to send out with teaching guides to schools on various subjects: Mississippi history, modern history, science, weather. In Mississippi, as in many states, the teaching of state history is mandatory in the secondary school curriculum. Dan Den Bleyker envisioned the videocassettes as an answer to the need for classroom materials. Northeast Historic Film compiled three videotapes from the Bangor Historical Society/WABI collection of Bangor, Maine, newsfilm selecting three topics—the Cold War, TV Commercials, and Transportation—based on a questionnaire circulated at the annual statewide secondary-school social studies conference. The forty-five minute videotapes, with paper descriptions of each story included, were made available to teachers free of charge with the stipulation that the teachers would report on their classroom use.

In New Hampshire, *The Granite State Sampler*, "a visual archive chronicling New Hampshire state history and government consisting of 12,000 still images and 17 motion sequences" was assembled on CAV laserdisc. The project was carried out by the Southeastern Regional Education Service Center (SERESC) and included placing videodisc players in schools.

Still images from the Wolfson Center's newsfilm collection on display in Miami.

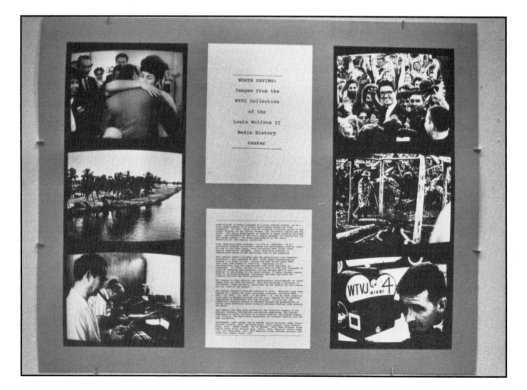

208

Visual Materials for Colleges and Universities. In Los Angeles, the UCLA Film and Television Archive developed research and curricular-related programs through its Archive Research and Study Center (ARSC). ARSC provides a wide range of services to both faculty and students at UCLA and to non-university researchers from the educational and creative communities.

In addition to organizing educational conferences and workshops, ARSC provides access to the Archive's holdings through an average of 9,200 individual viewing appointments every year. Since the opening of ARSC in 1989, the News and Public Affairs Collection (NAPA), in particular, has received increased attention from more and more researchers. ARSC provides on-site, non-circulating research viewing to the over 125,000 news programs in the NAPA collection.

Information about the Archive's collections is communicated through the university's MARC-based online information system, ORION. Access to the Archive database on ORION is available at any of the several hundred terminals on campus and via modem from off-campus.

The Archive also disseminates information about its programmatic activity through a quarterly newsletter, a bi-monthly calendar of all public programs, flyers and brochures—all of which are sent to a regularly updated and targeted mailing list.

The Public Affairs Video Archives at Purdue University, West Lafayette, Indiana, records, preserves and distributes both channels of the Cable Satellite Public Affairs Network (C-SPAN) exclusively for education and research. Institutional members receive catalogs of holdings and tapes on thirty-day loan for classroom use. The archive is licensed to provide tapes to educators only for educational and research purposes. C-SPAN retains all copyrights to its video programs.

Visual Materials for the Museum—Going Public. Videotapes and videodiscs are used in many cultural and historical museum settings integral to the exhibit, or as introductory or accompanying pieces.

The Japanese American National Museum in Los Angeles uses archival film in a three-screen laserdisc video presentation, *Through Our Own Eyes*, part of the museum's inaugural "Issei Pioneer" exhibit. There are three different nine-minute shows featuring scenes from various holdings from the museum's photographic and moving image archive. The video presentation was funded in part by a grant from the City of Los Angeles Cultural Affairs Department.

At the National Archives of Canada, *Beyond the Printed Word* is a public exhibition of newsreel and broadcast reporting in Canada at the National Museum of Science and Technology in Ottawa. It exhibits newsreels, radio and TV from public and privately-owned sources in English and French, covering 1897 to 1987. Interactive videodiscs contain 246 separate extracts, with an eight-hour total duration. The exhibition has become semi-permanent because of its popularity with visitors.

A media collection within a larger organization is often called on to contribute to the programs of other divisions. For example, Michele Kribs reports that she prepared a videotape on farming for an exhibit at the Oregon Historical Society. The completed videotape is also used by the society's education department as a rental.

The Mississippi Department of Archives and History uses a fourteen-minute segment of film transferred to tape in the state historical museum's civil rights exhibit.

Reference Materials. Many institutions serve researchers by making videotapes or reference prints available for on-site screening. Commonly, this is done in a designated

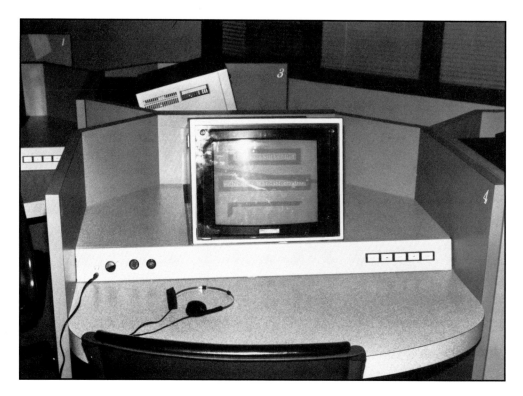

area, for example, the Museum of Broadcast Communications, Chicago, offers the A.C. Nielsen, Jr. Research Center where visitors may view tapes in twenty-six "study suites." This service is offered free of charge when the museum is open to members and non-members.

The Louis Wolfson II Media Center circulates videotapes from its collection to the public (with a copyright notice "burned" in) through the Miami-Dade Public Library System. The public can also make an appointment to view materials from the collection, in addition to the Center's regular screening programs.

Home Video. Smaller and specialized audiences can constitute significant potential markets for home-video compilations from archival collections. For the fortieth anniversary of television in Canada, the French television network of the Canadian Broadcasting Corporation assembled a series of eight TV programs from the 1950s and offered a four-cassette package at $59.95. This set of "Classiques des annees cinquante" has sold 30,000 copies in four months and a set from the 1960s is being planned.

ABC News and MPI Home Video market the Home Video Library of VHS videocassettes in categories of "Great TV News Stories," "ABC News Special Editions," "History of the 80s" and "Most Memorable Nightlines." Titles include eighty minutes of Jim and Tammy Faye Baker for $14.98, and *The Great Debates: John F. Kennedy vs. Richard M. Nixon* (sixty minutes) for $24.98.

Northeast Historic Film distributes *Maine's TV Time Machine*, a thirty-minute videotape compilation from a television collection, sold to the public, schools and libraries, and loaned through a membership "reference by mail" service. This half-hour compilation is accompanied by a printed guide, inserted in the cassette box, identifying all the stories by title and date.

Intellectual Preparation: Define Your Audience

There are many possible audiences for outreach. The preparation and level of content-things as fundamental as the language chosen, the length of program and type of collateral materials such as programs and guides—will follow from the audience you seek. Here are some types of audiences, with examples of institutions reaching them.

210

Archival footage from the Wolfson Center was part of this exhibition on Cuba at the Historical Museum of Southern Florida.

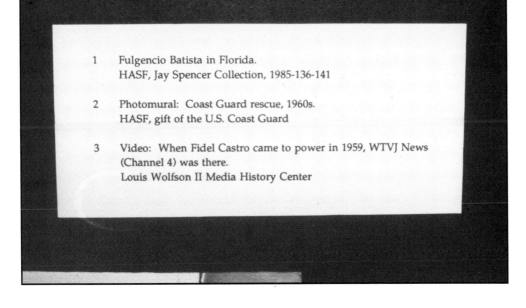

Credit provided for the footage.

1   Fulgencio Batista in Florida.
    HASF, Jay Spencer Collection, 1985-136-141

2   Photomural: Coast Guard rescue, 1960s.
    HASF, gift of the U.S. Coast Guard

3   Video: When Fidel Castro came to power in 1959, WTVJ News
    (Channel 4) was there.
    Louis Wolfson II Media History Center

Institutional Staff

Start within your organization. Keep your staff, board, volunteers and users up to date with your collections. Colleagues' enhanced knowledge may help in fostering commitment to your priorities and collections. Don't forget you have collections that may be very interesting, and fun, too.   A lunchtime videotape series can enlighten and enliven the work place. The Louis Wolfson II Media History Center, Miami, runs a twice weekly screening and seminar series, "Video Rewind." The archive is located at the Miami-Dade Public Library and events are attended by library personnel as well as the public. In recent years "Video Rewind" programs have also been presented at other venues throughout South Florida.

Your Members

If you are a membership organization, you have a responsibility to your members to maintain the quality of your programs. The Museum of Television and Radio, New York, publishes a members' newsletter announcing screenings and seminars. Members have access to services including the Members Reference Line. Members at the Contributing level and above have exclusive access to this telephone service, available weekdays, and may call with questions regarding radio and television.

This exhibition is on permanent display at the Wolfson Center.

To increase public awareness, the Wolfson Center set up this exhibit to display the variety of film and video formats which comprise its collections.

Other Groups' Members

Maxine Fleckner Ducy of the Wisconsin Center for Film and Theater Research, Madison, assembled a program for the annual meeting of the Office of Local History, part of the State Historical Society of Wisconsin. With Ducy's well-received program of television commercials, the director of the office met his objective of showing members that history encompasses recent culture and events.

Interested Public

The Museum of Broadcast Communications, Chicago, has exhibits and regular tours, and group tours can be arranged in advance. The National Jewish Archive of Broadcasting at The Jewish Museum, New York, presented "Ethnicity in Prime Time" as part of *Bridges and Boundaries: African Americans and American Jews* in collaboration with the National Association for the Advancement of Colored People. As one element in a larger schedule of events, it was included in the museum's printed program.

Special Interest Groups

There are innumerable groups—from civic to trade organizations—seeking programs, many of which pay honoraria or will make a donation to your organization. For example, Associated General Contractors of Maine requested a program from Northeast Historic Film—and were shown a bridge-building compilation which otherwise might not have found an audience.

Archivists and Related Professionals

Many archives send staff to conferences, including those of the Association of Moving Image Archivists, the Society of American Archivists, and others, to participate in committees and panels advocating the preservation of moving image materials.

Seminar and screening program at the Wolfson Center with students from Miami-Dade Community College watching *Eyes On the Prize II*.

Public Policy Makers

The Hawaii Moving Image Project, Honolulu, hosts screenings for the state legislature at the state house, complete with popcorn. These screenings inform lawmakers and their staffs about the project and the materials.

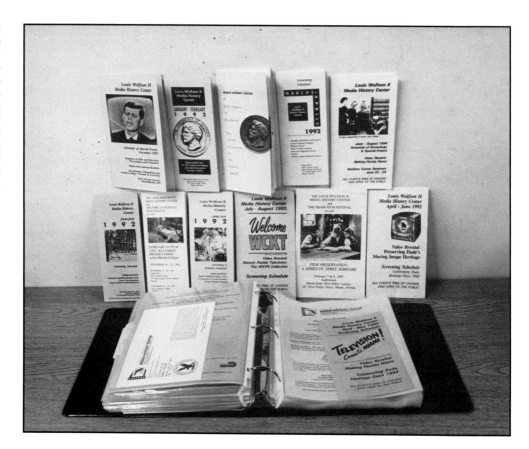

The Wolfson Center's "Video Rewind" programs are presented twice weekly at the Miami-Dade Public Library and increasingly at other venues throughout Miami and South Florida.

Researchers

This is a very broad category of people including academic researchers; trained film researchers for documentary, commercial, feature and other productions; news and other broadcast personnel; as well as students and independent researchers.

Dan Den Bleyker of the Mississippi Department of Archives and History reports that:

> In order to have the materials used, we must have the materials used. Before Blackside Incorporated used portions of our film in *Eyes on the Prize* we'd get an occasional local request for material. After Blackside used the collection, we literally were swamped with requests. The sudden increase in interest in the material, I think, can be traced to three factors. First, and I believe this to be the most important, the department was given credit by Blackside at the end of each episode in which our footage was used. This brought in many requests. Second, in January of 1986, the department sent copies of its newly produced newsfilm index to all public television stations in the United States as well as major archives throughout the United States. Third is word-of-mouth recommendation.

Collections that are as well-indexed and promoted as Mississippi's is may find that they receive a lot of interest from professional researchers. Den Bleyker goes on to point out that other research segments may be harder to reach. "There is one group that has not used the collection at all. This is the academics, particularly historians."

To help educate the academic world about using moving image media, John O'Connor at the New Jersey Institute of Technology produced a compilation for the American Historical Association, Washington, DC, for teachers on teaching history with film and television. It is available on CAV videodisc ($150) and on videotape ($50) with printed materials.

Cindy Martin of the Southwest Collection, Texas Tech, points out that her collection is particularly useful to academic researchers because it has manuscript material to back up the moving images, along with still photos and a full-time field representative who does oral history interviews. Even if your institution does not have these extensive resources, it would be useful to be able to refer researchers to existing complementary

Helene Whitson (San Francisco State University), Barry Sherman (Peabody Awards), and Steve Davidson (Wolfson Center) have addressed several professional groups on the work of archives.

resources. In turn, referrals may flow back to you from repositories of print and other materials.

Most states and provinces and some cities have film and television offices charged with assisting production in their regions. At the very least, they should know that your repository exists because they often serve as the first line of information for inquires about moving images. Perhaps a more fully-developed relationship may be worth exploring.

Children and their Parents

The Museum of Radio and Television, New York, has extensive public events targeted for various audiences including weekend screenings for children. Depending on your community, it is likely that there is a large body of potential users who will find out about you first through child-friendly activities. The Wolfson Media Center has shown children's television programs from the 1950s to the present, including material from its own collections as well as travelling exhibition programs from the Peabody Awards collection.

Funders

Special events for high-level members and prospective donors can be a form of outreach. The Museum of Television and Radio, New York, hosts breakfasts for its members.

If you provide preservation consultancy services, funders in your area (foundations, corporations) may also be potential clients for their own moving image collections. Any professional relationship your organization pursues and maintains builds your credibility, demonstrates your utility, and benefits the relationship over the long run.

Preparing Presentations

Consider whether you wish to prepare custom presentations for each event (this can be too time-consuming), or if you would rather offer a menu of standard presentations. Northeast Historic Film prepared a Presentations Sheet that describes half-a-dozen programs. It specifies the title, content and length of each program, the equipment required, and the fee.

The Maine State Library Association holds an annual conference each year in association with the state's Educational Media Association. The program committee had the presentation sheet on hand and selected a half-hour program for the lunch-time session. Two-hundred prime potential users of NHF's services (librarians and media specialists) were on hand for an introduction to the archive and a video presentation. The librarians participated in a question-and-answer session, and received handouts so that later they could contact NHF for programs and services on behalf of their individual institutions.

Some Selected Formats

Programs may be formed around outside speakers appearing in person: news personalities, communications scholars and other analysts.

Seminar Series

The Museum of Television and Radio organizes seminars, such as a series called "Sports Journalism: It's More than Just the Game." Four events moderated by Dick Schaap cost $50, or $38 for non-members. Another seminar featured "Peter Arnett: Reporting on the World" in a ninety-minute lecture and Q & A session.

The Louis Wolfson II Media History Center runs approximately ten seminar series a year with screenings and discussion. They give the public an opportunity to meet with producers and archivists around the country. The seminars are recorded on 3/4-inch U-matic and Hi8 videotape and are then available for subsequent programs or for individuals to view. Monthly screening schedules and postcards are mailed to over 3,000 individuals, broadcasters, education and cultural organizations. These are also distributed throughout the library system and all of South Florida. Press releases are also sent to mainstream, community and specialized publications as well as television and radio stations.

Symposia

A symposium, "Documents that Move and Speak: Managing Moving Images and Recorded Sound in Archives," sponsored by the National Archives of Canada, was held in association with the exhibition, *Beyond the Printed Word*. The symposium was intended for users (e.g., researchers, broadcasters) as well as administrators of moving image archives.

The Center for Southern Culture at the University of Mississippi sponsored a three-day symposium for journalists who have covered the civil rights movement. Dan Den Bleyker reports that while the symposium did not coordinate with his Department, it would have been an appropriate venue for exhibiting videotape from his collection.

University departments and divisions (history, communications, etc.) should be informed of your holdings and interest in collaborating on symposium materials. The state humanities councils can also help serve as clearinghouses as they often know of projects being planned and can help put your resources together with users.

Open Houses

Use a sample tape as an exhibit. The University of Baltimore library used a VCR and monitor to show a sample tape from the Abell Television Collections during open houses and public events at the library. This resulted in a number of research requests.

Roadshows

Plan a tour to present materials; create a theme and title. The Bishop Museum Archives, Honolulu, received funds from the State Foundation on Culture and the Arts to copy selected Hawaiian-content films from the collection onto new film stock and then videotape, and then to do presentations of such films in the community. The project director, DeSoto Brown, produced two fifty-minute videotapes, "Hawaii on Film: Selections from the Bishop Museum's Visual Collections" and "Hawaii on Film II: A Tour of the Hawaiian Islands." Each program was a compilation of clips preceded by a title, with music added. Brown reports, "Production was done at our local PBS affiliate, which gave us good rates, and was intentionally simple. Production costs were covered by the grant."

In the first year the videotape presentations were shown on Oahu, including at the Bishop Museum. In the second year they were shown on five different islands to senior citizens groups, on community college campuses and in public libraries. Scheduled public screenings at the Bishop Museum were advertised in the newspaper and through a membership mailing; a nominal $2 or $3 admission was charged. On the other islands admission was free of charge. Altogether there were thirty-five showings in the two years, reaching about 5,000 people. The well-regarded program, which was funded for preservation and outreach, has continued to receive state funding in subsequent years.

If your host or co-hosting organization is providing the hardware, make sure you talk about the details with them so you don't end up bringing 3/4-inch U-matic video while they only provide VHS equipment. There are a number of choices for hardware: the host institution's, your own (if possible, designate gear for traveling, as it will have a hard life), or from a rental house. Make sure the rental equipment providers understand what you want and when you want it, and be sure you know what it costs and who's expected to pay for it. Be sure you understand who is responsible in case of loss or damage. Check your institution's insurance coverage.

Most often you may be using video. For local events, Northeast Historic Film has used a twenty-seven-inch monitor which works well for about fifty people, as long as it is elevated. NHF puts the monitor on top of a five-and-a-half-foot high portable stand. Good quality sound is essential; use auxiliary speakers. If you employ video projection, you must be certain that the room can be made very dark. Obtain the best possible equipment and the services of a competent technician. Whatever system you use, test it before the audience arrives, and always check to make sure your tapes are cued.

A checklist of everything you'll need for the event is key; and make the list as foolproof as possible. If you're bringing equipment off site, it should list everything, including extension cords, three-prong adapters, and every other piece of hardware including the tape or film you plan to show, and the number of pieces of literature you will bring to hand out. The list will help make sure you get your stuff home, too.

There are many forms of communications available as outreach tools. Here are some being developed and others that are entirely commonplace.

National Bibliographic Utilities such as OCLC (Online Computer Library Center) and RLIN (Research Library Information Network) are beginning to consider accepting moving image entries. NAMID, the National Moving Image Database of the National Center for Film and Video Preservation at The American Film Institute, will assist archives in making their catalog records available to these bibliographic services. Data entered by archives into NAMID are protected. Archives participating in NAMID may have the option of requesting that their records be uploaded to RLIN at no charge. The catalog records, which are mapped to MARC, are in a communications format that can be exchanged among libraries and researchers. The Wisconsin Center for Film and Theater Research, through NAMID, is undertaking the application procedure for the records of an entertainment film collection. NAMID is an OCLC processing center and can do a tape upload to OCLC, another library information service with a very wide distribution. The Pacific Film Archives may be participating in OCLC with records uploaded from their collections by NAMID.

Finding Aids and Indexes are fundamental access tools. The Mississippi Department of Archives and History, Jackson, distributes a printed reference work, *Newsfilm Index: A Guide to the Newsfilm Collection, 1954-1971* (1985), and a second edition is being worked on. The State Historical Society of Wisconsin prepared *Madison Wisconsin Television Newsfilm, 1968-1972: A Descriptive Guide and Index to the Holdings of the State Historical Society of Wisconsin* (1991).

The Vanderbilt University Television News Archive in Nashville, Tennessee, produces printed abstracts with item-by-item descriptions of the videotapes in its collections. Indexes of the abstracts are provided to paying subscribers—mostly research libraries. The Vanderbilt University Television News Archive also distributes a brochure outlining its services, a ten-page sample copy, and a catalog of broadcast specials in the collections. John Lynch, director of the archive, notes that the most effective outreach method is to be cited by a scholar in footnotes and in the text of a scholarly paper.

ABC News published a CD-ROM that provides access to text describing news stories which may be used for production and research. It's important to update research aids and get them into the hands of users. The *ABC News Moving Image Collection CD-ROM Catalogue/1960-1989* contains information on 400,000 pieces of film and videotape from 1960 to 1989. The disc costs $49.95, and requires a CD-ROM optical reader and an IBM compatible personal computer.

Researchers and producers find descriptive aids essential in preparation of broadcast programs. Footage from this collection has been used in many documentaries. As broadcast credits appear on completed programs, word spreads about the source.

Directory Listings let people know you exist. *Footage 89* and *Footage 91* (hard copy and CD-ROM) published by Prelinger Associates, Inc., New York, describe North American film and video sources. Telephone directories are inexpensive and a basic resource. "Motion Picture Film Libraries" is a standard category in the Yellow Pages; your institution can be listed at no charge.

An Institutional Newsletter can let people know about activities, particularly if it contains a calendar of events. **Brochures** (less time sensitive) and **press releases** (about events, acquisitions and ongoing programs) can be very effective if they are succinct, well thought out and properly placed. Besides preparing releases for mass media, consider the publications of special interest groups. You can communicate with independent media artists, other archivists, librarians, etc., through their own journals. A good **article** can be very helpful; don't forget **reprints** of that article for the funders and your board and supporters.

In this age of databases and mail merge, it's a good idea to maintain and use your own **mailing list** of community contacts and individuals who have come to an event, subscribed to a service or communicated with your organization. It is an excellent idea to record the names and addresses of people who contact your institution, not just for your mailing list. If people are registering to come to an event, use that information— code the mailing list so that you know their interests. For a new audience, put out a "Sign Our Mailing List" sheet. Funders like to know that you can quantify and describe your user base. You may wish to get in touch with a user again in reference to their query, and someone who has called you is likely to be interested in your outreach activities at a later date.

Ethics of Outreach

As you plan new activities and new uses for your collections it is important to respect the structures established for use of your collections. You must abide by existing agreements, especially those restricting use, with the donors of your holdings. If changes in agreements are necessary, all negotiations must be final and paperwork signed before undertaking new uses.

Respect the communities involved. The legal rights holders may not be the only concerned parties. It is essential that you respect the cultural copyright of communities depicted in your moving images. Involve relevant community members in planning outreach. For example, if a new screening series is contemplated, consider forming or adding to a community advisory board to help plan the form of the screenings— including deciding where they are held—and assist in defining and reaching the intended audience. Don't forget that the location of your events is a big part of audience access: outreach may mean simply taking an established program to a new venue.

You may find that an increased investment of time by the advisory board results in benefits all around: your institution is proceeding responsibly, offenses are avoided, and a wider public is actively involved in promoting use of the materials.

As an institution safeguarding collections you have a responsibility to understand what the materials in your care mean to the community. The original creators are a part of this picture. For example, even if the newsfilm was donated long ago and no contact has ever been made with the original news gatherers, it is worth attempting to find them for purposes of annotation. There are many reasons to do background research on the people involved in creating the material. News gatherers may be your strongest supporters. After all, you're making sure that their life work is preserved. It is likely they will be interested in helping to record the highlights of their careers and untangle the technical history of your collections; this is an important curatorial project. (Annotating a contemporary collection with the help of super-busy news personnel is an equivalent challenge.) Camera people and reporters can be excellent adjuncts to your public programs, as live presenters, helping provide interpretive text for exhibitions, or as interviews in produced programs.

Finally, two cautionary notes:

First, understand the legal liabilities. Copyright infringement, libel and liability for personal injury are unpleasant topics. You need professional legal advice before, not after, you hear from someone else's lawyer. Suppose someone trips on your extension cords, or has a heart attack during a speech. It happens.

Second, consider all the ramifications of making your collection available in new ways. You may have the necessary legal rights to disseminate your materials in new and creative forms, but your community may not be ready for some kinds of outreach. A broad-based community advisory board can help. Adequate groundwork—and this takes imagination and a lot of listening—is essential.

A

Bibliography

(The following bibliography covers a broad range of topics related to television news archiving, including preservation practices, format stability and degradation, storage, new technologies, copyright and legal matters, automation, etc. It also provides a number of citations on specific television news archives and their collections. For sources on the subject of cataloging and descriptive standards, please see the detailed annotated bibliography at the conclusion of Chapter 9, "Cataloging," on pages 159-163 of the manual.)

Adams, William, and Fay Schreibman, eds. *Television Network News: Issues in Content Research*. Washington, DC: George Washington University, 1978. Includes a bibliography on the CBS lawsuit against Vanderbilt University (pp. 109-110).

Adelstein, P. Z., J. M. Reilly, D. W. Nishimura, and C. J. Erbland. "Stability of Cellulose Ester Base Photographic Film: Part I – Laboratory Testing Procedures." *SMPTE Journal* 101, n. 5 (May 1992): 336-346. Based on research by the Image Permanence Institute, Rochester Institute of Technology.

Adelstein, P. Z., J. M. Reilly, D. W. Nishimura, and C. J. Erbland. "Stability of Cellulose Ester Base Photographic Film: Part II – Practical Storage Considerations." *SMPTE Journal* 101, n. 5 (May 1992): 347-353.

Adelstein, P. Z., J. M. Reilly, D. W. Nishimura, and C. J. Erbland. "Stability of Cellulose Ester Base Photographic Film: Part III – Measurement of Film Degradation." *SMPTE Journal* 104, n. 5 (May 1995): 281-291.

Adelstein, P. Z., J. M. Reilly, D. W. Nishimura, and C. J. Erbland. "Stability of Cellulose Ester Base Photographic Film: Part V – Recent Findings." *SMPTE Journal* 104, n. 7 (July 1995): 439-447. Summarizes conclusions of recent research by the Image Permanence Institute on the fundamental nature of cellulose ester base film, including the expected long life – greater than 1,000 years – of polyester base films, the beneficial effects of lower storage humidities, and possible differences in manufacture based on a survey of films held in various film archives and manufactured in the 1930s and 1940s.

American Film Institute. *National Conference on Improved Management of Local Television Newsfilm Archives*. Final Report to the National Historical Publications and Records Commission, NHPRC Grant #87-57. Los Angeles: American Film Institute, National Center for Film and Video Preservation, 1989. 34 pp. plus appendices.

American Library Association. *Guidelines for Off-Air Taping of Copyrighted Programs for Educational Use: Thirty Questions Librarians Ask.* Chicago: ALA, 1982.

American Society of Cinematographers. *American Cinematographer Video Manual.* Second edition. Hollywood, CA: The ASC Press, 199?. Over 300 pp. All aspects of the video craft are covered. Special attention is given to imaging – including explanations of CCDs, luminance, color, contrast, exposure, lighting, lenses and formats – with other chapters including information about VTRs, waveform monitors, time code, and audio for video.

American Television and Radio Archives Act, sec. 113, 90 Stat. 2601-2602 (1976), 2 U.S. Code, sec. 170 (1976). Part of General Revision of Copyright Law, Public Law 94-553, October 19, 1976.

AMIA Newsletter. The *Newsletter of the Association of Moving Image Archivists.* Published quarterly. Los Angeles: AMIA, 1988 – .

Ampex Corporation. *A Guide to Media and Formats.* Second edition. Redwood City, CA: Ampex, Magnetic Tape Division, 1989.

Annenberg Washington Program. *Roundtable on Television Preservation: Rapporteur Summary.* Results of a colloquium convened by the Annenberg Washington Program, Washington, DC, May 19, 1989. 14 pp.

Archiving the Audio-Visual Heritage: A Joint Technical Symposium. Proceedings and papers from the 1987 Joint Technical Symposium held in West Berlin, May 20-22, 1987, organized by FIAF, FIAT and IASA. Thirty papers covering developments in the preservation and conservation of film, video and sound. 169 pp.

Association of Cinema and Video Laboratories, compiler. *The Association of Cinema and Video Laboratories (ACVL) Handbook: Recommended Procedures for Motion Picture and Video Laboratory Services.* Fifth Edition. Los Angeles: ACVL, 1994. Includes sections on "Film Laboratory Services," "ACVL Recommended Film Practices," "Release Prints," "Sound," "Storage of Motion Picture Film," "Video Services," "Glossary of Video Terms and Definitions," "American National Standard Nomenclature for Motion-Picture Film Used in Studios and Processing Laboratories," indexes to SMPTE test materials and SMPTE-sponsored standards and recommended practices, and a list of ACVL-member labs.

Atwater, Tony. "Consonance in Local Television News." *Journal of Broadcasting & Electronic Media* 30, n. 4 (Fall 1986): 467-72. A study of several television markets to explore duplication and non-duplication in local news coverage of national news stories.

Bashin, Bryan Jay. "The Great History Throwaway: How TV Stations are Destroying a Precious Resource." Research report prepared for the Center for Science Reporting [science news syndicate], Sacramento, CA, May 15, 1985. 10 pp.

Bashin, Bryan Jay. "How TV Stations are Trashing History." *Columbia Journalism Review* (May/June 1985): 51-52, 54. On the fate of historic local television news collections.

Bertram, H. Neal. *Theory of Magnetic Recording.* Cambridge: Cambridge University Press, 1994. Comprehensive text on the magnetic recording process; author is affiliated with the Center for Magnetic Recording Research at the University of California at San Diego.

Bertram, H. Neal, and Edward F. Cuddihy. "Kinetics of the Humid Aging of Magnetic Recording Tape." *Institute of Electrical and Electronics Engineers (IEEE) Transactions on Magnetics* 18, n. 5 (September 1982): 993-999.

Bertram, H. Neal, and A. Eshel. *Recording Media Archival Attributes (Magnetic).* Report RR-80-01. Redwood City, CA: Ampex Corporation, 1979.

Bertram, H. Neal, Michael K. Stafford, and David R. Mills. "The Print-Through Phenomenon." *Journal of the Audio Engineering Society* 28, n. 10 (October 1980): 690-705.

Boston, George, ed. *Guide to the Basic Technical Equipment Required by Audio, Film and Television Archives.* Written by the members of the Coordinating Committee for the Technical Commissions of the International Organizations for Audio, Film and Television Archives. Sponsored by FIAF, FIAT, IASA, ICA, and UNESCO. 1991. 104 pp.

Boston, George, ed. *Archiving the Audio-Visual Heritage*. Proceedings of the 1990 Third Joint Technical Symposium held at the Canadian Museum of Civilization in Ottawa, May 3-5, 1990, organized by FIAF, FIAT and IASA. Published by UNESCO and the Technical Coordinating Committee, 1992. 192 pp.

Bowser, Eileen, and John Kuiper, eds. *A Handbook for Film Archives*. New York: Garland Publishing, 1991. New edition of book previously published in 1980. 194 pp.

Boyle, Deirdre. *Video Preservation: Securing the Future of the Past*. New York: Media Alliance, 1993. 67 pp.

Brown, D. W., R. E. Lowry, and L. E. Smith. *Predictions of Long-Term Stability of Polyester-Based Recording Media*. National Bureau of Standards Institute Report 86-374. Progress report to June 1986. Washington, DC: National Bureau of Standards, 1986.

Brown, Harold, for the FIAF Preservation Commission. *Basic Film Handling*. Brussels: FIAF, April 1985. First edition. 46 pp.

Browning, Robert X. "Public Affairs Video Archive: The C-SPAN Persian Gulf Collection." *Film & History*, 22, nos. 1 & 2 (February/May 1992 [published 1993]): 57-62. Description of the content and availability of the more than 1,700 hours of videotaped programming related to the 1991 Gulf War.

Buechele, Lisa F., editor. *Newsfilm Index: A Guide to the Newsfilm Collection, 1954-1971, Mississippi Department of Archives and History*. Jackson, MS: Mississippi Dept. of Archives and History, 1985. 542 pp. The first published guide to a local television news collection; produced with grant support from the National Historical Publications and Records Commission. Includes "Index to Newsfilm Records," "Film Record Descriptions," "Chronological Index," and "Newsfilm Project Software Details."

Burdick, Patricia, Crystal Hall Cole, and Karan Sheldon. *Collections Guide: Moving Image Collections of Northeast Historic Film*. Bucksport, ME: Northeast Historic Film, 1995. 58 pp. Holdings listed in the following categories: Amateur Works, Drama, Independent Works, Industrial Works, Other Nonfiction, and Television. Indexed by subject headings and collection names.

Caniglia, Julie. "Video Archive Preserves Minnesota Memories." *The Independent* (January/February 1993), pp. 9-10. On the Video Archive Project, a collaboration of Intermedia Arts Minnesota, the Minnesota Historical Society, and KCTA-TV.

Cavanagh, Tom, Robert Herman, and Marvin Nolan. "Rewriting RP 103: Handling and Care of Magnetic Tape for Television." Engineering Committee Tutorial. *SMPTE Journal* 103, no. 10 (October 1994): 677-81.

Child, Dr. Margaret S., compiler. *Directory of Information Sources on Scientific Research Related to the Preservation of Sound Recordings, Still and Moving Images and Magnetic Tape*. Washington, DC: The Commission on Preservation and Access, September 1993. 14 pp. Includes descriptive listings of 18 national "Laboratories and Organizations" and numerous "Sources of Information."

Creech, Kenneth C. *Electronic Media Law and Regulation*. Second edition. Newton, MA: Focal Press, 1995. 426 pp. An overview of the major legal and regulatory issues facing broadcasting, cable and developing media, including copyright and licensing, invasion of privacy, and developing technologies.

Cuddihy, Edward F. "Aging of Magnetic Recording." *IEEE Transactions on Magnetics* 16, n. 4 (July 1980): 558-568.

Cuddihy, Edward F. "Magnetic Recording Tape: A Discussion of the Material Properties of Tape Having Relevance to the Storage, Performance, and Systems Effects." *Communication*, 1982.

Davies, Dr. David H., Ampex Systems Corporation. *Stability of Metal Particle Tapes*. Technical Article MI-0002. St. Paul, MN: National Media Lab, September 1993. 18 pp. Examines four potential problem areas – oxidation, corrosion by atmospheric pollutants, binder hydrolysis, and wear resistance to multiple passes – and produces data that verifies tape stability both in use and as a data archive media.

Davison, P.S., et al. "Aging of Magnetic Tape: A Critical Bibliography and Comparison of Literature Sources." *The Computer Journal* 11, n. 3 (1968). Scientific Documentation Center, Dunfermline, Fife, Scotland.

Dick, Ernest J. "An Archival Acquisition Strategy for the Broadcast Records of the Canadian Broadcasting Corporation." *Historical Journal of Film, Radio and Television* 11, n. 3 (1991): 253-268.

Eastman Kodak Company. *The Book of Film Care (H-23)*. Rochester, NY: Eastman Kodak, 1992. 84 pp. Revised and updated edition of perennial reference book on film care and preservation.

Einstein, Daniel. *Special Edition: A Guide to Network Television Documentary Series and Special News Reports, 1955-1979*. Metuchen, NJ: Scarecrow Press, 1987. 1069 pp.

Einstein, Daniel. *Special Edition: A Guide to Network Television News Documentary Series and Special News Reports, 1980-1989*. Metuchen, NJ: Scarecrow Press, 1996. 928 pp.

Eliassen, Meredith, compiler, for the San Francisco Bay Area Television News Archives. *A Guide to Emmy Award-Winning Programs for Northern California, 1974-1986*. San Francisco: San Francisco State University, J. Paul Leonard Library, 1990.

Environment Protection Agency. *Building Air Quality: A Guide for Building Owners and Facility Managers*. Washington, DC: EPA/NIOSH, 1991. Stock number S/N 055-000-00390-4. Information on how to develop a building profile to assist in preventing indoor air quality problems, and to identify causes and solutions to problems when they occur. Sections cover air sampling, heating, ventilating, air conditioning systems, moisture problems, and technical assistance resources.

Evans, Linda J., and Maureen O'Brien Will. *MARC For Archival Visual Materials: A Compendium of Practice*. Chicago: Chicago Historical Society, 1988. Produced with a grant from the National Historical Publications and Records Commission.

Feist, Rick. "What the Manual Didn't Tell You: Film/Tape Image Conversion." *The Independent* 15, n. 1 (January/February 1992): 23-37.

Film Preservation 1993: A Study of the Current State of American Film Preservation. Washington, DC: U. S. Government Printing Office, 1993. Report of the Librarian of Congress, in consultation with the National Film Preservation Board of the Library of Congress. Volume 1: Report (63 pp.). Volume 2: Los Angeles, CA Hearing (119 pp.). Volume 3: Washington, DC Hearing (133 pp.). Volume 4: Submissions (389 pp.).

Finch, Elsie Freeman. *Advocating Archives: An Introduction to Public Relations for Archivists*. Chicago: Society of American Archivists and Scarecrow Press, 1994. 108 pp. Includes practical advice on how to launch a fund-raising campaign, work with media, market programs, and train and use volunteers. The book aims to make public relations skills an integral part of archival management.

FOCAL International. Journal of the Federation of Commercial Audio-visual Libraries. Includes news from commercial/stock footage archives in the United Kingdom, other European nations, and the United States.

Fortson, Judith. *Disaster Planning and Recovery: A How-To-Do-It Manual for Librarians and Archivists*. New York: Neal-Schuman Publishers, 1992. Chapters include fire, water, wind, recovery, developing a plan, and managing risk. Includes sample disaster plans and the addresses of suppliers, national organizations, treatment centers, and publications.

Gasaway, Laura N., and Sarah K. Wiant. *Libraries and Copyright: A Guide to Copyright Law in the 1990's*. Washington, DC: Special Libraries Association, 1994. Includes chapters on audiovisual and nonprint works, educational copying, and international copyright.

Goald, Robert S. *Behind the Scenes at the Local News*. Newton, MA: Focal Press, 1994. 224 pp.

Gordon, Ann D. *Using the Nation's Documentary Heritage: The Report of the Historical Documents Study*. Supported by the National Historical Publications and Records Commission in cooperation with the American Council of Learned Societies. Washington, DC: NHPRC, 1992. 112 pp.

Harrison, Helen P., ed. *Audiovisual Archive Literature: Select Bibliography*. General Information Program and UNISIST, United Nations Educational, Scientific and Culteral Organization. Paris: UNESCO, February 1992. 153 pp. Prepared by Helen P. Harrison of the International Association of Sound Archives. Composed of three parts: 1) bibliographic references arranged by subject with limited annotations; 2) an author index; and 3) a subject index. Includes sections on: "History and Development of Archives"; the management of "Film Archives" and "Broadcasting Archives"; film, newsfilm, nitrate, and video "Materials"; "Preservation" and "Restoration" of moving images; "Legal Issues"; "Standards"; "Automation" in film and video cataloging; "Appraisal" of moving images; "Selection" of film and television materials; "Storage," "Handling," "Disaster Preparedness," etc.

Hartwig, Robert L. *Basic TV Technology.* Second edition. Newton, MA: Focal Press, 1995. 176 pp. Contents include sections on video system components, video recording standards and formats, digital technology, composite vs. component video, video compression, film chain projectors and video cameras, and an update on HDTV.

Image Permanence Institute. *The IPI Storage Guide for Acetate Film.* Rochester, NY: Image Permanence Institute, Rochester Institute of Technology, 1993. Includes a booklet, graph, table, and slide wheel presenting the results of IPI's research into the "vinegar syndrome" and its implications for film life expectancy and storage.

Inglis, Andrew F. *Behind the Tube: A History of Broadcasting Technology and Business.* Boston: Focal Press, 1990. Includes several excellent chapters on history of video recording technologies

International Federation of Film Archives. *Technical Manual of the FIAF Preservation Commission.* Brussels: FIAF, [ongoing]. A user's manual on practical film and video preservation procedures. Ongoing loose-leaf publication.

International Federation of Television Archives. *Minutes and Working Papers of the FIAT/IFTA Vth Seminar, 9-13 September, 1991, Turin, Italy.* Two volumes. Torino, Italy: RAI Radiotelevisione Italiana, 1992. 671 pp. Includes collected papers from working sessions on: (1) "Documentation," (2) "Use of Television Archive Materials," and (3) "Training and Personnel."

International Federation of Television Archives. *Minutes and Working Papers of the FIAT/IFTA VIth Seminar, 5th-9th September, 1993, Sofia (Bulgaria).* Torino, Italy: RAI Radiotelevisione Italiana, March 1994. 518 pp. Over 40 papers and presentations, including: "Video Tape Recording Archival Requirements," "Digital Betacam for Archive," "Report on Two-inch Tape Survey," "HDTV Today," "Video Tape Life and Obsolete Formats," "Selection of Non-Broadcasted Television Material," "FIAT Guidelines for Selection and Preservation of TV Programme Material – A National Archive Perspective," "The Resurrection of Archive Material – Restoring Old Data in New Stores," "Selection of Historical and Nostalgic Television Programming in the USA," and "Life After Death – The Fate of a TV Archive When a Broadcaster Ceases Transmissions."

International Federation of Television Archives. *Minutes and Working Papers of the FIAT/IFTA Conference. Internationales Bildungs-Centrum Bogensee, 3-8 September 1994.* Baden-Baden, Germany: FIAT/B.A.T.T.E.R.T. Verlag Baden-Baden, 1995. 299 pp. Included are papers on digital mass storage systems, new equipment for copying film to video, the vinegar syndrome in broadcast archives, documentation and information retrieval, the training of documentalists, audience reactions to vintage television programs, and a ten-year assessment of the use of videotape for off-air recording at the NFTVA, London.

International Federation of Television Archives. *Guide to Audiovisual Archives.* Seventh edition. Helsinki, Finland: YLE TV Archives for FIAT, February 1996. 177 pp. New edition of directory first published in 1990. Contains information on 110 FIAT members and 253 other organizations arranged by continent. Appendices include lists of broadcasters and other organizations worldwide, a bibliography, an alphabetical list of acronyms of international television and archival organizations, and a minimum data list of definitions of cataloging terms as recommended by the FIAT Documentation Commission.

Johnson, Dr. Steve. *Appraising AV Media: A Guide for Attorneys, Trust Officers, Insurance Professionals and Archivists in Appraising Films, Video, Photographs, Records and Other Audiovisual Assets.* Washington, DC: Copyright Information Services/AECT, 1993. 128 pp. Includes case studies, and chapters on the appraisal process, finding and working with qualified appraisers, and dealing with the IRS on appraisals. Appendices include lists of selected av media appraisers, selected professional associations, codes of ethics, IRS forms and publications, sample appraisal documents, and a bibliography.

Journal of Film Preservation. Brussels, Belgium: FIAF, ongoing. Published twice yearly by the International Federation of Film Archives.

Kallenberger, Richard H., and George D. Cvjetnicanin. *Film Into Video: A Guide to Merging the Technologies.* Newton, MA: Focal Press, 1994. 352 pp. Comprehensive, practical information on converting motion picture film to video, including telecine devices, video recorder formats, and planning for film and video transfers. One section discusses transferring video to film.

Kaniss, Phyllis. *Making Local News.* Chicago and London: The University of Chicago Press, 1991. 260 pp. Includes chapters on "The Historical Development of the Local News Media," "Commercial Pressures on Local News," and "Local Televison News."

Kesner, Richard, and Lisa Weber. *Automating the Archives: A Beginners Guide.* Chicago: Society of American Archivists, 1991. 8 pp.

Kies, Cosette. "Copyright Versus Free Access: CBS and Vanderbilt University Square Off." *Wilson Library Bulletin* 50 (November 1975): 242-246.

Kies, Cosette. "The CBS—Vanderbilt Litigation: Taping the Evening News." In *Fair Use and Free Inquiry,* edited by John Shelton Lawrence and Bernard Timberg. Norwood, NJ: Ablex, 1980.

Lee, William E., and Charleton C. Bard. "The Stability of Kodak Professional Motion-Picture Film Bases." *SMPTE Journal* 97 (November 1988): 911-14.

Lehtinen, Rick. "Archiving for Productivity." *Broadcast Engineering* (September 1991), pp. 86-90. Discusses automated video archiving strategies for television news divisions.

Lindner, Jim. "Sticking Point: A Tape-Restoration Primer and Tips for Preserving Your Videotapes. *Video Magazine* (February/March 1996): 50-52. Includes a thirteen-point tape preservation checklist.

Lindekugel, D. M. *Shooters: TV News Photographers and Their Work.* Westport, CT: Praeger Publishers, 1994.

Morrison, Fraser, and John Corcoran. "Accelerated Life Testing of Metal Particle Tape." *SMPTE Journal* 103, n. 1 (January 1994): 13-17.

National Archives and Records Administration. *Managing Audiovisual Records.* Second edition. Instructional Guide Series. College Park, MD: National Archives and Records Administration, Office of Records Administration, 1996. 19 pp. plus appendices.

National Archives of Canada. *Fading Away: Strategic Options to Ensure the Protection of and Access to Our Audio-Visual Memory.* Report of the Task Force on the Preservation and Enhanced Use of Canada's Audio-Visual Heritage, June 1995. 51 pp. In four parts: "Assessing the Situation," "Building an Audio-Visual Heritage," "Preserving the Audio-Visual Heritage," and "Accessing the Audio-Visual Heritage."

National Media Laboratory. *The Care and Handling of Tape.* VHS videocassette, 7 mins. Produced by AMPEX Recording Media Corporation; distrubuted free of charge by National Media Laboratory, St. Paul, MN.

Nemeyer, Sheldon. "Historical Note: Color News Film, 1965-1975." *SMPTE Journal,* v. 103, n. 2 (February 1994), pp. 112-113. Technical aspects and historical problems involved during the ten-year period when television news production shifted from black-and-white to color film.

Newborg, Gerald G. "Collection Snapshot: North Dakota Television Newsfilm Preservation Project." *Views: The Newsletter of the Visual Materials Section, Society of American Archivists* 8, no. 3 (August 1994): 4-5. Report by the North Dakota State Archivist on the completion of an NHPRC-funded project to preserve the Historical Society's television newsfilm collections.

News Library News: Bulletin of the News Division of Special Libraries Association 13, n. 1 (Fall 1990), 23 pp. Special issue on television news libraries. Articles include: "Canadian Broadcasting Corporation," by Jeannette Kopak and Leone Earls, "ABC News Research Center" by Madeline Cohen, "Cable News Network Library" by Kathy Christensen and Debra K. Bade, "NBC Reference Library" by Joan Levinstein, and "CBS News Reference Library" by Laura Kapnick.

North Dakota Newsfilm Preservation Project. *News Update.* Bismarck, ND: State Historical Society of North Dakota, September 1992. State Historical Society of North Dakota's occasional newsletter on the state's newsfilm and video preservation project.

Oakley, Robert L. *Copyright and Preservation: A Serious Problem in Need of a Thoughtful Solution*. Washington, DC: The Commission on Preservation and Access, 1990. 58 pp.

Patterson, L. Ray, and Stanley W. Lindberg. *The Nature of Copyright: A Law of Users' Rights*. Athens, GA: University of Georgia Press, 1991. 274 pp. Includes an examination of fair use issues; co-author Patterson represented the Vanderbilt Television News Archive in its 1970s lawsuit brought by CBS.

Prelinger, Richard, and Celeste R. Hoffnar, eds. *Footage 89: North American Film and Video Sources*. New York: Prelinger Associates, Inc., 1989. 795 pp. Includes detailed information on numerous local and national television news collections in the U.S. and Canada.

Prelinger, Richard, ed. *Footage 91: North American Film and Video Sources*. New York: Prelinger Associates, Inc., 1991. 246 pp. Supplement to *Footage 89* containing updates, corrections, additions and many new entries. Also available on CD-ROM.

Prelinger, Rick. "Archival Survival: The Fundamentals of Using Film Archives and Stock Footage Libraries." *The Independent* (October 1991): 20-24.

Public Affairs Video Archives. *1992-1993 Academic Consortium*. West Lafayette, IN: Purdue University, 1992. 24 pp. Introduction to the PAVA's academic access program, including finding aids and indexes to the C-SPAN research archive.

Ram, A. Tulsi, David F. Kopperl, Richard C. Sehlin, Stephanie Masaryk-Morris, James L. Vincent, and Paige Miller (Eastman Kodak Company). "The Effects and Prevention of the 'Vinegar Syndrome'." *Journal of Imaging Science and Technology* 38, no. 3 (May/June 1994): 249-61.

Redefining Film Preservation: A National Plan. Recommendations of the Librarian of Congress in Consultation with the National Film Preservation Board. Washington, DC: Library of Congress, August 1994. 79 pp.

Reilly, James M., Peter Z. Adelstein, and Douglas W. Nishimura. *Preservation of Safety Film*. Final Report to the Office of Preservation and Access, National Endowment for the Humanities, NEH Grant # PS-20159-88. Rochester, NY: Image Permanence Institute, March 1991.

Reilly, James M., Peter Z. Adelstein, Douglas W. Nishimura, and Catherine J. Erbland. *New Approaches to Safety Film Preservation*. Final Report to National Endowment for the Humanities, NEH Grant # PS-20445-91. Rochester, NY: Image Permanence Institute, April 1994.

Reilly, James M., Douglas W. Nishimura, and Edward Zinn for the Image Permanence Institute, Rochester Institute of Technology. *New Tools for Preservation: Assessing Long-Term Environmental Effects on Library and Archives Collections*. Washington, DC: The Commission on Preservation and Access, November 1995. 35 pp. Introduces the concept of the Time Weighted Preservation Index (TWPI), which provides a new way to measure and quantify how temperature and humidity changes affect the preservation quality of storage environments for paper, photographic and magnetic tape materials. Also describes plans for the development of a new Preservation Environment Monitor instrument.

Richards, David, and Edmund DiGiulio. "Film-to-Video Transfers: Time for a Change." *SMPTE Journal* 103, n. 2 (February 1994), pp. 85-93.

Richmond, Joseph C. *Transfer of Monochrome Video Information from Magnetic Tape to Motion Picture Film for Archival Storage*. Washington, DC: U.S. Department of Commerce, Bureau of Standards, 1978.

Rothenberg, Jeff. "Ensuring the Longevity of Digital Documents." *Scientific American* (January 1995): 42-47. On preserving, translating and interpreting digital bit streams; includes comparisons of the life expectancy and years until obsolescence of such common digital storage media as magnetic tape, videotape, magnetic disk and optical disk.

Saintville, Dominique, editorial supervisor. *Panorama of Audiovisual Archives*. English edition edited by Anne Hanford. London: FIAT/BBC Data Publications, 1986. 275 pp. Published with the assistance of UNESCO.

Sargent, Ralph N. *Preserving the Moving Image*. Washington, DC: Corporation for Public Broadcasting and the National Endowment for the Arts, 1974. 152 pp.

Schou, Henning, for the FIAF Preservation Commision. *Preservation of Moving Images and Sound*. Brussels: International Federation of Film Archives, September 1989. First edition.

Schreibman, Fay C. "Television News Archives: A Guide to Major Collections." In *Television Network News: Issues in Content Research*, edited by William Adams and Fay Schreibman. Washington, DC: Television and Politics Study Program, School of Public and International Affairs, George Washington University, 1978.

Schreibman, Fay C. "Searching for Television's History." Chapter 2 in *Broadcasting Research Methods*, edited by J. R. Dominick and J. E. Fletcher. Newton, MA: Allyn and Bacon, Inc., 1985. Pages 16-45. A guide to researching television history, with an appendix describing the collections of 24 television archives, their finding aids, and access facilities. Also provides a state-by-state list of museums and historical societies that hold local television news footage.

Semonche, Barbara P., ed. *News Media Libraries: A Management Handbook*. Westport, CT: Greenwood Press, 1993. Includes chapter on television news libraries by Jeannette Kopak of the Canadian Broadcasting Corporation describing the evolution of the CBC's English-network news library and computer system.

Society of American Archivists. *Code of Ethics for Archivists*. Chicago, IL: SAA, 1992. 4 pp. Revision of 1980 code.

Society of Motion Picture and Television Engineers. *Care and Handling of Magnetic Recording Tape*. SMPTE Recommended Practice RP 103, 1982.

Society of Motion Picture and Television Engineers. "Proposed SMPTE Recommended Practice, RP 131: Storage of Motion-Picture Film." *SMPTE Journal* 103, n. 3 (March 1994): 201-205. On the revision of RP 131-1985. Provides recommended environmental conditions for "active working storage," "medium-term storage," and "extended-term storage" (the latter previously known as "archival storage").

Society of Motion Picture and Television Engineers. "Proposed SMPTE Recommended Practice: Care, Storage, Operation, Handling and Shipping of Magnetic Recording Tape for Television." *SMPTE Journal* 103, no. 10 (October 1994): 692-95. On the revision of RP 103 - 1992.

State Historical Society of Wisconsin. *Madison, Wisconsin, Television Newsfilm, 1968-1972: A Descriptive Guide and Index to the Holdings at the State Historical Society of Wisconsin*. Madison: State Historical Society of Wisconsin, 1991.

Thomson, Patricia. "Sleuth: The Search for Television News Footage." *The Independent* (March 1988): 20-27. On the preservation, research and use of television news collections in independent and historical documentaries.

3M Company. "Videocassette Tape Physical Damage." *Retentivity*. Available from the 3M Company, Magnetic Audio/Video Products Division, 3M Center, Building 223-5N, St. Paul, MN 55101.

3M Company. "The Handling and Storage of Magnetic Recording Tape." *Retentivity*. Available from the 3M Company.

Tisch, Tom. "Cleaning Solutions for a Clean Environment: Developments in Motion-Picture Film-Cleaning Technology." *SMPTE Journal* 104, n. 8 (August 1995): 528-533. Film cleaning standardized on the use of methyl chloroform 37 years ago; as of December 31, 1995, this solvent was no longer manufactured. The article describes the search for effective film cleaning alternates that are safe to the film, the laboratory operator, and the environment.

United Nations Educational, Scientific and Cultural Organization, General Information Programme and UNISIST. *Curriculum Development for the Training of Personnel in Moving Image and Recorded Sound Archives*. Paris: UNESCO, 1990.

United Nations Educational, Scientific and Cultural Organization, General Information Programme and UNISIST. *Legal Questions Facing Audiovisual Archives*. Paris: UNESCO, March 1991.

Utz, Peter. "What's Happening to 3/4U?" *AV Video* (March 1992), p. 16, 127-129. Discusses prospects for continued use of the 3/4-inch U-Matic format in relation to S-VHS, Beta SP, and Hi8. Includes a detailed specifications and image equality comparison between 3/4-inch and S-VHS.

Van Bogart, Dr. John W. C. *Media Stability Studies Final Report*. Technical Report RE-0017. St. Paul, MN: National Media Lab, July 1994. 86 pp. An investigation of the stability of and estimate life expectancies (LEs) of various commercial magnetic tape media, including VHS, Hi 8mm, D8, D-1, and D-2.

Van Bogart, Dr. John W. C. *Magnetic Tape Storage and Handling: A Guide for Libraries and Archives*. Washington, DC: The Commission on Preservation and Access, June 1995. 34 pp. A joint project of the Commission on Preservation and Access and the National Media Laboratory, St. Paul, MN. Chapters include: "What Can Go Wrong with Magnetic Media," "Preventing Information Loss: Multiple Tape Copies," "Life Expectancy: How Long Will Magnetic Media Last," and "How Can You Prevent Magnetic Tape from Degrading Prematurely?" Appendices include "Estimation of Magnetic Tape Life Expectancies (LEs)," and "Resources for Transfer and Restoration of Video and Audio Tape."

Vitiello, Stephen, and Leanne Mella: "Facilities for Cleaning, Restoring, and Remastering Videotape." *The Independent* (October 1991): 28.

Vogel, Denis E. "Local Television News Holdings in Prefreeze American Television Stations." Unpublished paper presented to the Film and Television Archives Advisory Committee, October 1986. 6 pp. with charts. Results of a study to ascertain the existence and condition of local newsfilm collections at the 107 oldest American television stations that had been issued permits prior to the 1946 FCC freeze on station licensing.

Volkmann, Herbert, with Henning Schou, eds., for the FIAF Preservation Commission. *Preservation and Restoration of Moving Images and Sound*. Brussels: International Federation of Film Archives, 1986. 268 pp. Covers in 19 chapters the physical properties of film and sound tape, their handling and storage, and the equipment used by film archives to ensure permanent preservation.

Walch, Victoria Irons. *Standards for Archival Description: A Handbook*. Chicago: Society of American Archivists, 1993. 325 pp. Introductory guide to 85 standards (and the organizations that developed them), including USMARC formats, cataloging rules, thesauri, and standards for automated systems.

Watkinson, John. *The Digital Videotape Recorder*. Newton, MA: Focal Press, 1994. 288 pages. Provides in-depth information on current digital formats, including D1, D2, D3, D5, DCT, Digital Betacam, HD formats, as well as DVC the new 1/4-inch format.

Watkinson, John. *Digital Compression in Video and Audio*. Newton, MA: Focal Press, 1995. 256 pp. Explains the wide application of compression technologies, treating the subject from first principles without assuming any particular background for the reader. Theory is balanced with a range of practical applications to transmission and recording.

WGBH Educational Foundation. *Guide to the Administrative Records of the Lowell Institute, Cooperative Broadcasting Council, and WGBH Educational Foundation, 1945-1994 (1951-1991)*. Boston: WGBH, 1995. 54 pp. Processed by Claire Goodwin, Project Archivist, with a grant from the National Historical Publications and Records Commission.

Wheeler, Jim. "Videotape Storage: How to Make Your Videotapes Last for Decades...or Centuries." *American Cinematographer* 64, n. 1 (January 1983): 23-24.

Wheeler, Jim. "Long Term Storage of Video Tape." *SMPTE Journal* 92, n. 6 (June 1983): 650-654.

Whitaker, Jerry. "Preserving Technology." *Broadcast Engineering* (June 1984): 144-152. Describes five collections: the Ampex Museum of Magnetic Recording in Redwood City, CA, the Broadcast Pioneers Library in Washington, DC, the National Broadcast Museum in Dallas/Forth Worth, the Forest Hills Wireless Museum in Forest Hills, NY, and the Museum of Television and Radio in New York City.

Wilhelm, Henry, with contributing author Carol Brower. *The Permanence and Care of Color Photographs: Traditional and Digital Color Prints, Color Negatives, Slides, and Motion Pictures*. Grinnell, Iowa: Preservation Publishing Company, 1993. 744 pp. Covers all aspects of color film preservation and storage.

Woodward, J.G. "Stress Demagnetization in Videotapes." *IEEE Transactions on Magnetics* 18, n. 6 (November 1982): 1812-1817.

Wright, Belinda S., and David Bearman, compilers and eds. *1994-95 Directory of Software for Museums and Archives*. Pittsburgh: Archives and Museum Informatics, 1994. 95 pages. New edition of directory describes functions and features of over eighty software products. Includes essay "Trends in Software for Archives and Museums: 1994-95."

Yakel, Elizabeth. *Starting an Archive*. Chicago: Society of American Archivists and The Scarecrow Press, 1994. 106 pp. Designed for institutional administrators, archivists, and records managers. Provides both theoretical and practical approaches for the establishment of an archival program and discusses managerial, financial, and administrative implications involved. Includes descriptions of archival activities, samples of important archival policy documents and forms, and a current bibliography.

B

Photo Directory

All photographs in this manual are provided courtesy of the Louis Wolfson II Media History Center, with the following exceptions:

State Historical Society of North Dakota: pages 60, 62, 64.
Chicago Historical Society: page 74 (top and bottom).
San Francisco State University: pages 141 (top and bottom), 145, 146.

Reprints of all photographs (with the above noted exceptions) can be ordered by contacting the Wolfson Center at the address below. Please refer to page number and photo number when ordering.

Louis Wolfson II Media History Center
Miami-Dade Public Library
101 West Flagler Street
Miami, FL 33130
Phone: 305-375-1505
Fax: 305-375-4436

Page #	Caption	Photo #

Chapter 1

Chapter 2

Index

(Page numbers in italics indicate photographs.)

MISSION STATEMENT

AMERICAN FILM INSTITUTE

The American Film Institute is dedicated to advancing and preserving the art of film, television and other forms of the moving image.

AFI's programs promote innovation and excellence through teaching, presenting, preserving and redefining the moving image.

AFI NATIONAL CENTER FOR FILM AND VIDEO PRESERVATION

The National Center for Film and Video Preservation was established in 1984 by the American Film Institute and the National Endowment for the Arts. Its mission is to:

- Serve as the center for coordinating American moving image preservation activities on a national scale; in this role the NCFVP serves as Secretariat for the Association of Moving Image Archivists and for The Film Foundation.

- Establish ongoing relationships between the public archives and the film and television industry.

- Implement the National Moving Image Database (NAMID), which centralizes information on the film and television holdings of American archives and producers.

- Research and publish the *AFI Catalog of Feature Films*, which provides definitive filmographies on all feature-length motion pictures produced in the U.S. on a decade-by-decade basis.

- Locate and acquire films and television programs for inclusion in the AFI Collection to be preserved at the Library of Congress and other archives.

- Create broader public awareness of preservation needs.

MISSION STATEMENT

LOUIS WOLFSON II MEDIA HISTORY CENTER

The Louis Wolfson II Media History Center is one of the largest film and video archives of its kind in the country and is designated by the Florida Legislature as an official moving image archive. The Center was established in 1986 by Miami-Dade Community College, the University of Miami and the Miami-Dade Public Library.

The Center's mission, important to Florida and part of a broader national effort, is to collect, preserve, catalog and make accessible film and video materials which document Florida's history and culture. The Center's ever-growing collection began with an initial donation of newsfilm from WTVJ, one of the first television stations in the country. Now, the Center's collection spans over eight decades, dating from 1920s home movies, and contains millions of feet of film, thousands of hours of videotape, and materials donated by a variety of sources including television stations, production companies, corporations, organizations and individuals. Together these film and video materials not only chronicle the visual record and history of our community, they also provide a Florida perspective on national and international events and the issues that have impacted our lives and shaped the culture of our region.

The Center's activities include: preservation, collection and acquisition, cataloging, information and reference service, archival education, training and internship programs, screenings, exhibitions and seminars, academic and classroom use, provision of footage to film and video makers for new productions, and collaborations with other local, regional and national archives, museums, libraries and cultural organizations.

The Wolfson Center is utilized by the general public, researchers, students, educators, cultural organizations and film and video makers. Public access is available through screenings, seminars and exhibitions – all presented free at our facility or at other venues throughout South Florida. Other innovative forms of access include circulation of selected programming through the Miami-Dade Public Library System and our television program *Rewind*, which is broadcast twice daily. Collection queries and research requests from Florida, around the country and abroad are received on a daily basis. In addition the Center administers an annual film and video awards program which was established to underscore the importance of preservation and to recognize excellence in productions made in or about Florida.

Since its founding, the Wolfson Center has worked closely with the moving image archival community and other professional groups and organizations. The Center's coordinating role in the publication of *The Administration of Newsfilm and Videotape Collections: A Curatorial Manual* is the most recent example of its efforts to aid in the development of national level standards.